Advance Praise for *Teaching 2030*

"A fresh take on the real future of teaching, *Teaching 2030* delves into the myriad of issues that teachers face today and will confront in the future. Barnett and his colleagues pose bold ideas for recruiting and rewarding teachers. They point out how we should restructure accountability and more in order to provide our nation's children with the education they deserve."

—**Richard Riley**, former U.S. Secretary of Education
and former Governor of South Carolina

"*Teaching 2030* is a brilliant look at the future of teaching in America from the perspective of those who know most about what it is and should be: accomplished teachers. Working with Barnett Berry, himself a former teacher and one of the nation's foremost experts on teaching, these voices frame the issues and the possibilities with passion, knowledge, and insight. Everyone who cares about teaching and learning should read this book."

—**Linda Darling-Hammond**, Charles E. Ducommun
Professor of Education, Stanford University
and author of *The Flat World and Education*

"In this engaging volume, a notable and diverse team of accomplished teachers, and a researcher who advocates for them, explain why the teaching profession needs a dramatic overhaul and present an intriguing path to a more promising future. This provocative work is a welcome contribution to thinking about how we can get our kids the teachers they need."

—**Frederick M. Hess**, Resident Scholar and Director
of Education Policy Studies, American Enterprise Institute

"*Teaching 2030* is a remarkable, revolutionary picture of the future of our schools. Blasting the intellectual meltdown shaping too much of today's education policy, Berry and his colleagues reveal extraordinary opportunities to improve our schools and serve every student. Deeply respectful of teachers, *Teaching 2030* proposes how teachers and support professionals can help craft and take more ownership of their professions. This is an exciting and hopeful vision of possibility."

—**Dennis Van Roekel**,
president, National Education Association

"This is an exciting and provocative portrait of how teaching could look in 20 years, painting a picture of a profession centered on student learning. Barnett Berry and his colleagues make it clear that making this vision a reality is up to all of us."

—**Randi Weingarten**,
President, American Federation of Teachers

"*Teaching 2030* lays the groundwork for a bold vision for the teaching profession. In championing a student-centered profession, Barnett Berry elevates the voices of expert teachers on how to rejuvenate the educator workforce through policy and practice. He challenges us to rethink the 'brick-and-mortar' education career of the past and to envision the possibilities for creating the schools we need for the future."

—**Bob Wise**, former West Virginia Governor
and President of the Alliance for Excellent Education

"There is no other person in our country that captures the teacher voice like Barnett Berry. In his new book, Barnett works with 12 expert teacher colleagues in describing what teaching must look like in 2030 and what we need to do now. It is a call for policymakers to recruit the brightest and best to join our ranks and prepare them to lead the way for transforming the public schools. This is a must read for all practitioners and policymakers to ensure our schools are ready to prepare our students for 21st century careers."

—**Betsy Rogers**,
2003 National Teacher of the Year

Teaching 2030

What We Must Do for Our Students and Our Public Schools— Now and in the Future

BARNETT BERRY

and the TeacherSolutions 2030 Team

Jennifer Barnett	Kilian Betlach	Shannon C'de Baca
Susie Highley	John M. Holland	Carrie J. Kamm
Renee Moore	Cindi Rigsbee	Ariel Sacks
Emily Vickery	Jose Vilson	Laurie Wasserman

Teachers College
Columbia University
New York and London

Great Public Schools for Every Student

NEA Professional Library
National Education Association
Washington, D.C.

This book was generously supported by MetLife Foundation.

The box on p. 58 and Figures 4.1–4.3, 5.1, 7.1–7.11 are all reprinted here by permission of their publishers. Credit lines accompany the box and figures.

Published simultaneously by Teachers College Press, 1234 Amsterdam Avenue, New York, NY 10027 and the NEA Professional Library, 1201 16th Street N.W., Washington, D.C. 20036

Note: The opinions expressed in this publication should not be construed as representing the policy or position of the National Education Association. Materials published by the NEA Professional Library are intended to be discussion documents for educators who are concerned with specialized interests of the profession.

Library of Congress Cataloging-in-Publication Data

Berry, Barnett.
      Teaching 2030 : what we must do for our students and our public schools—now and in the future / Barnett Berry and the TeacherSolutions 2030 Team, Jennifer Barnett . . . [et al.].
          p. cm.
      Includes bibliographical references and index.
      ISBN 978-0-8077-5154-1 (pbk. : alk. paper)
      ISBN 978-0-8077-5155-8 (hardcover : alk. paper)
          1. Teaching—United States. 2. Public schools—United States. 3. Educational change—United States. I. TeacherSolutions 2030 Team. II. Title.
      LB1025.3.B4735   2011
      371.102—dc22   2010026444

Teachers College ISBN 978-0-8077-5154-1 (paper)
Teachers College ISBN 978-0-8077-5155-8 (hardcover)

National Education Association ISBN 978-0-8106-1878-7

Printed on acid-free paper
Manufactured in the United States of America

18   17   16   15   14   13   12   11   8   7   6   5   4   3   2   1

Contents

Acknowledgments

Coauthors' Acknowledgments

We are indebted to many teaching colleagues, students, friends and family, and the staff of the Center for Teaching Quality for their time, ideas, and encouragement as we've worked on this hopeful book about the future of teaching.

We are especially grateful to MetLife Foundation for its support of this work and steadfast belief in the value of a teacher "think/action tank" exploring the future of the teaching profession. We also appreciate the guidance and enthusiastic backing of our editor at Teachers College Press, Brian Ellerbeck, who from the start saw the value in our nontraditional approach to writing this book, and never wavered in his commitment to publish a new policy narrative with teachers' voices at its core.

Many experts in the field advised us and agreed to participate in our "Webinars" and online discussions, including Dennis Bartels, executive director of the San Francisco Exploratorium; Jon Snyder, graduate dean of Bank Street College; Ninive Calegari, founder of the Teacher Salary Project; Milton Chen, (former) executive director of the George Lucas Educational Foundation; Jillian Darwish and Monica Martinez of the KnowledgeWorks Foundation; Sandy Fivecoat, founder of WeAreTeachers.com; Wesley Fryer, teacher, instructional technologist, and award-winning education blogger; Heather Harding of Teach for America; Kevin Honeycutt, former art teacher and 21st-century education researcher; Rafiq Kalam Id-Din, founder of Teaching Firms of America; Susan Moore Johnson of Harvard University; Chris Lehmann, principal of the Science Leadership Academy in Philadelphia; Sheryl Nussbaum-Beach, charter member of the Teacher Leaders Network and founder of Powerful Learning Practice LLC; smart mobster Howard Rheingold; Andrea Saveri of the Institute for the Future; Zeke Vanderhoek, founder of the Equity Project charter school in Washington Heights, New York; and Sue Waters, an expert in mobile instructional technologies based in Perth, Australia. A special thanks is offered to education historian James Fraser, who gave extraordinary advice and helpful feedback as Barnett crafted an overview of teaching's past to serve as a prologue to its future.

Finally we thank our virtual colleagues from across the United States who participate in the ongoing 8-year policy discussion that takes place daily within the Teacher Leaders Network Forum. Their feedback and pushback as we honed the ideas represented in this book have been invaluable.

Barnett Berry's Acknowledgments

In my career I have been very fortunate to work with a number of colleagues who have taught me much about the teaching profession. Many have also become close friends. I am grateful for the wisdom about teaching and learning they have shared with me over the years, including: Mary Dean Barringer for her experience and knowledge of special needs as well as education entrepreneurship; Dennis Bartels for his expertise in human learning and professional networks; Rick Ginsberg for his deep understanding of the politics of education and the vagaries of social science research; Dwight Hare (partner in my first teacher labor market studies in the 1980s) for his scholarly focus and commitment to underserved students in rural America; Jon Snyder for his pedagogical insight and vision for teacher education; and Alan Wieder for his scholarly investigations and potent narratives into race, equity, and public education. The lessons learned from these colleagues have been profound, only exceeded by our deep and everlasting friendship.

My passion and quest for advancing teaching as a true profession began in graduate school under the mentorship of Julio George. Our professional and personal relationship continues to grow, and Julio still teaches me much today. After graduate school I was fortunate to begin my academic career at the RAND Corporation, under the guidance of the profession's foremost scholars, Arthur Wise and Linda Darling-Hammond. They taught me much then—and still do. Arthur continues to provide wise counsel to me as the Chairman of the Board of the Center for Teaching Quality.

My writing colleagues and I are deeply appreciative of the wisdom of Linda, our nation's #1 teaching policy expert and reformer, who provided us this past year with compelling evidence and powerful ideas and is an inspiration for all of us who seek to close student-achievement gaps. A close friend and mentor for more than 2 decades now, Linda has set the standard for those who truly seek to improve our public schools and transform the profession that makes all others possible.

The work of running a nonprofit and writing a book does not always go hand-in-glove. Our efforts to elevate teachers' voices through the TeacherSolutions 2030 initiative would not be possible without my colleagues at the Center for Teaching Quality—Brooke Adams, Alesha Daughtrey, Malinda Faber, Ali Kliegman, Melissa Rasberry, and Teresa Durn. We are making headway as an organization and would not be where we are without the deep commitment and guidance of our founding Board chair, Tom Lambeth. Deep gratitude is offered to my friend and colleague Ann Byrd, our chief operating officer at CTQ and an extraordinary teacher-leader in her own right. Ann is always there with insight from the classroom and was with us every step of the way, even when she wanted my attention on other matters of our organization.

And then there is John Norton, my TLN co-founder and friend of more than 2 decades, whose dedication to teacher leadership and voice is unsurpassed—literally. No one outside the profession can *hear* teachers better than John, and no one is more skilled at making sure their ideas and ideals are understood. This book, and all that it represents, would not have been possible without John.

Finally I turn to those I care about the most—first, to the memory of my father, Joe B. Berry, who taught me how not to separate caring for people from excellence in our work, and then, to my sister Roxanne Berry Corbett, who lives the life of respect for all others.

And then there is my extraordinary wife of 34 years, Meredith, who inspires and grounds me. Our life and love together serve as the bedrock for all that is good in my work. Meredith, an expert special education teacher of over three decades, does not let me forget any reality of teaching, emergent or otherwise. And finally, there are our beautiful children, Joseph and Evan, who, as young adults, already are making the world a better place for others to live. They fuel me every day. They make everything worthwhile.

PROLOGUE

We Cannot Create
What We Cannot Imagine

We are not soothsayers. So began my ongoing collaboration with a small team of highly effective American teachers eager to imagine a brighter future for students and the teaching profession. We quickly agreed not to make a vain attempt to describe the future of Teaching in 2030 with perfect clarity. But after more than a year of study, much of it online, we remain confident that we can identify present and emergent realities, examine expert predictions of future trends,[1] and apply our understandings of what works for student learning today to describe what will likely work—and be needed—in the schooling of tomorrow.

Using the virtual tools of the Teacher Leaders Network (TLN), a dynamic professional learning community supported by the Center for Teaching Quality (CTQ), we've studied the works of researchers and reformers, demographers and futurists—and the rich insights of teacher-leaders themselves. We've examined lessons of teaching's past. We've debated long and hard. We have not been afraid to challenge our own conventional wisdom; indeed, we've sought out divergent thinking and sharpened our own suppositions as a result. Ultimately we have come together, in harmony if not always in lock-step, about an expanded vision for student learning in the 21st century and for the teaching profession that will, in myriad ways, continue to accelerate that learning.

The teaching we imagine emerges from a student-centered profession driven by new tools, organizations, and ideals. Some of the concepts and principles that shape our vision come from the past, not the future. But they are principles yet to be achieved in most of our nation's public schools, where too many promises of educational opportunity remain unfulfilled. Our *collective understanding* is built from the need to transcend the long-standing dysfunctional debates over the status of teaching and the historical imperatives of gender, race, and class that have so often undermined efforts to ensure qualified and effective teachers for every student in America's system of public education. Our *collective vision* rests on four emergent realities: a transformed learning ecology for students and teachers, seamless connections in and out of cyberspace, differentiated pathways and careers, and "teacherpreneurs" who will foster innovation locally and globally. *Our collective hopes rely on six levers for change.* These include: engaging the public in provocative ways; overhauling school finance systems; creating transformative systems of preparation and licensing; ensuring school working conditions that we know promote effective teaching; reframing accountability for transformative results; and continuing to evolve teacher unions into professional guilds. We also agree that if teaching is to become the 21st-century profession that students deserve, then its unions must be transformed into results-oriented guilds in which effective teaching and learning are paramount. New policies, especially transformative ones, do not come easily. People need to take action. We conclude with seven actions steps to be taken by administrators, union leaders, policymakers, university presidents, community leaders, and parents and students, as well as our fellow teachers.

Our look ahead is a fast-forward to 2030—approximately 20 years from the publication of this book and well within the career reach of many teachers working in classrooms today, including a half-dozen members of our own writing team. Whatever the current stage of our education careers, those of us working on this project all agree: *The teaching profession must look very different in 2030 if all our students are going to be well prepared to meet the demands of the global economy and participate successfully in our nation's ever-evolving democratic way of life.*

My collaborators on this book teach in every region of the nation. They serve students through many teaching roles, at many grade levels, in urban, suburban, and rural schools. They span several generations: Some began teaching in the predigital 1970s, while others launched their careers in the new millennium. They include Jennifer Barnett (Talladega County, Alabama); Kilian Betlach (Oakland, California); Shannon C'de Baca (Iowa Online Learning); Susie Highley (Indianapolis, Indiana); John M. Holland (Richmond, Virginia); Carrie J. Kamm (Chicago, Illinois); Renee Moore (Cleveland, Mississippi); Cindi Rigsbee (Hillsborough, North Carolina); Ariel Sacks (New York, New York); Emily Vickery (Pensacola, Florida); Jose Vilson (New York, New York); and Laurie Wasserman (Medford, Massachusetts). (See the About the Authors section for the full bios of these outstanding teachers.)

As we envisioned the future, these 12 classroom experts and myself—a former teacher who advocates for the profession—also looked deeply at the history of public education in America and how that history has shaped current teaching policy. In particular, we examined the early 21st-century debates swirling around the landmark No Child Left Behind (NCLB) Act of 2002 and the more recent initiatives, such as Race to the Top—launched by the Obama administration around how best to identify, reward, and distribute highly effective teachers. We began testing out our ideas with more of our teaching colleagues from our virtual community, the Teacher Leaders Network. (See the About the Authors section for a listing of our TLN colleagues.) They deepened our vision for the profession's future and enriched our narrative with more voices from the classroom.

We all share the nation's sense of urgency about promoting high academic standards for all students and closing the achievement gap. And we believe that teacher evaluation must be results-oriented and new teaching effectiveness measures must be developed and used to transform the profession. At the same time, recalling Andy Hargreaves' insightful analysis of the current school-change wars, we are concerned that overly obsessive data-driven reforms can promote "a technocratic system of anticipatory surveillance where educators' energies are directed towards designing precise interventions that focus on meeting the next target, test, or outside inspection."[2]

The current tendency to exert tight control over the work of teachers, we believe, is closely tied to what sociologists say is teaching's long-time status as a "semi-profession." Rather than pursue a course that would result in a fully realized profession—one in which all teachers are fully prepared and supported as well as expected to make the best educational decisions for each individual student—many policymakers and school reformers continue to search for ways to somehow "teacher-proof" our classrooms. This attitude, I am convinced, is shaped more by past history than by any serious consideration of what the future holds for our students and our nation's public schools. And looking back often allows us to know how to move forward.

A Personal Aside

My own journey to create a 21st-century, results-oriented profession began in an inner-city high school in the late 1970s, where I taught a range of social studies courses to students not much younger than me. I was not prepared to teach them and had to rely on my wits and abundant optimism. I ran out of gas in 3 years, leaving the classroom to study the profession I left. After stints in a D.C.-based think tank and in higher education (and a brief foray as a top-level bureaucrat in a state education agency), I set out to build a nonprofit organization that has teachers and their voices at the center of our work.

My hope for the future of teaching is bolstered by my long-standing and still-expanding work and personal relationships with hundreds and hundreds of expert teachers across our great nation. They teach me much every day, and I will continue to learn from them.

My hope for the future of teaching is bolstered by my faith in America's capacity to create a public school system that manifests every child's right to learn and ensures educational excellence and equity for all of our students. I share this faith with my long-time friend, colleague, and mentor, Linda Darling-Hammond, whose 2010 book *The Flat World and Education* not only challenges us to make good on these democratic ideals but offers a wise and deeply researched plan to achieve them in the 21st century.

I recognize that not all Americans share my hopes. For some, successfully educating large numbers of other people's children threatens to blur the lines between the haves and have-nots and undermine the nation's socioeconomic pecking order. For others—including some school reformers—closing the achievement gap does not mean that we must grant all students access to a rich curriculum taught by expert, experienced teachers. For many critics of the current system, a regimen of drill-and-skill teaching, enforced by the next generation of standardized tests, will suffice for some students, including most of those who live in low-income communities. Today the politics of education are less than optimum. In fact, as David Simon—creator of the award-winning truth-telling TV series *The Wire*—posed poignantly, America has become "the land of the juked statistic,"—the "false quarterly profit statement," and the "impossible campaign promise," as well as the "hyped school test score."[3]

Accountability for student results is a must for the teaching profession. However, I believe tomorrow's teaching profession must be organized and supported to teach *all*, not just a few, students to understand ideas deeply and know how to create and apply knowledge on behalf of themselves and their communities. Achieving this goal will require more than relying on the results from *hyped* standardized test scores, built from early 20th-century conceptions of teaching and learning that have little to tell about what students know. Achieving this goal will require a greater investment in teaching and more opportunities for our nation's best teachers, using a growing knowledge base on how students actually learn, to lead the way. They are many and they are ready. They need to be supported and elevated.

For many of today's school administrators, union leaders, policymakers, and pundits, such a view challenges much of their conventional wisdom about how the public schools should be organized, what issues are addressed (or not) in collective-bargaining agreements, and what we mean when we talk about "transforming" the ways in which teachers are recruited, prepared, supported, and rewarded.

Developing a 21st-century teaching profession inevitably will mean a shift in resources toward developing and applying teacher knowledge—and away from the mega-billion-dollar industry that has grown up around lock-step instruction and high-stakes testing that narrows what is taught and learned. Such a shift will rattle more than a few cages—but this is what our students must have.

Teaching is hard work today. Unlike what many policy pundits suggest, teaching is also complex work. I predict it will be even harder and more complex tomorrow. The difference will be that the hard work of today is mostly performed in survival mode—draining the energy, creativity, and willpower of the teachers we need most. If the vision my teacher-colleagues and I set forth here can be achieved, the challenging work of tomorrow will energize, inspire, and empower the teachers of 2030, as they savor the success of their students and themselves.

—Barnett Berry

CHAPTER 1

The Teachers of 2030 and a Hopeful Vision

This book is about the teachers of 2030 and a hopeful vision for public education. Too many prescriptions for what has ailed the profession, today and yesterday, have been developed by those who know little of the ins and outs of how students learn and what teachers need to know and do in order to help them achieve.

We started out writing this book for those in the policy community who are weary of either/or arguments and are ready to hear a new message from our nation's most accomplished teachers. As we began our journey of study, reflection, debate, and writing, we also turned our attention to the many thousands of teacher-education faculty, from both traditional and alternative programs, who are responsible for preparing the next generation of teachers—and to the school administrators who will need to support teachers as pedagogical and policy leaders. Ultimately, as we considered what it really means to transform teaching into a results-oriented profession, we came to understand that we must also engage the American public. We must convince parents, businesspeople, and community leaders to think beyond tradition—beyond their own childhood experiences in school—and consider what it will mean for our students and for the nation when we fully embrace teaching as professional work and urge our best teachers to lead the way.

The first step along this path is to imagine a future that departs from the past. Our earliest work-group conversations focused on the challenges we faced in helping non-educators think about teaching in new ways. We agreed that while many Americans want our schools to be better, they often do not want them to look much different. We also agreed that too many policymakers hold simplistic notions of teachers' work and appear to assume that historical divides between administrators and teachers and management and labor are immutable. Given these public perceptions, we agreed that teachers themselves must create new narratives that define teaching as complex work and build new levels of trust among key stakeholders and

1

constituents. We understood and embraced the need to create incentives so that high-powered teachers can be recruited and rewarded when they meet head-on the inequities found in so many of our school communities. Finally, while we firmly believe that the future of teaching must be about far more than online learning, many of us have already experienced how new technologies can help close the achievement gap. But we also know too well how the lack of access and capacity to use those tools can widen the gulf between the educational haves and have-nots in our schools.

Our book is about tackling these challenges straight up, describing the emergent educational realities we see, and offering our best ideas about change that can pave the way for new thinking and action. As we tip toward a 21st-century teaching profession, our work begins, as it must, with students. This is why we teach and advocate for the profession that serves them.

Students of Today and Tomorrow

At the turn of the century, Marc Prensky suggested that students of today and tomorrow "do not just think about different things, they actually think differently."[1] Researchers have already documented how members of the emerging "iGeneration," born in the last 10 to 15 years and raised on mobile technologies and virtual reality games, learn very differently—and not just differently from their parents and teachers but from the slightly older members of what many call the "Net Generation," whose childhoods straddled the pre- and post-Internet era.

Writing in the *New York Times*, Brad Stone described today's toddlers as "children of cyberspace" who will themselves become "old fogeys" before they reach 30. An exploding evolution of technological change is "minting a series of mini-generation gaps, with each group of children uniquely influenced by the tech tools available in their formative stages of development," Stone suggested.[2] And if that is true, what does it say to policymakers and the public about our expectations for teachers in the decades to come? How will they do the work of teaching micro-generations? What varied roles will they need to play in a student learning-process that's constantly morphing?

Unfortunately the focus of today's education debates is mostly about "building" better schools and teachers using a slightly more sophisticated but still 20th-century blueprint for learning. Instead, the key conversation needs to be about creating a system that supports flexible learning environments and prepares teachers to fully serve the student of the moment by ensuring that teachers have constant access to professional learning— and the time built in to learn deeply.

"The resources of the Internet and search engines will shift cognitive capacities," say researchers for the Pew Internet & American Life Project, who interviewed nearly 900 Internet "stakeholders and critics" for the 2010 report *The Future of the Internet IV*. "We won't have to remember as much, but we'll have to think harder and have better critical thinking and analytical skills."[3] With less time devoted to memorization, people will have more time to learn new things—an important development, since 80% of the experts interviewed agreed with the prediction that "the hot gadgets and applications that will capture the imaginations of users . . . will often 'come out of the blue.'"

In the flattening world of the 21st century, American students will need to master knowledge and skills as never before. They must learn much more than the three R's of reading, writing, and math (and a smattering of science and social studies) now demanded of them by last-century standardized tests and top-down school accountability systems. The rules and tools of No Child Left Behind have reinforced an overreliance on traditional measures of student achievement and promoted a cautious curriculum and a timorous teaching style. Yet in the emerging workplace, most students—not just an elite few—must be able to find, synthesize, and evaluate information from a wide variety of subjects and sources. The continued exponential growth of knowledge in many fields, especially in science and mathematics, poses new challenges for keeping abreast—and undermines worn-out notions of the need to "cover" content defined by a classroom textbook and an overly prescriptive set of curriculum standards. At a time when more than 1,500 new books are published daily in the United States alone[4] (and you can publish your own for a few hundred dollars) no one can keep pace with the flow of new ideas. But students *can* gain the habits of mind, the learning skills, and the facility with digital tools necessary to process relevant information and determine what is useful and valid. Increasingly, some students and families are looking beyond their schools, seeking anytime/anywhere learning opportunities that better match their understanding of the future. Others—including many consigned to the dreary curriculum of "low-performing schools"—might join them if they were to have the necessary resources and teaching supports.

The information explosion, impelled by ever more powerful tools of access and connectivity, is changing human experience in permanent and profound ways. In a 2009 *Atlantic Monthly* article, futurist Jamais Cascio, a senior fellow at the Institute for Ethics and Emerging Technologies, argued that the array of problems facing humanity, from energy dependency to hunger and the spread of pandemics, "will force us to get smarter if we are to survive." This process is already underway, Cascio said, "across the full spectrum of how we understand intelligence." One key to this evolution, he believes, will be the development of resources that "help people find and assess information smartly."[5]

Today at New York City's School of One, middle school math students have their day organized on playlists—identifying lessons and offering access to virtual tutoring. Schools in the New Tech Network, especially those in rural areas where well-prepared teachers are in too short supply, are turning to Rosetta Stone and its interactive learning software to engage students in foreign languages. Researchers at the Institute of Play focus on digital and physical game design as a tool for 21st-century learning, and their New York City charter school Quest to Learn uses games as rule-based systems where students actively participate, use strategic thinking to make choices, solve complex problems, seek content knowledge, receive constant feedback, and consider the point of view of others.[6]

We believe educators must prepare themselves to meet every learner in an expanding educational "free market," leveraging their teaching skills and knowledge as wise and caring guides who help students through a potentially bewildering world of technology-driven learning opportunities. But we also believe educators must prepare themselves to meet every learner in America's evolving democracy, which is framed by overwhelming information overload and widening socioeconomic divides. And it is Internet technology itself that will spread teaching expertise, as well as allow teachers to know their students and families more deeply in an increasingly complex economic and social order.

Students are not the only ones seeking out anytime education for themselves. Internet technologies are providing unprecedented opportunities for professional growth, as educators connect with one another beyond school walls. Teacher-created virtual networks are breaking down bureaucratic control over staff development and making it possible for any teacher to learn from successful colleagues without regard to physical boundaries, the clock on the classroom wall, or the budgetary decisions of the central office.

In most cases, this surge in teacher networking and student online learning is taking place outside the purview of school system decision makers and apart from the daily instructional life of the school. A 2008 report from the Forum on Education and Democracy said it well:

> The need for major transformation to create a 21st century learning system has been undermined by [an] inconsistent approach—one that has stimulated innovations on the margins, while maintaining a compliance-and-control regulatory approach that holds the bulk of the system in place, trapping most schools within the constraints of a factory model designed a century ago for another purpose.[7]

In 20 years, we imagine that a lot will have changed. It must.

"Imagineering" the Future:
Learning and Teaching in the Year 2030

In 2030, interactive media environments and immersive learning games have long since created students with a new profile of cognitive skills, requiring teachers to teach much differently.[8] Advances in cognitive science and human brain-scanning techniques have spawned new teaching methodologies that diagnose and remedy literacy difficulties in children and adults. Teachers, who are recruited for their diverse teaching skills and strategically prepared, help groups of students, in both virtual and brick-and-mortar venues, to mutually support each other's learning, promoting a high level of interaction and collaboration that is flexible, democratic, and person-centered.

Virtual tools and networking, just coming of age in the early years of the century, have now opened borderless learning territories for students of all ages, anytime and anywhere. The progressive education movement, which stalled in previous eras, is now fueled by networking technologies and open-source software. As a result, empowered well-prepared teachers routinely synthesize a multitude of Internet tools for teaching and learning—co-mingling text, images, audio, video, simulations, and games in ways reflective of how re-wired students develop and use knowledge. Ray Kurzweil's early 21st-century vision of brain cybernetics and nano-machines that would allow human users to vastly expand their cognitive abilities has proven prescient. Early on, Kurzweil helped launch multi-sensory tools so learners can access virtually any text or curriculum, including print, electronic, and web-based documents. Now, not only are students benefitting directly from such technologies, but many teacher-leaders have begun to use tools like "experience beaming"[9] to spread their teaching expertise more readily to fellow practitioners, underscoring the value of pedagogical experts in a society and an economy that rests on information science.

Indeed, in the year 2030, we can see that America's teaching profession has fully arrived, and once-beleaguered public schools are reaping the benefits of all students having access to talented, well-prepared, and highly supported educators. As a result, the structure of the profession looks very different than it did 2 decades ago, at the height of the dysfunctional debate over how to recruit and identify effective teachers and principals. The battle over the role of university-based teacher education and alternative certification—and the controversy over how to evaluate and reward teachers—has pretty much ended.

School districts are no longer faced with the dilemma of whether to search for traditional college-prepared teachers who will teach for a career or to pursue nontraditional candidates who enter with limited preservice education and choose to stay in the classroom for just a few years. They now do both—and care far less about the source of their teachers than the qualities they bring. School districts give careful attention to who is recruited, how much training the new teachers will require, and how they will be organized and supported to serve students and their school communities. In 2030, our nation's policymakers, think-tank analysts, and leaders of professional teacher guilds have figured out how to remove cumbersome state procedures that may inhibit talented individuals from entering teaching—while also avoiding preparation shortcuts that undermine a teacher's readiness to teach, especially in our highest needs schools. Universities, school districts, nonprofits and community-based organizations are working together to recruit and develop teachers for high-needs schools, which are still very much with us. But now high-needs schools, once routinely labeled as hard to staff, have become "easy-to-staff" learning environments.

In 2030, policymakers, administrators, and teacher unions are no longer arguing over whether to use standardized-test-score data to assess teaching effectiveness. In the mid 2010s, under new leadership from a collective of researchers and teacher-leaders, an ingenious array of student assessments were instituted that both drive instructional change and ensure public accountability.

New data and statistical tools—descendents of software concepts like the Quantified Self—and the pervasiveness of personal learning environment (PLE) strategies[10] have led the way for gathering, disseminating, and producing information among and by teachers—eroding long-standing walls between what students learn, how teachers teach, and how the public knows whether schools are improving. Idea marketplaces, inspired by early trendsetters like Teachers TV and Wireless Generation, have demolished the long-standing isolation of America's teachers and created endless opportunities for good teaching to be seen, critiqued, and emulated.

In 2030, Teaching Is Understood as Complex Work

For much of its occupational history, teaching was defined as "women's work," whereby females were primarily expected to nurture children while working for mostly male administrators at below-market wages.[11] As a result, teaching fell prey to a range of competing factors, interests, and ideals. Teachers were expected to be authoritarian with their students but always subservient to political, bureaucratic, and school managerial authorities on matters of policy and practice. While they were often admired for service to children, they bore the brunt of a widespread disdain for public education and were frequently belittled for their assumed lack of intellectual ability.

Teachers were so familiar and so visible, historian David Labaree observed, that what they knew seemed to be "all too common."[12] Having experienced teaching for years as public school students, many Americans concluded that patience and persistence, not professional knowledge, made for a great teacher. An old adage, attributed to H. L. Mencken, framed the public view of teaching for much of the 20th century: "Those who can, do. Those who can't, teach."

In 2030, teaching has come to be seen as complex professional work. In his prescient 2002 book *Smart Mobs*, virtual collaboration expert Howard Rheingold described how groups of people would soon use digital networking tools to "gain new forms of social power, new ways to organize their interactions and exchanges."[13] In the decades since, teachers have come to do just that. Using the latest connective technologies, they are identifying their most effective colleagues and capitalizing on a wide variety of virtual professional learning opportunities. In the first decade of this century, global social networking projects like Classroom 2.0, created by Web-entrepreneur Steve Hargadon, began to model the Internet's potential to bridge cultural and geographical divides and offered powerful examples of what people can do and learn without traditional organizational structures.[14] By 2010, pedagogical entrepreneurs were just beginning to demonstrate the power of web-based professional development to de-isolate teaching, visualize how good teachers teach, and offer cost-effective ways of spreading exemplary practices across a once-fractionated world of educators.

The fruits of those labors have been realized in 2030. About 15% of the nation's teachers—more than 600,000—have been prepared in customized residency programs designed to fully train them in the cognitive science of teaching and to also equip them for new leadership roles. Most now serve in hybrid positions as teacherpreneurs, teaching students part of the day or week, and also have dedicated time to lead as student support specialists, teacher educators, community organizers, and virtual mentors in teacher networks. Some spend part of their nonteaching time working closely with university- and think tank–based researchers on studies of teaching and learning—or conducting policy analyses that are grounded in their everyday pedagogical experiences. In some school districts, teachers in these hybrid roles earn salaries comparable to, if not higher than, the highest paid administrators.

These expert teacher-leaders, thanks in part to viral networking, have become well known to growing numbers of parents, business and community leaders, and policymakers. They are honored for their ability to use a wide array of instructional tools, built on brain research and neurological advances, to design personalized, learner-centered experiences and environments for the diverse students who still populate America's public schools. These teacherpreneurs will be identified by a dramatically different National Board Certification process that hones in on the "Goggled learner" and teaching in high-need schools.

These specially trained teacherpreneurs are groomed for a long career in teaching. As the leaders of their profession, they are expected to support and develop a wide array of classroom practitioners, many of whom may transition to other careers during their working life. Master teachers also work closely with content experts, online mentors, and teaching assistants who—with the right supervision—contribute significantly to a teaching and learning enterprise that extends beyond the conventional school day.

The once-vexing struggle to secure qualified and effective teachers for all of America's 65 million students has been resolved. No longer is the "teacher quality" debate focused solely on measuring the effectiveness of individual teachers in isolated classrooms. Doing so is necessary, but wholly insufficient. Most policymakers are equally interested in how teachers grow professionally and spread their knowledge to others. In 2030, education accountability systems place a premium on how teachers are strategically assembled as teams, both in their brick-and-mortar buildings and in virtual settings where they work with peers, mentors, and coaches. In 2030, curriculum and instruction drive accountability and results, not the other way around as has been the case for much of education's convoluted past.

Policymakers have, finally, rejected top-down social engineering strategies like No Child Left Behind that (however well intentioned) ultimately sapped initiative and stymied innovation. Instead, school accountability focuses on multiple measures of student learning that are in sync with the teacher knowledge and performances known to promote intellectual, social, and emotional growth. Accountability systems have also expanded their oversight to assess how effectively district administrators, nonprofits, community colleges, and universities support teachers and principals. In an extraordinary reversal of past top-down policy control, distributed reputation systems powered by the Web have created a "currency of trust" that allows teachers and other education stakeholders to hold policymakers more accountable for how well they govern and finance public education.[15]

In 2030, New Trust Remakes Teaching and Learning

In 2030, new levels of trust among key stakeholders and constituents have created new levels of cooperation. Consequently, the debilitating struggle among reformers, administrators, and unions over hiring, tenure, and merit-pay policies has all but vanished from the political scene. Teachers who have always worked in environments that promote collaboration and continuous improvement now lead their unions. They have evolved into something akin to professional guilds—leaving behind that part of their mission that once required them to fight for teachers to earn a decent middle-class living, work under reasonable conditions, and not be hired or fired on the basis of administrative whims. This has been possible because school boards and administrators—long tied to 20th-century industrial thinking—now accept teachers as knowledge workers in a 21st-century profession.

In 2030, school boards and administrators typically craft contracts with teachers for teaching in their physical buildings as well as in the virtual world, creating new ways to utilize and compensate teacher talent. Teachers can earn far more money than ever before, and many are in a position to negotiate their own personal services contracts with school districts and partnering learning agencies. With the support of their professional guilds, these teacherpreneurs are highly valued and well paid for their custom pedagogical expertise—not to enrich themselves at the expense of their colleagues, but to elevate the profession that makes all others possible.

New visions of the linchpin role of education and schools in America's future prosperity are providing teachers with numerous options for entrepreneurial activity. Some participate in the global trade in pedagogy. Others may choose to serve their local communities more deeply—bridging school, family, and neighborhood. Increasing numbers of teacher-leaders are recognized and rewarded for spearheading efforts to integrate social, academic, and health services in school buildings that now serve as 24/7 community centers, educating and supporting both children and adults. Drawing on decades of evidence from full-service intervention strategies like the Harlem Children's Zone, policymakers have embraced the need to connect academic improvement to a wide range of early childhood programs, parent training and engagement, and social and health services. Governmental budgets at the federal, state, and local levels are now connected—merging ideas, funds, people and initiatives across P–12 and higher education as well as social and health care sectors.

In 2030, the principal's job has become more doable. Policy makers have finally realized that public schools can no longer afford for their highly skilled principals and teacher leaders to perform routine administrative duties. Building managers are now more likely to handle the business of running schools, and governments have restructured finance formulas and organizational configurations so that staff and auxiliary personnel can carry out the many critical custodial tasks associated with public education. (Yes, in 2030, parents still need good and safe places for their children to learn while they work to earn a living.) Principals themselves are more engaged as leaders of teacher-leaders, because principals also teach students. They now are far more likely to be selected on the basis of their pedagogical expertise and ability to manage schools driven by teacher leadership. Indeed, in many places the word *principal* is no longer a noun, but an adjective describing the most effective teachers who are expected to lead their colleagues.

To earn a prestigious slot as the leader of a high-needs school, principals must successfully complete a 2-year residency and pass a rigorous performance assessment. Before they enter a residency program, principal candidates must demonstrate that they are highly effective teachers who can lead in a collaborative environment. Principals are rewarded, first and foremost, on the basis of how well they develop and utilize classroom teachers who have assumed hybrid roles as leaders of school improvement initiatives and community engagement efforts.

In 2030, the world of teaching offers bright, ambitious, and caring individuals an unparalleled opportunity to develop personally and professionally. Is this vision of the future overly speculative? We don't think so. In fact, absent the inevitable advances in technology over the next 20 years, most everything that needs to be done to realize this vision is being done now—somewhere in the world.

For example, in 2008, with great public fanfare, educator and successful business entrepreneur Zeke Vanderhoek launched a New York City charter school where some teachers are paid more than the principal. More teacher-leaders are also beginning to create their own "charter-like" schools—often in high-needs communities—where work rules and student achievement are not incompatible. Lori Nazareno, a National Board–certified teacher and charter member of the Teacher Leaders Network, has launched the Math and Science Leadership Academy (MSLA) with a number of colleagues in Denver—and with full support of the local union. MSLA is an entirely teacher-led school that promises to close the achievement gap through the use of technology tools, data-informed teaching practices, inquiry learning, parent engagement, and active student participation in the local community.[16] Other teachers, like Milwaukee's Roxie Hentz, have taken on much-needed roles as community organizers and developers of "future human capital." Hentz founded the successful afterschool program "Teen Approach" to help bridge school experiences and community life by engaging children ages 8 to 14 in programs "that build character and promote a healthy spirit, mind and body." These early efforts have inspired us to believe strongly that performance pay for teachers needs to promote the development of teacher activism in the service of students and not just on the results on any narrow band of academic achievement measures.

And what about teachers who are meeting students "wherever they are"? The evidence of accelerating educational connectivity across the globe is indisputable.

- Shannon C'de Baca, a member of our Teachers of 2030 writing team, is a winner of the prestigious Milken Award and host of the PBS series "The Missing Link in Mathematics." She not only teaches high school science online for the state-supported Iowa virtual school network, she also mentors novice teachers in Afghanistan and other eastern nations via the Web—all from her home near Los Alamos, New Mexico.
- Vicki Davis, a teacher and the IT director at Westwood Schools in Camilla, Georgia, has co-created, with teacher Julie Lindsay currently at Qatar Academy, three award-winning international wiki-centric projects, the Flat Classroom project, the Horizon project, and Digiteen. Their efforts have linked more than 500 students from both public and private schools in Australia, Austria, Bangladesh, China, Japan, Qatar, Spain, and the United States.
- In Westport, Connecticut, frustrated math teachers have abandoned the 1,000-page Algebra I textbook and created their own custom-designed online curriculum to help their students understand key topics in depth.[17] To increase student engagement, after designing the content they use an education service in India "to jazz up the algorithms and problem sets with animation and sounds."
- Through projects like the Global Challenge, Taking It Global, and Global SchoolNet, teachers who work with nonprofit entrepreneurs are offering online learning opportunities to underrepresented K–12 students throughout the world as they develop and propose solutions to complex social and economic problems from global warming to the future of energy.

These are a few examples of thousands of trailblazing efforts by Digital Age teachers who are not waiting for someone else to change the world. Teachers are also working in their own schools and districts to accelerate the 21st-century teaching and learning process. For example, at

High Tech High in San Diego (part of a network of California high school charters), teachers lead students to select an area of specialization (engineering, art and design, multimedia, etc.) and then employ technology to research issues and develop products that cut across subject matter disciplines. Senior projects—not standardized tests—provide a comprehensive approach to student and teacher accountability. The HTH network, now spanning grades K–12, is developing its own teacher preparation and credentialing program, because neither universities nor short-cut alternative certification approaches are meeting the schools' teacher-supply needs.

In other communities, school-university partnerships, often driven by the support of nonprofits, are creating urban teacher residencies (UTRs). These UTRs offer intensive, paid full-year internships designed to deeply prepare new recruits with the expectation that they will serve as long-term teachers and change agents for the challenging schools in which they are intentionally placed. In the early 21st century, both the Academy for Urban School Leadership (in Chicago) and the Boston Teacher Residency programs began to produce higher student achievement and more-stable teaching forces in their respective communities. Soon we will develop alternative, high-quality teacher residencies for our nation's rural schools—which are often neglected by our nation's policymakers.

Everywhere we look, we catch sight of powerful teaching and learning practices that can help transform our nation's public schools. That said, it is also true—and sadly so—that in the United States today, no state or school district has yet managed to assemble all the pieces of a 21st-century teacher development and leadership system. One key obstacle to achieving this goal is American society's seldom acknowledged "elephant in the schoolhouse"—the pervasive educational inequities that have, so far, undermined efforts to ensure that every student, every hour of the day, has access to qualified and effective teachers.

In 2030, Confronting Educational Inequities

We are not Pollyannas. Our vision and hopes for a fully realized teaching profession rest on policymakers finally confronting the shameful reality of our nation's long-standing system of educational haves and have-nots. Even in the public sector, money talks in America. Schools in communities with access to more resources can pay for better prepared and supported teachers, who in turn can teach more effectively. In some metropolitan areas, teachers can earn twice as much teaching in a prosperous suburban district than in a nearby high-needs urban one. In some states, new school districts are carved out of high-population counties specifically to take advantage of this fact. If many effective teachers choose a higher salary and better working conditions, who can blame them? They are certainly following cultural norms found in other helping professions.

No matter what definition we might use for a qualified teacher—certification, subject matter knowledge, college pedigree, pedagogical training, academic ability, or experience—there is research to document that less qualified teachers are more likely to be found in schools serving greater numbers of low-income and minority students.[18] It is also true that novice teachers and those with less preparation are more likely to be teaching in schools identified as "underperforming." In 2009, it was estimated that about 12% of America's high schools have become "dropout factories," accounting for 50% of the nation's students who do not graduate and are destined to be underemployed. Researchers at the Center for the Social Organization of Schools found that schools with high concentrations of minority students are overrepresented in that group—nearly 60% of high schools that enroll more than 90% African American or Hispanic students met the "dropout factory" criteria.[19]

Developing new measures for good teaching in the digital age and installing new systems of preparation and pay for those who teach are important. But it will take more than the smart use of technology—or even a ubiquitous network of highly effective teachers—to overcome the historical inequities that still plague our nation's public schools.

While educational equality serves as a bedrock of democracy, it has been illusive in America. The landmark 1954 *Brown v. Board of Education* decision reflected, in part, our nation's official recognition that state laws establishing separate public schools for Black and White students denied Black children equal educational opportunities. Even so, a decade after *Brown*, virtually all African American students in southern schools were still being taught in all-Black schools, and almost three-quarters of Black students in northern schools were still enrolled in predominantly minority schools.[20] Although the percentage of "minority" students in predominantly minority schools declined in the late 1960s and 1970s, that trend began to reverse in the 1980s and 1990s. By 2000, almost three-quarters of the nation's Black students were once again being taught in predominantly minority schools. As our TeacherSolutions 2030 colleague Renee Moore has noted, the culturally attuned Black teachers who served in segregated schools have been replaced by novices who often do not bring much understanding of the children they teach and do not remain long enough to get to know them well and teach them effectively. Today, minority students and children who live in poverty (especially in increasingly segregated charter schools) are most likely to be taught by new recruits who are White and middle-class. While many are imbued with energy and commitment, for the most part these novices have not been prepared to perform well in high-demand school environments and have had insufficient access to effective peers who could "positively influence academic learning."[21]

In one way or another, inequities in the opportunity to learn have existed for generations, begetting what Gloria Ladson-Billings has labeled an "educational debt."[22] Poor children and those of color have systematically been denied access, not just to effective teachers, but also to the best curriculum and facilities and to a quality of health care that advances learning at school and at home. More than 4 decades of research evidence has proven that out-of-school or "complementary learning" opportunities are powerful predictors of student achievement and overall social-emotional development.[23] Yet poor children and those of color are still much less likely to receive the comprehensive array of out-of-school supports they need.

Without adequate teaching, supports, and resources, students taught in high-poverty schools have lower achievement.[24] Why are we surprised to learn that many of these schools have become "dropout factories"? They are stark evidence of our society's frequent failure to do what it takes for every child to succeed. And while many choose to blame students or families for the problems in these schools, we now have research documenting that *even non-poor students* who attend high-poverty schools have lower achievement than their counterparts in low-poverty settings.[25] Plainly put, these are the schools that affluent America has been willing to ignore.

An early 21st-century census report estimated that 22% of U.S. children were living in poverty (50% higher than in the early 1970s),[26] and more than 3 million Americans were homeless, one-half of them children.[27] More than 46 million Americans lacked health insurance, with one in five children in poverty having no coverage whatsoever.[28] The economic recession of 2008 (which has continued for several years through the writing of this book) has created an even wider gulf between the "haves" and the "have-nots." By early 2010, media outlets were focused on a 9% unemployment rate, but few analysts noted the disparity between the 3.2% rate for high-income professionals and the almost 31% rate among those who typically earn less than $20,000 a year. "While there is now, finally, a great deal of talk among the politicians and in the news media about unemployment," *New York Times* columnist Bob Herbert wrote in February 2010, "there is still almost a willful refusal to focus on just who is suffering the most from joblessness and underemployment."[29] And under recession pressures, states are slashing child care budgets, forcing many low-income parents to unduly "reconcile the demands of work and parenting."[30]

Many families with fewer resources at home have little or no access to preventative health care. As a result, students from low-income families arrive at school far less ready to learn, both from a health and a developmental perspective. In their 2006 book, *A Vision for Universal Preschool Education*, Zigler, Gilliam, and Jones reported that 30 to 40% of children entering kindergarten do not have the social and emotional or language skills necessary to be successful in school.[31] Well-designed schools, strong principals who are instructional leaders, and effective teachers who have the right supports can help narrow these achievement gaps—and they have in some cases. But they cannot do it alone and, especially, not at the scale needed to turn around the estimated 30,000 schools currently identified as low performing.[32]

A 21st-century teaching profession will only make a meaningful difference in the lives of students if our nation's policymakers address a comprehensive set of reforms—in how schools are financed; how education, social services, and health care agencies work together; and how teachers are recruited, developed, rewarded, and retained. Action on this agenda is imperative. As our interconnected world gets smaller, our schools have even more challenges to meet. They must help students understand and work with culturally diverse people, across national boundaries, using tools and methods unimagined when their parents entered the workforce. If we as society, as Linda Darling-Hammond has so poignantly posed, do not get serious about the flat world and education,[33] then prosperity in the world of the future will be available to a much smaller number of Americans than we can even claim today.

Tipping Toward a 21st-Century Profession

The Year 2030 will be here in no time. And a great deal must change for teaching to emerge as a profession ready to meet the challenges of the mid-21st century. We are optimistic that it can.

The change we imagine and expect will not necessarily emerge in lockstep, linear fashion. Digital tools will certainly help spread pedagogical expertise in ways completely outside the experience of many teachers today. We expect that Web and wireless technologies will encourage more and more smart networking among teachers, promoting idea sharing, mentoring, and video-based critiquing of teaching practices. These phenomena will, to some degree, trump the archaic and rigid school structures that undermine efforts to elevate teacher expertise today.

But what we foresee will require more than another explosion of new technology and innovation. We imagine social change of a very high order, transforming a narrow conceptualization of teachers' work—one that has produced more than a century of claustrophobic teaching policy—into an absolute realization that teaching is a subtle and intricate profession that must be supported by an equally subtle and intricate policy approach.

As a team of forward-looking teachers, researchers, and advocates we are hopeful about the possibilities of a tipping point. Malcolm Gladwell has described how social epidemics can take hold quickly and unexpectedly, behaving in atypical and often counterintuitive ways.³⁴ In Gladwell's estimation, it does not take much of a *thing* to mushroom into *something* that has vast social consequences. One concept he postulates is the Law of the Few, where a limited number of talented and committed individuals can lead the way in taking an idea to scale—from small start-up to widespread movement. Another is how *salesmen* (charismatic individuals with powerful negotiation skills), *connectors* (who link people and ideas and span "different worlds"), and *mavens* (information specialists who broker ideas and actions) can spur innovation in short order. As change agents, foremost in our sights is the prospect of organizing a critical mass of teachers, parents, administrators, researchers, reformers, legislators, community leaders, nonprofit organizers, and students themselves around a reform agenda that will finally produce fundamental improvements in American teaching and learning.

Emergent Realities Shape the Teaching Profession of 2030

In our TeacherSolutions 2030 journey of research, discovery, debate, and learning we have grappled with a prodigious amount of evidence and numerous ideas. As we began the writing process, we first sorted out our assignments by topics critical to any profession—recruitment, preparation, induction, evaluation, continued professional growth, and, of course, compensation and career pathways. This approach ultimately proved to be too linear—too 20th century. After more consideration we landed on the concept of *emergent realities* as an organizing framework.

We chose *emergent* because the future of education is *already being shaped* by the rapid escalation of global communications, economic and demographic realignment, and technological innovation. The trendlines are visible, and the prerequisites for transformation are already beginning to surface in dynamic schools and classrooms and among dedicated professionals throughout the nation. We added *realities* because we are not dealing in fantasy or utopian thinking, but *building on ideas and ideals that are already influencing public education and student learning opportunities*—both here and abroad. In fact, we are sanguine about the future of teaching and learning, especially given the powerful systems of teacher development already in place worldwide (e.g., in Singapore and Finland) and the role classroom experts play as leaders in some international education systems known for "teaching less, testing less, and learning more."³⁵

Those of us who teach children, tweens, and teens on a daily basis experience their enormous collective potential and remain hopeful about public education's prospects. But we are not gazing at the future through magical or rose-colored glasses. Among the realities that cast shadows on the future is the devastating economic recession, which is sapping the forward momentum of many school districts. America's financial meltdown and subsequent state and local budget slashing has also had a disquieting effect on teachers' morale and their capacity to teach effectively. The negative impacts of larger class sizes and more out-of-field teaching assignments are magnified by increasingly mobile students who move from school to school as their parents search for new or better employment and affordable housing. These conditions—class sizes that jump from 25 to 45; having to teach subjects for which one is not prepared; more and more transient students—can severely limit the readiness of many schools to help all students meet achievement markers. These same conditions have not, generally speaking, limited the willingness of many policymakers and pundits to blame teachers when test scores lag. Indeed the mass media, fueled by the blogosphere and ideologically driven think tanks, has frequently identified teachers as the *chief cause* of public education's problems, with little thought given to tapping into classroom experts as a source of solutions.

Despite this current context, we see the real possibility of a brighter path ahead. As we have examined societal trends and considered the most robust ways in which education could respond to likely future events, we've shaped our thinking around four emergent realities:

Emergent Reality #1 focuses on students and a more personalized system of learning necessary for them to develop and use skills demanded by both the global economy and the need to sustain a democratic way of life in a world increasingly controlled by technology. It foresees *a transformed learning ecology for students and teachers* whereby digital tools provide a surfeit of choices for instant and accessible information, communication, and self-expression. While these tools will change the way students learn and teachers teach and can bridge old divides over the purposes of schooling, they will not go to scale without a transformed school-accountability system that promotes powerful professionalism and a culture of joint responsibility among teachers, administrators, parents, and policymakers as well as students.

Emergent Reality #2 foresees *seamless connections in and out of cyberspace* where virtual collaboration and new technologies expand learning opportunities beyond geographical limits and the traditional 8 a.m. to 3 p.m.

school day. The Internet's infinite capacity for connectivity is exploding the millennia-old–single-teacher paradigm. By 2030, the outdated concept of bells and block schedules will have morphed into dynamic study groups. Integrated courses will be the norm, and expert teachers will engage students in interactive global learning communities using 3D Web environments, augmented reality, and mobile devices that we can only begin to imagine today. At the same time, and perhaps counterintuitively, our unstable economy and the spread of volatile, uncertain, complex, and ambiguous (VUCA) communities[36] will push the brick-and-mortar school to become even more important in the future of many communities. Many educators will assume more-diversified roles and their teaching will connect more directly to the hub of the community and the comprehensive services some students and their families will need.

Emergent Reality #3 foresees *differentiated professional pathways* along which teachers develop specialized skills and work in flexible roles that contribute to the educational enterprise. We imagine a profession built on the concept of hybridization, with many expert teacher-leaders who are specially prepared and paid as change agents, both working closely with students and playing other roles that advance learning. Teachers with different capabilities will join in collaborative teams to maximize the strengths of their respective (and diverse) preparation, experience, and knowledge as they teach in both in brick-and-mortar and online settings. And as the labor market becomes more complex, in general, the teaching profession of 2030 will promote the idea that talented individuals can enter, advance in, exit, and re-enter via multiple paths. At the same time, teaching will continue to have an ample core group of highly effective, career teachers who guarantee quality and stability by serving in a variety of leadership roles.

Emergent Reality #4 foresees the evolution of *teacherpreneurism and a future of innovation.* Teaching will become an adaptive profession that empowers and rewards members who develop their pedagogical talent, spread and "sell" their expertise, and find innovative solutions to the challenges their students face. The concept of "teacherpreneurism" is not primarily about making more money (although we find little reason to deny expert teachers the opportunity to participate in the marketplace, so long as their activities serve the best interest of students). Coining the term *teacherpreneurism* is our way of distinguishing between the current "education entrepreneur" (who may chalk up a year or 2 of teaching experience before entering the school reform marketplace) and the concept of deeply expert professionals applying their know-how and creativity to drive the schools of the future.

Many of the building blocks for what we imagine and seek to create can be found scattered throughout the population of teachers and schools. But how does America begin to take its 21st-century learning systems to scale? In this book, we pinpoint several critical *policy levers of change*—or catalysts for a new reform framework—that will have to be engineered if our vision of the profession's future is to be achieved a mere 20 years from now. Fully engaging these change levers will require steady work and some serious heavy lifting on the part of union leaders and administrators, parents and students, business leaders and policymakers—and the hundreds of thousands of teacher-leaders.

In closing, we lay out specific action steps that need to be taken in order for a teaching profession, worthy of the new millennium, to be realized. But before we describe in some detail our emergent realities, powerful policy levers for change, and the kinds of actions policymakers, practitioners, and the public must take, we turn to a brief overview of teaching's past, serving as a prologue to 2030. One cannot carve out the best path to the future without fully knowing the roads traveled in the past. But we hope our readers will never lose this thought: This important work cannot be done unless our nation's most effective teachers today are heard, understood, and embraced.

CHAPTER 2

A Very Brief History of Teaching in America

Why revisit the past in a book about the future of the teaching? Because we won't know how to get where we need to go until we understand where we've been.

Bookshelves are filled with historical accounts of America's teaching profession. They tell a stormy and convoluted story, documenting more than a century of struggle to determine who will teach what and how, under what conditions, and at what cost. Since the late 19th century, teaching in America has evolved from a short-term occupation for unmarried women who earned very little, into a career for those who are satisfied with stable, middle-class incomes and pensions that guarantee retirement without falling into poverty. Teaching's complicated history includes long-standing control by laypersons, a lack of clarity and rigor in becoming a teacher, and limited prestige and income—restricting the professional possibilities of its members.[1] As a result, the best teachers have struggled to stave off administrative and political demands for them to teach as they are told.

In the modern era, teacher unions have sought to better control conditions that might undermine their members' ability to perform their jobs effectively. Collective bargaining, which only took root in the early 1960s, set a standard for defining teachers' economic interests along industrial union lines. For more than a half-century, that industrial standard has provided equity and security, but it has not significantly advanced the status of teachers in terms of their being recognized and rewarded as experts about learning. Sociologist Dan Lortie pointed out almost 4 decades ago that teaching's egg-crate structure historically has isolated teachers from their colleagues and reinforced an egalitarian culture in which everyone tries *not* to stand out.[2] Teachers have not been expected or encouraged to be superstars or experts but, rather, average faces in the crowd.

When schools have come under pressure to produce better student test scores, administrators have expected teachers to teach in more predictable and routine ways to ensure tangible results in short order. In times of shortage, policymakers have filled classrooms with underprepared teachers, exacerbating the need to follow a scripted curriculum and solidifying the image of teaching as *work on the margins*, too uncomplicated to justify well-paid professionals.

Perhaps most important, teaching's standing in American society has been delimited by its sheer conspicuousness. As David Labaree has noted, teachers are "way too familiar and too visible, and what they know seems to be all too common."[3] The vast majority of Americans have attended public schools and have observed at least 12 years of classroom teaching—creating in many a false sense of expertise about the work teachers do. Very few of us are exposed so persistently to the professional practice of doctors, engineers, lawyers, nurses, or architects as we are to teachers.

In many Americans, familiarity with the occupation of teaching breeds a perplexing mix of affection and contempt. Teachers are often admired by parents for their service, but just as often take the brunt of deep disdain when public education is being criticized. And while they are typically appreciated for working with "the next generation," teachers are frequently mocked for their assumed lack of intellectual prowess and their perceived inability to compete in the larger labor market. In sum, our nation has held complicated and contradictory views of the occupation of teaching for most of its history—perhaps a reflection of America's long-standing biases against those who serve children as opposed to those who serve adult enterprises.

Horace Mann created the first normal school to formally prepare teachers in the mid-1800s. In the many years since, teachers have seen their salaries and working conditions improve, and they are better educated than ever before. Yet policymakers—who control decisions about who enters teaching and how teachers are developed and rewarded—have never made the substantial political and financial investments necessary to fully professionalize teaching. As a result, at a time when technology and global connectivity are transforming society, the inner-workings of a teacher's job haven't changed much at all.

Here is how that came to be.

From Women's Work to Industrial Age Automatons

The history of today's public school teacher traces back to Colonial times when community leaders turned to pious individuals who would ensure that our nation's youth could read the *Good Book*. As the occupation of teaching began to take shape in America, "teachers were chosen not for any instructional skills, but for their religious background, moral character, and political affinity with the family or community that hired them."[4]

Up until the mid-1800s, most teachers were young white men who were expected to teach for a few years, often as they prepared for careers as ministers or lawyers. Teaching was "transient" work, given that it was seasonal and paid very little. As the industrial age emerged and higher education expanded, new career paths for men developed, and women began filling the ranks of teaching. Feminine dispositions seemed more in sync with the new expectation that students needed nurturing as well as salvation. In fact, some historical accounts claim that teaching was a substitute for marriage, and in most cases, one of the best female employment opportunities.[5] If a woman did not choose to teach, her alternatives typically were becoming a domestic servant or mill worker. The "feminization of teaching" took hold, and by the early 20th century, almost four out of five teachers were women.[6] And since the time when women began to dominate the teaching workforce some 150 years ago, the occupation's "image, status, and desirability" has been suspect in American society.[7]

Other historical trends have shaped teaching's past and current status. Teachers often came from provincial and working-class backgrounds. Only in the 1950s and 1960s did most states actually require elementary teachers to earn a college degree—and many who did were the first children in their families to attend and graduate from college.[8] Few were selected for their intellectual attributes. Teaching students basic skills was thought to be something many adults could do, and if some were better at it than others, that "was more a matter of innate talent than of training."[9] Perhaps this is why the popular adage "Teachers are born, not made" has endured—undermining efforts to compel serious investments in teacher education.

As industrial and business employment became commonplace, the custodial responsibilities of schools grew and the occupation was labeled as "women's work" or "social housekeeping."[10] Scholars have long traced the connections between a female teaching workforce and the top-down mandates of male administrators determined to control the curriculum and "keep women in their place."[11] Female teachers were expected to move in and out of teaching as they established their own households and focused on rearing their own children.

The common-school movement of the mid- to late-1800s increasingly focused on systematizing public education. Age-grading and a rigid course of study framed teaching as the public schools began to serve an increasingly diverse set of immigrant children. Teaching and learning became "preeminently fitted to deaden the soul and convert human beings into automatons,"[12] and teachers themselves were expected to function like factory hands.[13]

As demands on teachers mounted, so did the stress of their jobs. Yet the National Education Association (NEA), founded in the mid-19th century, initially organized only male education leaders, primarily superintendents and college professors. In the early 1900s when classroom activist Margaret Haley led a demonstration on teachers' economic conditions at a NEA national convention, she was viewed as an "unwelcome guest."[14] Under Haley's leadership, teachers began to call attention not only to low and inequitable salaries but also overcrowded classrooms, overwhelming workloads, and rigid rules for how teachers were expected to teach. In 1921, Denver and Des Moines were the first cities to offer single salary schedules so that teachers would no longer be paid on the basis of gender, administrative caprice, or unreliable merit pay measures but on academic preparation and years of experience.

Thorndike Beats Dewey in the Early Struggle

In the mid-1800s, many high schools created "normal" departments to train teachers for the common schools, where growing numbers of children were being prepared to work in America's industrializing economy. Horace Mann, then secretary of the Massachusetts Board of Public Schools, believed that more formal teacher education was key to more efficient and effective public schooling. In 1839, the first state-supported normal school opened in Massachusetts. By 1870, 40 state normal schools were operating across the nation.

In another prelude to today's policy debates, the Horace Mann–inspired normal schools were thought by some to waste too much time on teacher preparation. Some local education agencies created teacher institutes, which offered a truncated way to prepare teachers. The curriculum varied widely, most notably covering the subject matter taught in the local schools and "a few lectures on principles and methods of good teaching given by successful teachers." The institutes were a much less expensive way to train teachers and for the most part "respond(ed) to the practical exigencies of rural life."[15] Angus and Mirel tell us that "professional educators despised these institutes," in part, because "they threatened the image of professionalism that the educators were attempting to promote for teaching." We see a similar situation today in the struggle over the merits of university-based teacher education versus shortcut alternative-certification programs.

By the early 1920s, about 25% of the nation's primary school teachers had yet to earn a high school diploma, while fewer than half had completed 2 years of college.[16] It was around this same time that teaching's split personality began to show. Progressive educators, who drew on intellectuals such as John Dewey, tried to "usurp teacher-centered schooling in favor of experiential learning."[17] University lab schools became hotbeds of progressive ideas. Teachers were expected not just to deliver information but to guide students' opportunities to explore, discover, construct, and create knowledge, appealing to their unique interests and abilities and large capacity for learning.

But during the same time period, Fredrick Taylor's theories of scientific management exerted even more control over the public classroom. Taylor, an efficiency expert whose ideas were used to jump-start output in American factories, led many educators to treat students like assembly-line workers. John Franklin Bobbitt, a traditional educationist who drew upon Taylor's theories, maintained that student learning should be managed like production goals in a steel mill, such as, "add[ing] at a speed of 65 combinations per minute, with an accuracy of 94%."[18]

These rigid theories of learning were intensified by Edward Thorndike, who in the early- to mid-20th century laid the scientific foundations for modern educational psychology. Thorndike believed that students were limited in what they could learn, and that learning was incremental and linear. He took a narrow view of student achievement, with school outcomes focused on results of standardized tests. Education's cult of efficiency quickly took hold[19]—further bolstered by the work of IQ-test creator, Lewis Terman, and the growing popularity of instruments designed to sort and label students on the basis of their "native" intelligence.[20]

In the 1930s, researcher and reformer Ralph Tyler led the well-documented Eight-Year Study, which found that students from "Dewey-like" progressive schools, compared to their counterparts in Thorndike-like traditional schools, fared far better academically and socially over time. Teachers in the progressive schools were better prepared, and they were far more creative in their teaching.[21] However, the landmark study[22]—still cited today—had little long-term systemic impact.

World War II depleted the ranks of qualified teachers even further, and district administrators were able to downgrade hiring standards in order to fill classrooms. As late as the 1950s, about 50% of the nation's teachers still did not possess a 4-year college degree[23]—in part because policymakers and administrators worried that if job qualifications were raised, higher salary costs would follow.

Weak preparatory programs, rather than testing, became the basis for credentialing.[24] In 1954, the National Council for the Accreditation of Teacher Education (NCATE) was established to address the "hodgepodge" of training programs that were proliferating across the country, with the expectation that all programs would come to meet common standards.[25] However, the NCATE process to this day has remained voluntary for the nation's colleges and universities that prepare teachers. As a consequence, since *all* institutions of higher education do not have to be held accountable to the common standards, NCATE historically has not achieved its potential as one of several powerful quality-control tools needed to advance teaching as a full profession.

In 1957, the Russians launched *Sputnik*—which quickly became a symbol of America's weakening position in science and technology, as well as education. *Sputnik* was seen as a threat to the nation's military superiority and to political freedom. The resulting near-hysteria provided an opportunity for school reformers to "bang the drum" for more investments in both education programs and new approaches to teaching and learning.[26] One year later Congress approved $1 billion for the National Defense Education Act (NDEA). An array of programs ensued to replace textbook teaching (especially in math and science) and promote a more activity-oriented pedagogy whereby students would not just memorize facts but learn the structures and procedures of the subject matter discipline.

NDEA also spurred new investments in public school teachers, with federal funding for college scholarships to recruit teachers into high-need fields and fellowships for prospective teacher educators who would prepare new recruits for public school teaching. But just as before, the aspiration for a more-ambitious pedagogy soon waned as talented individuals proved difficult to recruit, preparation and support did not keep up with the curricular demands, and more-traditional educators and policymakers fought off attempts to weaken scientific management's stranglehold on teaching and learning.

As historian Ellen Condliffe Lagemann has noted: "One cannot understand the history of education [and the teaching profession] in the United States during the 20th century unless one realizes that Edward Thorndike won and John Dewey lost."

"The Great Society" Looks to Teaching for Answers

The pendulum of school reform—and efforts to professionalize teaching —continued to swing back and forth in the next decades. President Kennedy's vision for America (and the sympathy for his ideas after his assassination in 1963) translated into a wave of social reforms, including not just the Civil Rights Act of 1964 but also new investments to improve life in urban America, combat poverty, and upgrade education. With the *Brown* Supreme Court decision of 1954 as a legal rationale to end school segregation and inherent inequities in educating our nation's minority students, President Johnson's plan for "the Great Society" included a spate of federal interventions aimed at public schools and the teaching profession. In

1965, the Elementary and Secondary Education Act supplied the first federal dollars for precollegiate education with a laser focus on high-poverty schools. The Higher Education Act provided new funding programs to prepare teachers for such schools—most notably the Teacher Corps.

Launched in 1966, the Teacher Corps borrowed from the Peace Corps model, placing idealistic young college graduates into urban (and some rural) schools. Many of the new recruits came from elite universities and also brought cultural experiences quite different from the students they were serving. With only 2 months of training, teams of interns, supported by a master teacher, taught in high-poverty settings while working toward certification and an advanced degree in education. The Corps members were expected to not only teach but also work in the surrounding community. Over its lifespan, the program grew to include more than 100 universities and 250 school districts. The Corps members frequently clashed with education-school professors whose theories and methods did not match up well with the challenges faced by students in high-poverty communities.[27] While a large number of these idealistic young adults stayed in teaching, many became "disillusioned" and "regressed" to teacher-centered instruction.[28] They never became the teacher change-agents the ambitious reforms required.

During the same time period, new research findings began to undermine efforts to invest in teaching as a means to improve society. In 1966, sociologist James Coleman released his influential report, *Equality of Educational Opportunity*, suggesting that school funding and other inputs like teacher quality had little effect on student achievement.[29] His analysis suggests that socioeconomic class and family background mattered much more, raising serious questions in the minds of policymakers about the likely return on investments in teaching and learning.

Later analyses revealed that Coleman's statistical models did not account for the strong correlations between students' backgrounds and their schools' resources, thereby making it difficult to detect an independent effect of schooling (and teacher quality) on achievement.[30] In fact, a reanalysis of the original data set used by Coleman and his colleagues found that going to a high-poverty school, or a highly segregated African American school, had a profound effect on achievement outcomes *irrespective* of an individual student's poverty or minority status.[31] At the time, however, Coleman's report, with its "no effects" finding, created huge policy ripples and gave fuel to critics of public education and the teaching profession who were already promoting the idea that schools and teachers had little effect on student achievement. The impact of this report on subsequent events in American education cannot be underestimated, and its legacy remains today.

The Civil Rights Movement continued to focus on ending inequities in the ways White and Black (and, later, Latino) students were taught. However, few public policies were ever put into place to ensure that all students would have experienced and qualified teachers, including in America's most impoverished districts. And while researchers in the 1980s began to point to some characteristics of effective schools that were able to close the achievement gap, most of their attention was given to the role of principals, not teachers, in paving the way to success.[32]

Unions Ascend as Teaching Pressures Mount

As some researchers and policymakers questioned the role that schools and teachers could play in overcoming the ill-effects of poverty on student achievement, teacher unions were beginning to mobilize and take action at unprecedented levels.[33] After being in business for a half-century, the unions turned more militant, taking cues from blue-collar counterparts in other industries. In 1962 about one-half of New York City teachers, under the leadership of early organizers like Albert Shanker, went on strike.

Shanker, longtime head of the United Federation of Teachers (UFT) in New York City (1964–1986) and the American Federation of Teachers (AFT) nationally (1974–1997), has been called by some the George Washington of the teaching profession. He believed that teachers should firmly establish and enforce standards among their ranks.[34] However, as the son of a seamstress active in the International Ladies Garment Workers Union, Shanker was also motivated to organize teachers in response to low salaries, autocratic administrators, and working conditions that undermined the profession and the capacity to serve students and families effectively.[35]

Since the 1960s, union leaders and administrators have engaged in industrial-style, adversarial collective bargaining, resulting in periodic labor-management tensions but also standardized work rules. Collective bargaining worked well for union leaders who wanted equal treatment of teachers who had varying degrees of skill and marketability—and for administrators who sought uniform rules for their growing school-bureaucracies. For a host of economic and political reasons, modern teacher unions have shaped their bargaining efforts around the concept of teachers as industrial or craft workers, not as professionals who have established high standards for membership.[36] While organized teachers did not trust administrators to evaluate them fairly, they also wanted "no part of judging their fellow union members."[37] Doing so would break up their solidarity. And it suited many administrators for teachers to remain in a subservient position to them, with top-down evaluation ensuring that the "hired hands" would ultimately be held in check.[38]

Unions have often been characterized as focusing on adult issues and not on the needs of students. However, even in the early, most militant days, the unions sought to change conditions that undermined members' ability to teach effectively. As long ago as the early 1960s, union leaders were arguing that certain school conditions were demoralizing to teachers. They pointed to non-teaching chores, inadequate textbook supplies, and rote lesson plans prepared for visiting administrators as extra burdens that could easily be eliminated. It was clear, of course, that school administrators did not want teachers to act like independent-minded and autonomous university faculty. They wanted employees to do what they were told without debate—an attitude that, over time, generated more and more support among teachers for union representation.

By 1975, about 22% of all public school teachers were covered by collective-bargaining agreements,[39] and 241 teacher strikes took place nationwide.[40] Researchers cite several reasons why collective bargaining began to grow in the 1970s, including escalating inflation that eroded teachers' salaries, burgeoning school bureaucracies that weakened teachers' decision making, and changing social conditions that made teaching a more challenging job.[41]

While in its early years the NEA was very reluctant to engage in collective bargaining, it ultimately had to do so in order to compete with the AFT for members. The competing unions began fighting over representation—further splintering an already fragmented semiprofession. By 1980, the percentage of teachers under collective-bargaining agreements grew to 45%, then to 60% by the mid-1980s.[42] (In the early 21st century, unions represent about two-thirds of the nation's more than 3 million teachers, a percentage that has been stable for some time now.)

Angus and Mirel have claimed that rising "teacher militancy and aggressiveness" began to trump the professional-standards movement during this period.[43] From the union perspective, there was ample reason to fight for workplace prerogatives like tenure—which was often bargained in order to make a low-paying career more job-secure, as well as to "protect teachers from the whims of autocratic principals and patronage allocating administrators."[44]

In 1970, fewer than 27% of the American people believed that the teacher unions had too much power.[45] That outlook has shifted over the decades since, as the popular press increasingly cast teacher unions as willing to protect members at the expense of a much-needed focus on student achievement. One analyst noted in 1999, "Many Americans [became] uncomfortable with militant, striking teachers, and remain so today, eroding public sympathy for teachers."[46] In recent years, researchers have noted that unions are generally portrayed as "stand(ing) in the way of reforms needed to attract new teachers, compete successfully with charter schools, and meet state and federal accountability demands."[47]

Critics of public schooling often associate the collective action of unions with ongoing efforts to professionalize teaching and give more voice about instruction to millions of classroom teachers.[48] That is a gross and sometimes deliberate oversimplification. As a new generation of teachers emerges—one without trade unionist roots—current union officials often find themselves struggling to lead a membership that is "divided along generational lines." While millions of union members cannot be easily sorted into just two camps, researchers are finding that many older veterans still put "basic" job protections first while many new millennium members are looking for opportunities to "grow as a professional" and wonder why poor teachers are protected.[49]

While recent polls show that Americans have unfavorable opinions of teachers' unions, they hold teachers themselves in high regard,[50] do not support the privatization of public schooling,[51] and say they are willing to invest more in teaching as a profession.[52] But public opinion often does not figure into the debates over education, particularly those related to the teaching profession.

Professionalism Versus Deregulation in the Late 20th Century

As unions were beginning to make more of a mark on school policy in the early 1980s, the National Commission on Excellence in Education, working under the auspices of President Reagan, issued a landmark report criticizing the public schools—and, in particular, university preparation programs, the academic ability of the recruits they trained, and how teachers were paid.[53]

A Nation at Risk, released in 1983, repeated the clarion call to arms first heard after *Sputnik* and with even stronger language. The Commission suggested that "if an unfriendly foreign power had attempted to impose on America the mediocre educational performance that exists today, we might well have viewed it as an act of war." The report called for less pedagogical preparation (and more subject matter coursework for prospective teachers) as well as merit pay that would financially reward individual teachers for improving test score performance. The report also called for dismantling the by now sacrosanct single-salary schedule for teachers, based on credentials and experience, which ensured uniformity and reinforced the egalitarian culture of teaching. The Commission's recommendations about merit-based compensation were intended to raise the ire of teacher unions, and they did. Over the next several years, states intensified efforts to measure schools and teachers, using standardized tests, and to implement a new generation of merit-pay plans.

In the mid-1980s, like earlier, teachers were seen as a problem to be fixed—not as a source of solutions to what ailed public education. No doubt the criticism of teachers contributed to a 71% decline in the proportion of freshmen planning to pursue elementary or secondary teaching careers—from 21.7% in 1966 to 6.2% in 1985.[54] While some part of the decline certainly had to do with the opening of a larger labor market for women and minorities, other factors were in play—including runaway inflation in the 1970s that cut deeply into teachers' capacity to make a decent living and, in the 1980s, teacher bashing at unprecedented levels.

The education community responded to *A Nation at Risk* with rhetoric of its own and ideas about how to improve teaching and teacher education. In 1986, Carnegie Corporation of New York released *A Nation Prepared: Teachers for the 21st Century*, which recognized the important public school challenges to be overcome but also pushed on the idea that teachers were more the solution than the problem. *A Nation Prepared* called for more rigor in teacher education and also for the establishment of a National Board for Professional Teaching Standards (NBPTS), mirroring both the substance and credentialing procedures of more-established professions like medicine and architecture. Carnegie also called on schools to be restructured so that those teachers who passed muster on advanced certification exams would have opportunities to lead their colleagues and earn salaries (at least for the most accomplished practitioners) that were competitive and on par with other professionals.

In 1987, the National Board for Professional Teaching Standards was created, fueled by support from Carnegie, other foundations, businesses, and the federal government. After years of development, in 1993–1994 the NBPTS offered and granted its first advanced certification, using "state-of-the-art" assessment tools that "go far beyond multiple choice examinations" used by many states and "take into account the accumulated wisdom of teachers."[55] The assessments, designed for 24 different subjects and student grade levels, were built from content-specific and student-development-specific teaching standards, mirroring the rigors of an Architect Registration Examination. As the new system rolled out, it became possible in many states and districts for National Board–certified teachers (NBCTs) to earn substantially more salary (as much as 12% in North Carolina), albeit not on par with other professionals. Teachers who seek national board certification almost uniformly voice that the process is the best professional development they have ever experienced. This sentiment holds for teachers who certify as well as those who do not.[56]

In the late 1980s, the Holmes Group, an alliance of education school deans, responded to criticisms of preservice programs with its own reform agenda, revealed in a trilogy of reports published over a 9-year period. These reports called for teachers to be prepared inside of K–12 schools and for university faculty to be rewarded for helping them do so. But the reforms were driven more by the needs of universities, not school district partners, and as a result little changed.

In 1996, the National Commission on Teaching & America's Future (NCTAF)—a blue-ribbon panel of policymakers, business and civic leaders, top teacher-union officials, accomplished teachers, and other key education stakeholders—issued a major report that galvanized national attention around the importance of teachers in raising student achievement. Chaired by then-governor James B. Hunt of North Carolina (also the founding chair of the NBPTS) and led by education scholar Linda Darling-Hammond, NCTAF assembled new evidence on the teaching quality and student learning debate, pointed clearly to promising policies and practices, and assembled state and local partners to begin putting together a comprehensive approach to teacher development.

The report, *What Matters Most: Teaching for America's Future*, proposed five interlocking recommendations: (1) getting serious about standards for both students and teachers by creating performance-based systems of teacher licensing and advanced certification; (2) reinventing teacher preparation and professional development by creating extended preparation programs and results-oriented–education-program accreditation; (3) fixing teacher recruitment by streamlining hiring procedures, eliminating barriers to mobility, providing incentives for teaching in shortage areas and fields, and creating high-quality pathways into teaching for mid-career entrants; (4) encouraging and rewarding teacher knowledge and skills by creating evaluation and compensation systems that reward expert teachers, removing incompetent teachers (through peer review), and allowing teachers to share their skills without leaving the classroom; and (5) creating schools that are organized for student and teacher success by flattening hierarchies, reallocating resources to teaching, and redesigning roles.[57]

These were not necessarily novel ideas—but nowhere before had such a compelling and coherent narrative been constructed. Within months of the release of the report, 12 states had agreed to join in the NCTAF partnership to implement its policy recommendations. Several more followed. As the 20th century drew to a close, American teacher professionalism—at long last—seemed to be on the rise.

However, much like other reforms, the NCTAF movement ultimately stalled—in part due to the departure of Darling-Hammond in 2002, which left the organization without its charismatic founder at a time when the federal No Child Left Behind legislation was beginning to take education-reform's center stage. The lack of major progress on NCTAF's ambitious agenda left the cause of teacher professionalism in a vulnerable state, with pushback from several quarters. This included unions that had a vested interest in protecting long-standing work rules and conservative education think tanks that sought to ensure schools would be staffed with less expensive and compliant teachers.

As the 21st century dawned, the new school reform priorities of President George W. Bush and other strong supporters of the No Child Left Behind Act of 2002 slowed efforts to professionalize teaching, while also spotlighting problems in the teacher supply system. NCLB helped raised public awareness of the achievement gap as well as unequal distribution of qualified teachers. However, the NCLB testing regime brought on more lockstep teaching and learning (as advanced by Thorndike, not Dewey) in schools. And NCLB did not erase the outmoded policies that continued to leave millions of students underserved. Funding also proved problematic when much of the new federal teacher-quality dollars were used to back-fill shrinking state and local budgets.[58]

As implemented, the law's Highly Qualified Teacher (HQT) provision proved to be more of a low bar for states to clear than a lofty goal to achieve. Focused more on content background than high across-the-board teaching standards, the HQT rules actually opened the gates for alternative certification, allowing new recruits to enter with little professional training. As a result, the number of fast-track teachers going into the nation's most challenging classrooms increased dramatically, as district administrators struggled with growing teacher shortages and rapid staff turnover in high-needs schools.

Six years after the passage of NCLB, there was only limited evidence that low-income and minority students had any greater access to highly qualified teachers.[59] An Education Trust report, released in 2008, revealed that nationwide about 40% of all core subject area classes in high-poverty, high-minority middle schools were staffed by out-of-field teachers.[60] But even an in-field teacher may not have the pedagogical skills to teach—especially given the growing numbers of special needs and second language learners filling America's classrooms. While the Bush administration was promoting the idea that a teacher's content knowledge, not pedagogical training from a university, was what mattered for student achievement, somewhere between 10% and 20% of the nation's public school students had identified learning-differences and another 15% did not speak English as their primary language.[61]

Many Bush administration policy supporters also argued that teachers needed to be freed from onerous rules developed through school district and teacher union collective bargaining. During the early 2000s, charter schools, which did not have to hire certified teachers or adhere to specific working conditions (like the number of hours a teacher was expected to work a day), grew in importance to policymakers who sought to break up the perceived monopolistic practices of university-based teacher education programs and unions. Despite the absence of any convincing evidence that teachers in private or charter schools outperformed public school teachers, opponents of strong teacher organizations saw a "free market" for teacher labor as the surest way to end the tenuous controls teacher unions still exert over salary and working conditions. It was also a way to redirect resources that were being expended in order to certify teachers, including investments in advanced credentialing programs like the National Board for Professional Teaching Standards. Former assistant secretary of education Chester Finn, advocating from his post as president of the Thomas B. Fordham Institute, argued that states should insist teachers possess subject knowledge before they enter teaching and not much else—and then "hold schools accountable for their results, with teacher performance judged by what students learn."[62]

Finn and his allies, including many free-market economists, had their effect. Alternative certification efforts began to pick up steam— promoting the idea that capable college graduates, with only a few weeks of pedagogical training, could become successful public school teachers—even for those students in schools characterized by high poverty. One of the most well-known alternative-route programs, Teach for America (TFA), was initially launched in the early 1990s. By early 2010, TFA was placing over 4,000 bright, young recruits annually for 2-year teaching stints in some of the nation's highest needs schools—locales that traditional teacher-education graduates tended to avoid. Researchers continue to debate the extent to which TFA recruits, when compared to their more traditionally prepared counterparts, produce higher achievement gains.[63] But the organization has definitively put much-needed heat on university-based teacher education schools to change their recruitment and placement strategies. In effect, TFA has challenged traditional programs to demonstrate that they can produce graduates who are both willing and fully prepared to meet the needs of students in high-poverty schools.

While TFA is the most high-profile supplier of new teachers who enter the classroom through nontraditional routes, many more alternative training programs emerged in the early 21st century. In 2009, a total of about 62,000 teachers enrolled in nearly 600 alternative programs. Most of these recruits were trained for a few weeks before assuming full classroom teaching duties and were expected to eventually earn full certification by taking courses in the evening after the workday.[64] In most instances, that education coursework focused solely on classroom management and how to teach a particular district's prescribed curriculum.[65] Few of these alternative programs provided any substantive and consistent form of induction support to their new recruits once they began teaching.[66]

In the early 2000s, the Carnegie Corporation of New York (once again) made a major investment in university-based preparation. Teachers for a New Era (TNE) funded 11 universities over 5 years to ratchet up quality control by: (1) measuring the quality of their training program on the basis of the student learning growth in the classrooms of the teachers they graduated from the program; (2) engaging the arts and sciences faculty fully in the development of new teachers, and (3) supporting the teachers they produced during their first 2 years of full-time professional teaching. As part of that support, the novice teachers were to have access to mentoring with respect to the clinical skills necessary for effective classroom teaching.

TNE yielded some notable local successes. But the TNE universities, as a group, had no plan to spread any lessons learned outside their own inner circles. And while some of these trailblazing IHEs produced powerful evidence on the effects of teacher education on student achievement, none of the data could be aggregated across sites and generalized on a large scale. There was no marketing strategy for universities to tout their changes and improvements at a level anywhere near the well-funded and highly effective promotion of counterefforts that could more quickly recruit teachers in direct response to school district needs. Much like in the past, few state policies were enacted to replicate and institutionalize the quiet successes of some of the individual TNE universities and their partner school districts.

As the first decade of the 21st century drew to an end, criticisms of teacher education continued to grow, even though graduates of university-based programs were becoming more academically qualified than in the past.[67] Researchers continued to struggle to definitely determine the kind of pre-service training that made a difference for student achievement.[68] Meanwhile, advocates of education deregulation continued to fight against investments in university-based preparation, which was portrayed as part of a teacher-professionalism "cartel" that avoided proving itself in the "competitive arena." The deregulators also feared that *professionalism*, as defined by many university faculty, would promote teachers as "shapers-of-school-improvement" as opposed to "instruments-of-school-improvement."[69] With university programs focused on empowerment, teachers would no longer be "workers," they would be "bosses." From a historical perspective, one might conclude that the deregulation advocates would be satisfied if less-prepared teachers enter and leave teaching quickly, keeping teacher salaries low and limiting the potential impact that highly professionalized teachers could have on what is taught—and how it is taught—in our nation's public schools.

Looking Forward—with Some Hope and Audacity

In 2009, President Barack Obama and his education secretary, Arne Duncan, launched a $4.35-billion Race to the Top (R2T) investment aimed at turning around low-performing schools to make all students "college-ready." In doing so, the federal government committed to its largest discretionary-funding program ever. The Obama administration expects states and districts to adopt standards and assessments that prepare students for college and the global economy; to build data systems that measure student growth and success; and to recruit, reward, and retain effective teachers and principals and make sure they work where they are needed most.

In part, the early efforts of the Obama administration drew on the agenda of the Democrats for Education Reform (DFER)—which emphasized the expansion of charter schools, alternative certification, and high-stakes accountability for teachers. For DFER supporters, charter schools are necessary to break up the education establishment, freeing crusading educators from the entanglements of teacher-tenure laws and union work-rules. DFER also focuses on alternative certification of a type that prepares teachers more inexpensively and for the specific curriculum that school district administrators, not university professors, want to be taught. Finally, DFER adherents want to keep a tight focus on standardized test scores as the primary measure for whether teachers will be judged effective or not—and even whether they will be eligible for pay raises. While the DFER agenda has honed in on a number of progressive ideals often associated with the Democratic Party, its strategy—much like that of the Bush administration—has been to push hard against the teacher unions, whose leaders remain deeply skeptical of pay and evaluation reforms that—while needed—might also reopen the door to capricious personnel decisions made by administrators.[70]

By early 2010, there were signs that the Obama administration was not satisfied to define school reform efforts so narrowly. The federal government began to invest in Promise Neighborhoods, a full-service school strategy that suggested to deregulation advocates that "bad teachers" are not the primary problem in underperforming schools. The administration also launched an effort to create more-nuanced performance assessments that could drive the kinds of robust student-learning goals so many teachers sought to achieve. Recognizing that NCLB's byzantine accountability structure created perverse incentives for states to lower academic standards and for teachers to teach to the test, the Obama administration has also set forth audacious goals to develop smarter ways to measure students' progress toward college readiness—assessments that are designed not to target teachers, but to help them target effective instruction. The administration's 2010 National Educational Technology Plan provided a framework for leveraging "current technologies to implement sophisticated learning, teaching, and assessment anyplace and anytime, lifelong and lifewide," and in doing so, establishing a "strategic vision of a redesigned K–20 formal educational system."[71]

However, the rhetoric of Obama administration's teaching policies did not always match reality. For example, in a number of cases the testing and evaluation policies continued the practice of bashing and "wounding" educators, even highly effective ones.[72] The kind of vision posited by Obama's "technology plan" did not get much attention by USDOE officials who crafted Race to the Top criteria. Teacher unions and their leaders, who invested heavily in electing President Obama, began to sharply criticize his policies, especially those related to measuring teacher effectiveness with the same standardized tests and value-added statistics embraced by the Bush administration. Despite the warning from the scientific community about the instability of the tests and models in determining effective (and ineffective) teachers,[73] the Obama administration plowed ahead, advancing most of the DFER policies. Despite growing evidence that merit pay plans rarely promote higher student achievement,[74] the Obama administration put more emphasis on test score-based indicators as the key strategy to advance teaching effectiveness reforms. While some union leaders began to work with the administrators on local reform efforts, others expressed very grave concerns, questioning the motives behind the Race to the Top policy approach and even whether the President supported public education."[75]

Twenty years from now, historians will begin to determine whether the Obama administration simply continued a century-long policy cycle that effectively marginalized classroom teachers as agents of school reform—or ultimately found the levers of change that were needed for the teachers of 2030 to become the architects of a fully realized results-oriented profession committed to every child's success.

CHAPTER 3

Emergent Reality #1:
A Transformed Learning Ecology
for Students and Teachers

For more than 2,000 years there have been vigorous and often vitriolic debates over how people learn. From the Greeks (including Socrates, Plato, and Aristotle) to the Romans (and the Catholic Church), from Renaissance thinkers to 19th century psychologists, differences in both fact and opinion hinged on the purpose of education and what counts for learning. Over the past 100 years or so, learning theory has been divided by a very active and distinct academic fault line—with behavioral psychology and cognitive psychology grinding against each another and producing periodic tremors through the world of education. Do humans learn knowledge by way of a stimulus-response mechanism (driven by rewards and punishments) or when they are prompted to construct knowledge from information they receive, interpret, and use? Is teaching a science or an art? Is learning best measured by objective, standardized tests or by what students produce and demonstrate? Should the teacher's role be the purveyor of knowledge (behavioral) or the facilitator of learning (cognitive)?

This disagreement over how people learn (like so many education debates) produces a lot of unnecessary heat. Teachers spend their lives along these fault lines, and they know from daily experience that it is pointless to take sides when the debate is about whether to *only* follow discreet, lockstep strategies for all students (behavioral) or to *only* "scaffold" learning using strategies determined by individual differences in student experience, culture, and language (cognitive). Smart instruction offers a blend, tailored to the content and the situation. And in the near future, the marriage of brain research and technology will make instruction smarter and more tailored than ever before.

Our teacher-colleague Emily Vickery describes a powerful vision of a new learning ecology for students and teachers.

The creation of personalized learning experiences will grow more sophisticated, challenging current and future teachers to redefine what should be learned and what learning is. The content to be learned will often be determined by market demand. In an environment where "attention" is among the most valuable commodities, the most successful teachers will be those who have learned to effectively allocate student attention in the most efficient manner, taking the least amount of time. Successful teachers will become masters of a curation economy (in which "curators" are employed to find, sort, select, recommend—and teach—"contextual quality content"). Teachers will be sought after for their expertise in editing and filtering digital content as they customize learning experiences. Master teachers will be those who can gather, filter, and distribute customized, meaningful learning via various deliverable designs based on advances in learning theory.[1]

According to Marc Prensky, the new skills and patterns students develop from hours and hours a day spent text messaging, gaming, and surfing the web both benefit and challenge learning as well as teachers. Prensky notes,

One key area that appears to have been affected is reflection. Reflection is what enables us, according to many theorists, to generalize, as we create mental models from our experience. It is, in many ways, the process of learning from experience. In our twitch-speed world, there is less and less time and opportunity for reflection, and this development concerns many people. One of the most interesting challenges and opportunities in teaching "digital natives" is to figure out and invent ways to include reflection and critical thinking in the learning (either built into the instruction or through a process of instructor-led debriefing) but still do it in the digital native language. We can and must do more in this area.

We are all aware of today's students who—as Prensky noted—are "accustomed to the twitch-speed, multitasking, random-access, graphics-first, active, connected, fun, fantasy, quick-payoff world of their video games, MTV, and Internet" and are "bored by most of today's education, well meaning as it may be." Indeed, as a recent Gates Foundation–funded survey discovered, most students drop out of school not because they are performing poorly academically; they do so because they are bored.[2]

The skills students are developing as a result of new technologies and ways of communicating are seldom, if ever, comprehensively addressed in our public schools. But they must be. Teachers need to accommodate for and capitalize upon the parallel processing abilities, graphic awareness, and desire to stay connected with peers of the "net generation"—both as a way to engage students and to advance learning.

Sarah Henchey, a young 6th-grade language arts teacher in Hillsborough, North Carolina, is a member of Teacher Leaders Network. She told this story:

> Earlier this week, I was spending time with a group of friends. Our ages ranged from 27 to 33. We're all college educated but from diverse cultural, social, and economic backgrounds. As we discussed a current political issue, the need to consult an informational source became a must. With a few strokes on an iPhone, we had our answer and were able to dig deeper into our conversation.
>
> With the accessibility of information increasing daily, students do not see our formal curriculum (or teachers' interpretation of said curriculum) as very relevant or engaging or even necessary to their daily lives. For example, one of my 6th-grade teammates conducts weekly map quizzes for the first 18 weeks of school on the locations, capitals, climates, etc., of European countries. Do students need to be able to recall these facts to be successful in today's world? We need to teach them to become curious and critical questioners and use tools to access today's information-rich world and make sense of it, accurately and fairly.

Sarah's comments resonate with social-trend experts interviewed by the Pew Internet and American Life Project. "Holding in your head information that is easily discoverable on Google will no longer be a mark of intelligence, but a side-show act," said Alex Halavais of the Association of Internet Researchers. "Being able to quickly and effectively discover information and solve problems, rather than do it 'in your head,' will be the metric we use." The policy question, suggested futurist and educator Howard Rheingold, "is whether people will learn and be taught the essential literacies necessary for thriving in the current infosphere: attention, participation, collaboration, crap detection, and network awareness . . . [I] am not optimistic about the rate of change in our education systems, but it is clear to me that people are not going to be smarter without learning the ropes."[3]

We agree with Dr. Rheingold that the rate of change *must* accelerate. At the same time, we see many opportunities for teachers and schools to quicken the pace of 21st-century learning and to make sure students "learn the ropes" associated with essential new literacies. Projects like ThinkQuest,[4] sponsored by the Oracle Foundation, are opening up large-scale, education-oriented social networks that promise student privacy and safety plus the excitement of learning collaborations with new friends around the world. Other projects have a "think globally, act locally" focus, like Remix World, a popular social networking site, created by Chicago's Digital Youth Network, to "give students tools to be engaged, articulate, critical, and collaborative [and to] facilitate the ability to become creators—designers, builders, and innovators—who can envision new possibilities."[5] We might also cite Dr. Rheingold's own work in developing a "social media classroom" web platform, which he imagines can be "an all-purpose tool for educators who seek to use social media in pursuit of a more participative pedagogy."[6]

We also found compelling evidence that the iGeneration students we are now teaching can and do learn via educational gaming. The research and development around learning games seeks to increase student interest while promoting deductive reasoning, collaborative problem solving, digital literacy, and content knowledge.[7] Web environments like the Harvard-developed River City interactive web simulation for middle-grades science help students develop scientific inquiry and 21st-century skills and use built-in assessment tools to measure that learning.[8] A game-based learning activity developed by the Ontario educational television network is teaching younger children (age 6 to 10) democratic values as they assume the role of dragons seeking to restore freedom to their kingdom.[9] MIT's Games-to-Teach project[10] has demonstrated the viability of using young people's fascination with massively multiplayer online role-playing games (MMORPG) to engage them in interactive learning. The project developed a suite of conceptual frameworks designed to support learning across math, science, engineering, and humanities curricula, then worked with game experts to produce 15 game concepts "with supporting pedagogy that showed how advanced math, science and humanities content could be uniquely blended with state-of-the-art game play." One example, *Revolution*, had participants interact in a virtual world where they experienced the social, economic, and political realities of the American War for Independence—playing the roles of farmers, slaves, Royalists, merchants, politicians, and other 18th-century characters.

We are confident that learning theorists and innovative curriculum designers will continue to build on these early applications of the Web's powerful connectivity—and at an evermore rapid pace, hastening the day when school and teacher buy-in will be inevitable and irresistible. And we don't discount the relentless pressure that will be applied by iGeneration students who are already impatient with outdated teaching methods. Bill Ferriter, a 6th-grade teacher in Raleigh, North Carolina, and author of the digital-learning-oriented blog the Tempered Radical, calls these students "Googled learners." In a Teacher Leaders Network discussion Ferriter wrote:

> Do you ever wonder if they're impatient because they know that they can learn faster and easier outside of school than they can inside of school? Do you think they feel like school is holding them back—and that their impatience will become intolerance by the year 2030 unless we make dramatic changes between now and then?
>
> I see a rebellion in the future—students demanding that the more interactive, individualized, and responsive learning environment they are used to beyond school be mirrored in their institutionalized learning environments.
>
> And honestly, I don't think it's going to take 20 years for the sparks to fly.

The digital revolution is radically transforming our world. The facts are compelling:

- With more than 400 million active users,[11] Facebook would be the third largest country by population in the world behind China and India.
- There are well over one trillion unique URLs in Google's index[12]—and nearly 500 million searches per day in the United States alone.[13] The Google library of scanned books has surpassed the 10 million mark.[14]
- More than 24 hours of YouTube video is uploaded every minute.[15] At top YouTube competitor Hulu, viewers watched more than 1 billion video streams for a combined 97 million hours—in a single month.[16]

These are early 2010 figures. By the time you read them, they undoubtedly will have been surpassed. Our students don't find them remarkable; this is the only world they know.

Many labor prognosticators expect a great deal of "job churn" in the next two decades, with a distinct advantage to be given to prospective workers who can expertly navigate and interpret the Internet. "As we build a new foundation for economic growth in the 21st century," said a July 2009 report from the President's Office of Economic Advisors, "the nation's workers will be better prepared for ever-changing opportunities if they have strong analytical and interpersonal skills."[17] The message for educators could not be clearer: *We must teach students how to determine fact from fiction in the mega-information age.* At the same time, we must help them develop the diagnostic and organizational know-how that will enable them to create, communicate, and collaborate in an interconnected world with a complex global *and* local economy.

Our colleague Bill Ferriter is growing these skills among his middle school students through projects like "Do Something Funny for Money Day." The "tweenagers" at his school raised several hundred dollars (while observing behavior protocols they helped develop)—which they then invested in Kiva, the microlending website that allows citizens to make small loans to individual entrepreneurs in the developing world. Ferriter shaped lesson plans that guided his students through the process of deciding what they wanted to support with their microloans. He described the project's purpose in a handout he shared with teachers in his school:[18]

> Once we've raised funds, students will work in groups in their social studies classes to select individuals in Kiva to fund. We'll study the project that each small businessman/woman has proposed to determine whether it is likely to benefit the community. We'll study the countries that we are making loans to and explore the kinds of challenges that people face when trying to improve the quality of life for their families.
>
> We'll study the organizations that are supporting the loan recipient to decide how safe our loaned funds will be. We'll discuss microloans and the financial literacy concepts behind loan agreements and terms. We'll track the loans that we make by location and by nation. We'll study the Kiva partners that we have in each loan project and track the countries that they come from.

Ferriter's plan, which blends an array of traditional and 21st-century skills into a service-learning framework, models the kind of teaching expertise we believe must become commonplace among teachers of 2030.

Learning from Isaiah, Ziad, and Many Other Students

What we ask of teachers and students is changing—and needs to change—in every discipline and at every grade level. In math and science, teachers are already using the iPad and iTunes so students can generate a deeper understanding of quadratic equations and learn the periodic tables.[19] But they are also doing much more.

Our co-author John M. Holland, a national board–certified early childhood educator, describes the teacher-student learning interaction in ways that are refreshingly different, from the end goal of having a student provide bits of information on demand via a standardized achievement test—or, for that matter, having a teacher facilitate learning based on anything that might interest a child. In John's account of his interaction with preschooler "Isaiah," we can see the advantages that accrue when teachers have the freedom to meet an individual child's needs through the application of accumulated teaching skills and classroom experience. This is the face of teaching and learning in 2030 as we envision it: deeply personal, highly differentiated, and still—as learning is today—dependent on the expertise of great teachers.

> Isaiah was struggling with writing his name. He held the crayon without a problem. He could make straight and curved lines, but he couldn't seem to master the curve in the *S*. Whenever he sat down during our daily journal time he refused to try to write his name.
>
> My one-sided conversation went something like this:
>
> "Move the crayon up and then down."
> "Try to make it smooth. That's close, but now try again like this."
> "Let's try it with my hand on yours."
> "Isaiah, please quit stopping me from moving your hand."
>
> I tried getting him to trace over an *S* written with a highlighter. I showed him how to draw an *S* in the air. None of these tactics was working. Then at some point I noticed that he liked to make noises to designate action, especially when he was playing with cars in the block area. The next time he was struggling to write his name I tried something new. I showed him how to move the crayon around the *S* but make it sound like a race car.
>
> "EeeeeAwawwa."
>
> A smile with ears looked up at me. It worked. He had so much fun he forgot he couldn't make an *S*. We played the same game with all of his letters, and over time the noise-making disappeared. I had succeeded in teaching Isaiah to write his name.

My solution did not come from a textbook, at least not one I have read. It came after I'd tried every technique passed on to me in teacher-education, by other teachers, or collected in a workshop. None of them impressed Isaiah. I am sure other pre-K teachers have discovered what I call the "matchbox car" writing method, but I'm pretty confident it hasn't been researched and proven to be a best practice. I had an inspiration in what Malcolm Gladwell would call a "blink" of an eye.[20] I had been thinking about helping Isaiah consciously and unconsciously for several days when the solution just came to me. I would call the ability I used to come up with the solution "creative problem solving."

The tired but eternal debate over whether teaching is an art or a science perpetuates a false dichotomy. Art and science are two branches of the same tree of understanding. Each serves in its unique way to light reality.

For those who might think that Isaiah and John's shared learning moment is the typical classroom experience, consider the portrait of another one of our colleagues, Shannon C'de Baca. Shannon was a Milken Award–winning science classroom teacher before becoming a "virtual teacher" for Iowa Learning Online, where she teaches high school students who are widely dispersed across the state. Shannon works daily with students whose brick-and-mortar learning environments failed to support the type of personal learning that John's story emphasizes:

Ziad is 15 years old and sees no point in school. Her schedule is packed with courses she thought sounded interesting, but they lost their appeal when the rules and structure limited the pace and style of her learning. She reads ahead and does all the teacher requires, but Ziad finds no rewards for her creative thinking or extra work. Her private folder is packed with essays and questions she would like to share, but with 35 students in her science class, there is little time for one-on-one interactions with her teacher.

Six months ago, Ziad began to cause trouble. She got lots of attention—and a hefty suspension for misbehaving. She decided to enroll in an online science course to pass the time and keep up with her coursework while suspended. In her virtual course she talks live over the Internet with her teacher three times a week, posts her thoughtful and creative questions in an online class discussion forum and submits extra work regularly to her teacher, who provides timely feedback. She is able to share not just what she knows, but who she is.

Four-year-old Isaiah and 15-year-old Ziad are at two different poles of the education system, but—specific developmental needs aside—what they require to be successful learners is much the same. Isaiah and Ziad need teachers who have the opportunity to observe their unique gifts and interests and connect their learning to these individual attributes. They need teachers to serve as models of critical thinking and trusted guides in learning, so that they will risk venturing down new or previously unfruitful intellectual paths—not an easy task for a toddler or a teen.

If you have any doubts about the needs and desires of students, you can try asking them yourself. Our coauthor Laurie Wasserman did just that. Laurie is a national board–certified teacher (NBCT) entering her 4th decade as a special education teacher in Massachusetts. She asked 6th-graders throughout her school what traits a teacher of the future should have so students can learn more. Laurie was astonished to see some normally recalcitrant students pore over their written responses, several of them requesting to extend a brief classroom activity into a multiday project. Their words paint a portrait of teachers and learning opportunities that are highly personalized, evolving, and even fallible. These students recognize that 21st-century skills are the product of a process of learning, unlearning, and relearning, and they expect their teachers to serve as models at every step of the journey. Laurie writes:

> Teachers of the future, according to 12-year-old Callie, need the attributes of her best teachers today. As she described her third- and 4th-grade teachers, she said: "One thing that made them amazing teachers is that we were never, ever bored. They thought of fun projects, we learned games at recess, and yet I learned through them more than in a classroom where you just sit and the teacher reads out of a textbook. This year I have an English teacher in 6th grade that I think is the best teacher I ever had. It's hard to even understand why, but I guess it's just that she does projects. She cares about what we think, and she's just so darned nice. To be a good teacher, you need to listen to your students and to care about what they say."
>
> Teachers of tomorrow will need to "know what you know and know what you don't know," said Amanda. They must "always help whoever needs help and give extra time for whoever needs it. Always be ready for questions and not do the same thing day after day; it gets boring."

More advice for educators of 2030: "I think teachers will need to lay down the law, but be a mentor and a friend. When kids can trust the teacher, they feel safe and well taken care of. Share your knowledge. You will be wrong sometimes, but everyone makes mistakes. Be funny, do projects, keep your class interested. Tell stories about your mistakes. It will make the kids feel less self-conscious."

The teaching we are talking about goes well beyond behavioral or cognitive psychology and the debate between "memorizing the facts" versus "constructing your meaning" sorts of learning. We are talking about a new ecology of learning that recognizes how the emergence of ubiquitous networked learning will create an insatiable demand for highly adaptable teaching experts like John, Shannon, and Laurie. Canadian educator George Siemens calls this new ecology "connectivism," an environment in which teachers are challenged to rapidly "actuate known knowledge at the point of application"[21] (see box).

Siemens' ideas about the future of teaching are not only "out of the box," but out of the entire frame of reference of many policymakers and educators today. In a 2010 essay, he writes,

> Social and technological networks subvert the classroom-based role of the teacher. Networks thin classroom walls. . . . The largely unitary voice of the traditional teacher is fragmented by the limitless conversation opportunities available in networks. When learners have control of the tools of conversation, they also control the conversations in which they choose to engage.

As the captive-audience model of schooling loses its dominance, the ability of teachers to fully engage learners and add value to the "limitless" Internet experience will become paramount. "I've come to view teaching as a critical and needed activity in the chaotic and ambiguous information climate created by networks," Siemens says. "In the future, however, the role of the teacher, the educator, will be dramatically different from the current norm."[22]

The Obama administration's technology plans have the rhetoric right:

> In connected teaching, teaching is a team activity. Individual educators build online learning communities consisting of their students and their students' peers; fellow educators in their schools, libraries, and after-school programs; professional experts in various disciplines around the

---

Principles of Connectivism

- Learning and knowledge rests in diversity of opinions.
- Learning is a process of connecting specialized nodes or information sources.
- Learning may reside in nonhuman appliances.
- Capacity to know more is more critical than what is currently known.
- Nurturing and maintaining connections is needed to facilitate continual learning.
- Ability to see connections between fields, ideas, and concepts is a core skill.
- Currency (accurate, up-to-date knowledge) is the intent of all connectivist learning activities.

"Connectivism presents a model of learning that acknowledges the tectonic shifts in society [in which] learning is no longer an internal, individualistic activity. How people work and function is altered when new tools are utilized. The field of education has been slow to recognize both the impact of new learning tools and the environmental changes in what it means to learn. Connectivism provides insight into learning skills and tasks needed for learners to flourish in a digital era."
—G. Siemens

---

world; members of community organizations that serve students in the hours they are not in school; and parents who desire greater participation in their children's education.[23]

But America's schools, teachers, and students continue to be buffeted by the "chaotic and ambiguous" climate shift Siemens describes. For the most part, the policymakers and reform activists who steer public education's course, including those leading Obama's education reform initiatives, still operate from a 20th-century construct of teaching and school. Unless decision makers recognize the tumultuous change looming on learning's horizon and act accordingly, our public school systems will become increasingly ineffective and out of touch. While many affluent individuals will likely have the resources and know-how to thrive in this new learning environment, many of our most vulnerable children and families will not. To fully participate in 21st-century life and work, high-needs students must have the support of adaptable, responsive, and highly effective teacher leaders. It's the job of today's decision makers and reform advocates to make sure we have such leaders tomorrow.

Confronting the Limitations of
20th-Century Standardized Tests and Accountability

Many of our TeacherSolutions 2030 team members work in high-needs schools. We can testify that a national reform agenda which set out a decade ago to bridge achievement gaps and sharpen the focus on student learning outcomes is collapsing under the weight of overly rigid sanctions and "turn-around" regimes. Many students and teachers are caught in the vise grip of an educational Catch-22, as policy advocates who favor lockstep instruction vie with the proponents of inquiry learning and 21st-century skills. The NCLB measures of progress implemented over the last decade have proved to be woefully inadequate. In many high-needs schools, they have narrowed what is taught to the limited content and skills required to achieve passing scores on outdated standardized tests.

Our coauthor John M. Holland contends that the negative effects of NCLB will not keep great teachers "from an unwavering commitment to meet an individual child's needs through the application of his accumulated teaching skills." But making such a commitment often requires extraordinary efforts from individuals who must constantly swim against a strong tide to teach well. How many teachers have such endurance? And how much productive learning time is lost in the struggle to resist counterproductive educational policy?

Some researchers have found that the NCLB accountability system has actually *decreased* the cognitive demands of classroom instruction and reduced the time available for the exploration and reflection that, not only promotes creative problem solving but helps establish the powerful learning relationships described by Laurie Wasserman's adolescent students.[24] Studies have consistently shown that "instruction focused on memorizing unconnected facts and drilling skills out of context produces inert rather than active knowledge which does not transfer to real world activities or problem solving situations." Most of what is learned this way "is soon forgotten and cannot be retrieved or applied when it would be useful later," points out Linda Darling-Hammond in her recent book *The Flat World and Education*.[25]

The business maxim that "what is most inspected gets respected" holds true in schools. Investigations of high-stakes testing practices in Arizona, Florida, and Texas have found that "under pressure to show improved performance, teachers often prepare students by spending substantial instructional time on exercises that look just like the test items, reverting to worksheets filled with multiple choice questions and drill based on recall and recitation that they feel will prepare students for the tests."[26] California's 8th-grade history and social science exam prompts students to recall

Eighth-Grade California Standards Test, History and Social Sciences, Released Questions, 2003–2008[27]

Which development most enabled early peoples to form permanent settlements?

   A. advances in agricultural production
   B. the creation of democratic government
   C. the spread of monotheism
   D. advances in written language

The legacy of ancient Greek myths and epics, such as The Iliad, *continues to provide people with*

   A. accurate descriptions of historical events.
   B. heroic figures and great adventures.
   C. real life stories about everyday people.
   D. objective studies of ancient civilizations.

The stories from Marco Polo's travels encouraged Europeans to

   A. journey to Asia in search of wealth.
   B. abandon the feudal land system.
   C. launch the Crusades against Muslims.
   D. isolate themselves from foreigners

relative important facts, but the test's construction often forces teachers to pursue an intricate classroom game of trivial pursuit.

We can do better. A description of questions on the College Work and Readiness Assessment, a test commonly cited as a paragon for 21st-century skills from the Council for Aid to Education:

> When 9th-graders at St. Andrew's School, a private boarding school in Middletown, Delaware, sat down last year to take the school's College Work and Readiness Assessment (CWRA), they faced the sort of problems that often stump city officials and administrators, but rarely show up on standardized tests, such as how to manage traffic congestion caused by population growth. "I proposed a new transportation system for the city," said one student describing his answer. "It's expensive, but it will cut pollution."
>
> Students were given research reports, budgets, and other documents to help draft their answers, and they were expected to demonstrate proficiency in subjects like reading and math as well as mastery of broader and more sophisticated skills like evaluating and analyzing information and thinking creatively about how to apply information to real-world problems.[28]

The U.S. Department of Education, in the early years of the Obama administration, is drawing on two multi-state consortia to revamp how students are tested, offering in 2010 almost $350 million in grants to "develop assessments" that accurately measure how much a child has learned each year and ensure the student is ready for college or a career after high school.[29] Other nations have figured this out, as revealed by the biology exam (see Figure 3.1) given in Australia.

FIGURE 3.1. Victoria, Australia, High School Biology Exam[30]

When scientists design drugs against infectious agents, the term "designed drug" is often used.

A. Explain what is meant by this term.

_____

_____

_____

Scientists aim to develop a drug against a particular virus that infects humans. The virus has a protein coat and different parts of the coat play different roles in the infective cycle. Some sites assist in the attachment of the virus to a host cell; others are important in the release from a host cell. The structure is represented in the following diagram:

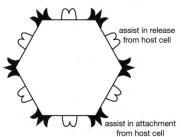

The virus reproduces by attaching itself to the surface of a host cell and injecting its DNA into the host cell. The viral DNA then uses the components of the host cell to reproduce its parts, and hundreds of new viruses bud off from the host cell. Ultimately the host cell dies.

B. Design a drug that will be effective against this virus. In your answer outline the important aspects you would need to consider. Outline how your drug would prevent continuation of the cycle of reproduction of the virus particle. Use diagrams in your answer. Space for diagrams is provided on the next page.

C. Before a drug is used on humans, it is usually tested on animals. In this case, the virus under investigation also infects mice. Design an experiment, using mice, to test the effectiveness of the drug you have designed.

When teachers point out these issues, it is not our intent to shy away from accountability that measures student progress. But if accountability systems focus on the wrong things, if they put too much emphasis on what can be easily and cheaply measured using traditional standardized tests, then we shouldn't be surprised when our schools produce more students ready to work in mid-20th-century American corporations and factories than in 21st-century global marketplaces. A recent study by the Center on Education Policy, a nonpartisan think tank devoted to measuring the impacts of No Child Left Behind, found that almost 50% of all elementary schools have cut back substantially on time spent teaching science, social studies, arts, music, and physical education. Instead, they have focused almost exclusively on the math and literacy content emphasized by the NCLB testing regime.[31] In one study in Texas, a state known for its rigid accountability rules, teachers reported that they could not teach social studies and science until March, after high-stakes tests were administered.[32]

The evidence about the adverse side effects of NCLB-style accountability is growing. And that evidence is no longer just being whispered about—like the pharmaceutical ads on television that downplay the deleterious aspects of the latest "wonder drug." Even NCLB's early champions are having to come to terms publicly with the law's negative impacts on curriculum, instruction, and school morale. "These types of [standardized] tests are useful for meeting the proficiency goals of the federal No Child Left Behind Act (NCLB) and state accountability systems," an Education Sector report commented recently. "But leaders in business, government, and higher education are increasingly emphatic in saying that such tests don't do enough. The intellectual demands of 21st-century work, today's leaders say, require assessments that measure more-advanced skills, 21st-century skills."[33] In her recent book *The Death and Life of the Great American School System: How Testing and Choice Are Undermining Education*, education scholar Diane Ravitch frankly admits that her early enthusiasm for No Child Left Behind was misplaced. "I too had drunk deeply of the elixir that promised a quick fix to intractable problems," she wrote. In 2009, after carefully reviewing the research on NCLB's effects, she reversed her stance. "It is the mark of a sentient human being to learn from experience, to pay close attention to how theories work out when put into practice." And the practice of K–12 standardized testing has emerged as an industry that costs $2.6 billion a year.[34]

As we write this book, the Obama administration is in the midst of its "Race to the Top" competition. Much talk abounds about new assessments. But, the R2T eligibility requirements demonstrate the administration's continued faith in an NCLB-style assessment system that uses narrowly focused standardized tests to make sweeping judgments about student progress. Dr. Ravitch wrote that "as we seek to reform our schools, we must take care to do no harm." We certainly agree—and we question whether inside-the-Beltway policy analysts know "harm" when they see it. How much do the makers and shapers of education policy actually understand about the students teachers are teaching today?

TLN member Ellen Berg, a charter school teacher from San Diego who has also taught in inner-city St. Louis, offers this reflection on theory versus practice.

> I have one kid I teach in mind who is my litmus test for any testing and accountability reforms proposed by policymakers. When Z was born, his mother was told he would never walk and would probably need to be institutionalized. There was no hope that he would ever read or write, because he was profoundly disabled. Z's mom refused to accept this as so. She worked with him, and Z learned to walk and talk. She enrolled him in our charter school as a 1st-grader, and we wrote an IEP that gave him resource time and an in-class aide. He was included in all of the field trips and treated with respect and high expectations by students and teachers. His mother also exposed him to tons of things—dance (she is a therapeutic dance instructor), trips, hiking, etc. Her husband died when Z was an infant, and she was definitely not wealthy, but her time and resources were put into Z. And although Z made academic progress, you could never chart his proficiency or growth with current standardized tests and the statistical formulas in use today.
>
> In 4th grade, Z learned how to read quite suddenly. That was my first year at the school, and the staff was in full celebration. He was never supposed to read—his IEP has a list of disabilities half a mile long—but here he was, reading and writing. Fast forward to my 8th-grade class: Z was reading grade-level text and fully comprehending it. His writing was probably at a 5th-grade level, but as the year went on, he went from describing his weekend or the weather to writing stories with dialogue—an abstraction that was initially difficult for him. I credit his reading success in part to the peer learning system we set up and students' regular sharing of their own writing with each other.
>
> Z is now in high school and progressing well. Throughout his time with us, our belief was that we should never limit Z; let's offer things to him and see what he does with it. Z's mother refused to accept the recommendations of the "experts" or

take too much stock in standardized tests as a measure of his progress. So did we.

Some might argue that Z is an extreme case whose issues would be "accommodated" by the accountability system. But the underlying lesson here is that every child brings something different to the table—there is no "average" learner, and by assuming there is, policymakers immediately limit expectations for students ("we know you can't learn this") and for teachers ("we can't teach that child but so much"). Research on best practice says that as teachers we should approach each child as a unique learner and respond to what we find out about their learning needs. Standards are important not in the abstract but *in the context of each child.* And if the system says, "we can't trust teachers to make those kinds of professional judgments," then policymakers, teachers, and other stakeholders had better work together on policies that will build such trust. Because we really can't predict any individual child's exact "adequate yearly progress" in advance. *We need knowledgeable and skillful teachers who can push that progress to the limit. And that is the context within which teacher-accountability systems should be designed.*

Improve Measures to Improve Teaching and Learning

Bill Ferriter, an award-winning middle school teacher and coauthor of a user's guide to professional learning communities published by Solution Tree, had an opportunity to sit in on a student assessment in Denmark. What he observed was the country's only formal high-stakes test, an eight-hour exam given once at the end of 10th grade. It was quite different from the high school "exit exams" that have emerged in U.S. states since the passage of No Child Left Behind. Here's an excerpt from Bill's report:

> Denmark's final exams are probably the most responsible system of student assessment that I've ever seen in action. Here's how they go:
>
> 1. Classroom teachers put together a collection of readings and audio recordings related to content studied during the course of the school year. In the sessions that I observed—both English exams—there were packets of materials on 20 different topics ranging from racism and role models to terrorism and global warming.
> 2. Also included was a list of related lessons that students had completed on the topic in their regular classes. These

lists included things like articles read, videos watched, and seminars completed. While the supporting materials for each lesson were not included, these lists allowed students to dig into their background knowledge while attacking new texts.

3. Each student arrived at a prescheduled time, entered the examination room and randomly selected a number corresponding to one of the predetermined topics. Then, he/she spent 20 minutes studying the new materials: taking notes, filling out reading guides, listening to recordings, and planning a personal response to the topic that they'd selected.

4. After 20 minutes—a time period that was closely monitored—the student returned to the assessment room where his/her classroom teacher was waiting with a teacher of the same grade level from a school in a nearby town. The rest of the assessment consisted of an ongoing conversation between the student and the assessors about the topic selected.

5. The assessors carefully listened to each student, looking for evidence of reflective thinking and for the ability to connect new texts to previous materials or experiences. While students did the majority of the talking during the 20-minute assessment period, both assessors asked prodding questions to challenge students and to test the depth of their knowledge about the topic selected.

6. When the students finished working through their thoughts, they were asked to leave the examination room. Then, the assessors—guided by a predetermined rubric—engaged in a 10-minute conversation with one another to determine the student's level of mastery.

7. To ensure that final scores weren't biased, the outside assessor—who had no relationship with the student being tested—took the lead in the conversation and in determining the score given, but both teachers interacted with each other and came to general consensus around each bullet point on the rubric. If there had been disagreement, the school principal would have been called in to determine a final score.

8. Finally, the student returned to the room to receive feedback from both teachers. Suggestions for future work were offered, compliments were given, and the final score was awarded.[35]

This approach to assessment—asking students both to demonstrate *what* they know and explain *why* they know it—creates important expectations for both the learner and for their teachers, all the way down to the earliest grades. It says to everyone, "We will not just inspect the breadth of learning but its depth." Our coauthor Renee Moore, a literature and writing teacher, offers an example from her own high school practice:

> For years, one of my favorite classroom assessments has been to tie my opening activity of the semester to my final exam (composition). Students start the class by telling me (in writing) about their past experiences with writing, types of writing they have done (in and out of school), and their views on what constitutes good writing. For the final exam, I ask them to revisit that piece and explain what has changed as a result of their experiences in this class. They have to document examples of growth. I have an exit essay that can be graded using the rubric adopted by the English faculty, and I also give them a tool that guides them through the reflection on what they learned and why. Student work samples like these (which can be digitized, stored and analyzed over time) are also extremely valuable to me as evaluations of my own work and of how the class can be improved or changed.

We are impressed with the performance assessment framework supported by the Council of Chief State School Officers developed under the leadership of Linda Darling-Hammond and now being advanced by the Smarter Balanced Assessment Consortium, led by, among others, former Maine superintendent of education Susan Gendron (see box on next page).

In the future, Renee argues, alternative assessments like this should not only become the norm but should be developed collaboratively by teams of teachers within the school.

> Writing is one of the best ways to measure depth of learning. Writing-based assessments can also serve as evidence that students know history and science as well as how to write and communicate. By developing and reviewing the results of assessments together, we not only open our work to the scrutiny of others but can have important conversations about what we mean by quality student work and "deep" learning. This effect can be further magnified by evaluating the results of assessments, not only among teams of teachers, but also with students and the public.

The Council of Chief State School Officers has been working with researchers and stakeholders to develop a set of principles for a 21st-century student assessment system. These principles were released to the public in early 2010:

1. Addressing the depth and breadth of standards as well as all areas of the curriculum, not just those that are easy to measure
2. Considering and including all students as an integral part of the design process, anticipating their particular needs and encouraging all students to demonstrate what they know and can do
3. Honoring the research indicating that students learn best when given challenging content and provided with assistance, guidance, and feedback on a regular basis
4. Employing a variety of appropriate measures, instruments, and processes at the classroom, school, and district levels, as well as the state level (e.g., multiple measures that are both formative and summative)
5. Engaging teachers in scoring student work based on shared targets

Source: Darling-Hammond, L. (2010). *Performance counts: Assessment systems that support high-quality learning*. Washington, DC: CCSSO. Retrieved April 7, 2010, from http://www.ccsso.org/publications/details.cfm?PublicationID=381. Reprinted by permission.

Renee, who teaches in the rural Mississippi delta, knows from long experience that "a single, one-size-fits-all test will not capture the growth in academic achievement among the diverse students I teach."

> The purpose of my classroom writing assessment is so students and I can measure the amount of individual progress made by each writer. They all start from different points and end with various levels of current proficiency as writers. I can generate reports, based on our school-adopted rubrics and learning outcomes, that show where each student is in relation to those outcomes and how far each student has moved over the course of the semester.

And Renee gets right to the heart of professional trust:

> If the scoring instruments that I'm using within my classroom are of high quality, then I as an ethical, professionally trained expert should be able to use those instruments to evaluate my students' work accurately and fairly. Why is that too big a leap for us to make in thinking about all classroom teachers? We make exactly that assumption for doctors, professional sport

referees, and auto mechanics. Do some of them make mistakes in their judgments? Yes. Are some of them unscrupulous or inept. Yes. Do we question the entire enterprise because it includes imperfect assessments or poor performers? No.

We're asking the right policy question when we ask "how can we better prepare the nation's teachers to conduct, evaluate, and use formative and summative assessments—and to share that information in a format usable by parents, schools, employers, and other interested parties." This is the broad vision of accountability we need.

Other nations routinely assess their public students with a range of tests developed and scored primarily by teachers. And these assessments are trusted. A number of scholars have also shown how relatively low-stakes tests that require students to demonstrate deep content understanding can promote the higher orders of teaching necessary for serious academic achievement. As Linda Darling-Hammond has noted:

> A critical issue for learning is the extent to which assessments focus on valuable content and generative skills that enable transfer of what is learned to new problems and settings, rather than focusing on lower-level skills of recall and recognition alone. Also, teachers' abilities to learn from the assessment information make a difference for whether results translate into more productive teaching or simply result in failure and stigma for struggling students. These understandings have been a driving force for assessment reforms in high-achieving countries in Europe and Asia, as well as in some states in the U.S., but they have been overlooked by many policymakers.[36]

The Forum on Education and Democracy has reported that student assessments in high-achieving countries demand "evidence of actual student performance on challenging tasks that evaluate standards of advanced learning." The assessments push students (and teachers who teach them) to demonstrate how they can "organize information to solve problems, frame and conduct inquiries, analyze and synthesize data, and apply learning to new situations." This approach is so sensible one wonders why we've missed it in America. Perhaps because it would have required the American public to accept learning as a science and agree to invest more in developing our teacher workforce to take full advantage of these understandings—a concept that directly challenges our nation's traditional views on schooling and teachers' work.[37] By 2030, we predict, those traditions will be historical artifacts.

A Different Kind of Accountability

As we've said, radical changes in the way the people of the world communicate are driving the creation of a new learning ecology, which will inevitably drive new forms of assessment and accountability. Julianna Dauble, a 5th-grade teacher in Washington State, participates in TLN's New Millennium Initiative, aimed at developing tomorrow's teacher leaders. She writes:

> The amount of information available at every moment of our lives is overwhelming us in 2010. People tune out objective facts and listen to talking heads expounding opinions guised as truth. While troubling, it will result in a shift in how we access information . . . and opinion forming will be a process of intense study of an issue. In 20 years the "core academic standards" will be unique to each student (and) mastery of each standard will be determined in an on-going way as students discover their talents and niche in society through self-designed/self-chosen projects and areas of study.

With new tools and technologies and more time for teachers to use them, Julianna suggests, we can create both new assessments and accountability measures to match them. More and more, students will be expected to apply what they are learning in authentic real-world situations, and built-in assessments will be a natural part of that process. Already many forward-thinking educators and advocacy groups are asking questions like this one posed by our TLN colleague Bill Ferriter: "Aren't we holding kids back when the only assessments we ask them to perform are paper and pencil measures that no one outside our classrooms will ever see?"

In many U.S. schools today, the curriculum is a mile wide and an inch deep—pushing teachers to rush through topic after topic to "cover" the content. As a result of this mad race, more students may score a bit higher on the standardized test (and keep their schools off the failing-school list), but they seldom learn anything deeply. On the other hand, high-scoring nations teach and test far fewer topics each year—and the results show.[38] In a new learning ecology, the essentials of learning will have less to do with specific content and more to do with understanding knowledge systems—learning how to access information, investigate and evaluate it, and think deeply about it—all in the context of problem solving and creation.

As the new learning ecology evolves, the tried and now not-so-true "Carnegie unit" of counting students' course completion and seat-time must finally be put aside. The Carnegie unit (named for the foundation that financed a study of higher education more than a century ago) was an attempt to break down the rigidity of a classical or general education in secondary schools. It has been a source of increasing frustration for many educators, as Renee Moore describes:

> Everything about the American education system is time based. Case-in-point: the measure of secondary student accomplishment for generations has been the "Carnegie unit." The unit, developed in 1906, measures the amount of time a student has been enrolled in a subject. For example, a total of 120 hours in one subject—meeting 4 or 5 times a week for 40 to 60 minutes, for 36 to 40 weeks each year—earns the student one "unit" of high school credit. A predetermined number of units constitute the minimum amount of preparation that could be interpreted as 4 years of academic or high school preparation. Under such a system, what matters is, not so much what is taught, how it is taught, or how well it is learned, but how much time is spent on each subject.

The rigidity of the Carnegie unit as an organizing framework for learning has been identified as a barrier to innovations in teaching and school organizations and a crutch for policymakers and administrators who want easy ways to "count" learning. Back in 1966, a Portland superintendent lamented that the "Unit" had let administrators off the hook when it came to demonstrating the "continuous educational progress of each student" and provided them the "luxury of doing nothing about modifying educational programs."[39]

Our TeacherSolutions 2030 team has a better idea for the digital age—the *potential learning unit*. In a world where technologies are making the transfer of information increasingly efficient, yet potentially overwhelming for developing learners, we would argue that meaningful human interactions, informed by research around how individuals learn best, need to replace time as the central unit of learning. We like the term potential learning (PL) units. PL units define not a random measure of arbitrary time but *the explicit outcome of such interactions*. Learning environments—whether brick-and-mortar schools, virtual schools, teacher professional-development environments, or software learning tools—should be designed to increase the frequency and impact of educational experiences that can be measured by PL units.

Teachers are not the only professionals questioning the preponderance of fact-oriented curriculum standards and bubble-in multiple choice tests that reinforce 20th-century approaches to schooling. In early 2010, the National Research Council began work on a new generation of science standards that will promote thinking and reasoning skills around disciplinary and cross-disciplinary core concepts. *Education Week* reported that "two central goals of the project are to focus science instruction on a smaller set of critical concepts and to ensure that students don't just learn facts and figures, but gain a deeper conceptual understanding of science that is grounded in thinking and reasoning skills." Thomas E. Keller, a senior program officer at the NRC's board of science education, told reporters that "the research is pretty clear that helping kids answer the right fill-in-the-bubble [questions] doesn't make them science-literate."[40]

This big idea—deeper conceptual understanding grounded in thinking and reasoning skills—begs for a new framework for measuring student progress, co-designed by effective and insightful teachers. As our coauthor John M. Holland says, teachers "must have a hand in creating 21st-century accountability tools that make sense. Because the quality of our teaching should be assessed on the basis of our ability to help every student grow and learn, future student assessments should also reveal how effective we are at making the right learning decisions for each student we teach."

In this actual student prompt, TLN member Ken Bernstein, an award-winning high school social studies teacher in Maryland and blogger at DailyKos, offers a powerful example from his government classroom of how deep conceptual understanding can be assessed:

> We have just finished a unit on the presidency. Draft a question that would require a student to demonstrate a deep and reasonably complete understanding of the functioning of the presidency in the modern world, with respect to separation of powers and checks and balances. It should be answerable with real world examples that we may have covered in the unit, or of which the student may have independent knowledge. Then answer that question.
>
> Now, having answered the question, evaluate how well it required you to demonstrate your understanding, what skills it required you to apply, and what it did not require you to do. Then evaluate your own response.

Between now and 2030, we predict that advances in learning theory and new metric tools that can capture nuanced information about student achievement gains will finally make this kind of accountability possible on a large scale.

Darling-Hammond, in her 2010 report for the Council of Chief State School Officers, asserted that:

> Technology can be used to enhance these assessments in three ways: by delivering the assessments; in online tasks of higher order abilities, allowing students to search for information or manipulate variables and tracking information about the students' problem-solving processes; and in some cases, scoring the results or delivering the responses to trained scorers/teachers to assess from an electronic platform.[41]

With the support of 21st-generation, voice-driven web-based smart phones and "killer apps," teachers will keep a running record of students' academic progress using a range of data—constantly analyzing what works and what does not. These assessments, driven by real-world tasks such as how students design a mid-21st-century school building or develop a community garden and implement a business plan to sustain local food sources, will be linked to an array of more-sophisticated achievement tests that teachers create alongside psychometricians and scholars. The design of these cutting-edge tests will be influenced by the now-demonstrated connections between the emotional and instructional climates for learning and student outcomes.

A New Learning Ecology for Teachers Too

In the learning environments of 2030, we expect to see not only students having regular interactions with community members, subject area experts, and peers from other locales, but also to see teachers having similar interactions about content, curriculum, pedagogy, and assessment with distant teacher colleagues, researchers, and other experts. As we consider how the teachers of 2030 must learn to teach, we have been impressed by the accumulating evidence from Deborah Ball and other scholars that teachers need to not only know content but to teach a student who is unfamiliar with the subject matter. This confirms our own understandings, and we recognize the need to draw on this new line of research in light of the changing learning ecology of students.

Our coauthor Emily Vickery notes that shifting market forces and the constant ramping up of interactive media and communication will continue to solidify an "attention economy" and spur the teaching profession "to redefine itself or become obsolete."

> Attention economics, Wikipedia tells us, "is an approach to the management of information that treats human attention as a

scarce commodity." As networks "learn" a person's behavior and preferences, content will become more personalized. In an attention economy, this personalization will become more and more valuable. Our "professional friends" on our networks become not only a source of information but also have the potential to act as filters—in essence channeling our attention. This applies not only to student learning but our own professional learning.

Researchers have documented the benefits of online professional learning that can be experienced anytime, anywhere,[42] while providing teachers instant access to a network of colleagues who have useful skills and knowledge.[43] We know from experiences with our own mostly virtual Teacher Leaders Network that the challenge for online community developers is "fostering among participants a sense of belonging, trust, and support, all of which are necessary for effective learning."[44] We foresee that new Web tools that both drive and are driven by the attention economy will help create a new learning ecology for teachers to promote ownership, trust and support; and actually help turn schools into organic knowledge organizations that encourage a high degree of creativity, adaptability and emergent collaboration.[45] Already in 2010, TeacherTube has created an online community to share instructional videos; Classroom 2.0 is connecting tens of thousands of K–12 teachers with weekly networking opportunities, and the avant-garde group Virtual Pioneers[46] has established an international network of social studies teachers interested in teaching students inside virtual worlds that depict historical eras.[47]

TeachScape provides extensive professional development, drawing on a blend of facilitated online, face-to-face, and classroom-based learning experiences through which teachers "dig into the research, observe exemplary teaching, practice approaches modeled in the case studies, collect samples of student work, and reflect on what they are doing (collaboratively)."[48] In 2010, TeachScape's web-based platform offered a wide range of functionality including tools to manage curriculum and provide "instant dissemination" of curricular modifications; assessment tools to guide instructional planning and decision making; "persistent access" to data for students, class, schools, and the district; and applications for using handheld devices to build a picture of a school's instructional activity.[49] Teachers.TV assembles engaging videos and practical resources and has established an active online community for teachers in the United Kingdom and the United States to "widen their skills, develop their practice, and connect with others in the field." By early 2010, Teachers.TV had already put together 3,500 video lessons that are used for grade-level teams to collectively learn how to teach specific topics (e.g., climate change, fractions, etc.) with "inspiration" and for master teachers to induct teaching assistants into their schools.[50]

Well before 2030, inspired by the entrepreneurial efforts of organizations like TeachScape and Teachers.TV, we'll see online treasure troves of the most effective teaching strategies—codified with emerging research on effective teachers and the conditions under which they can teach successfully. This transformational process will not only lead to more firmly establishing what counts for effective teaching but what effective teachers look like in practice and why. We predict that along a parallel line, associations and services led by expert teachers will offer nuanced feedback as they coach colleagues based on live and recorded classroom observations via the Internet. A novice physics teacher in rural America will no longer have to teach solo, with no master teacher on hand to provide just-in-time advice, feedback, and critique. Access to teaching expertise from afar will be a resource that can be customized to the needs of particular teacher communities, with learning and discussion built in, all created as part of ongoing, in-depth, needs-driven professional development.

Some teachers today are creating videos of their lessons with digital cameras and uploading the footage for use with mentors and trusted colleagues. In 2030, teaching "voyeurism" will be the norm. Thanks to policy incentives that reward teachers for revealing both the weaknesses and the strengths of their teaching, a new generation of teachers will find it normal and comfortable to share the artifacts of their practice with other educators—and even with parents and the public. Easily accessible databases, driven by semantic Web applications, will make it easier for teachers to upload and share specific bundles, images, data, commentary, and analyses with colleagues, students, and family members.

We understand the giant leap that this vision of shared practice via the Internet implies. The MetLife Survey of the American Teacher: Past, Present and Future (2008) found that only 15% of our colleagues had participated in any online professional network. Less than 60% had communicated virtually in any way with peers outside of their district. A mere 40% had taken an online course, while only 28% had ever written or read a blog on teaching. But these practices (or the lack of them) will change quickly as teachers born into the iGeneration seize the fiber-optic reins of teacher leadership over the next 2 decades. These trailblazers and the generations of teachers that succeed them will think nothing of sharing a student performance-clip with a parent or chatting with a colleague via a mobile device while observing her new lesson plan as it rolls out live in a physical classroom miles away—or in an avatar environment deep in cyberspace.

Our coauthor Jose Vilson, who grew up in the "Net Generation," teaches math in a high-needs New York City middle school. He writes about how new technologies could bring teachers together around new forms of collective assessment and accountability:

> Imagine that a student can instantly place [his or her] portfolio project on their handheld personal computer (HPC), and the permissions on that portfolio project are set for specific users, i.e., the teacher, the principal, the ELL coach and administrators, and even a trusted outside expert, mentor, or parent. If, ultimately, the teacher needs or wants to share the portfolio project, he can simply forward it to someone else. If the student portfolio should be made completely public, the software strips all personal identity information from the assessment product, and it's easily shareable throughout the Internet for feedback, evaluation or training purposes. Using technologies that are already emerging today, teachers and administrators can make comments directly on the portfolio project or link related portfolios, rubrics, demonstrations and data.
>
> I can imagine that the teacher might post the "anonymized" student product on [his or her] professional blog or within a virtual learning network. In 2010, we already see a not-so-secret movement in education where teachers establish blogs specifically to reflect and discuss their classroom experiences, thereby participating in an informal but powerful form of professional development as other educators interact in a "critical friend" role. Some teachers today have even taken on the arduous task of putting up whole lessons and multimedia demonstrations of their work, giving others free rein to dissect and criticize their methodologies. Imagine that this use of connective technologies becomes standard practice in the not-distant future (instead of unusual and even controversial). Not only will this method of improving teaching practice be cost-effective, but teachers will become empowered in the process by taking control of their professional learning.

We recognize the road that the teaching profession will have to travel, but we will get there, with new-millennium teachers leading the way—supported by veteran yet innovative teachers from previous generations. Unlike some policy pundits of today, our team is convinced that the teachers of 2030 will require *more* pedagogical training, not less. As Jose asserts:

No matter what technological advancements we experience as a society, educators will still need to concentrate on pedagogy, shaping our teaching around the needs of each child. Future technologies will constantly create demands on teachers to adapt sound pedagogical principles to new teaching methods and strategies that best meet the needs of students who are experiencing those technologies as natural ways of learning.

Now and in the future, effective teaching will be about organizing, whether it be the classroom and cyberspace environment; the knowledge, information, and activities in which students are engaged; or the interactions among students, colleagues, and other professional support personnel in the service of learning. By 2030, professional training for teachers will routinely include how to work in multiuser virtual environments (MUVEs), helping students engage in open-ended, collaborative inquiry and using their virtual work products to assess academic progress.[51] As more students have formal opportunities to learn in MUVEs, it will become even more important for teachers to understand how students process visual, aural, verbal, or tactile information. Indeed, the teachers of 2030 will need to be experts in the science of learning generally. Neuroscientists today are reporting that learning actually changes the physical structure of the maturing brain and that for serious learning to occur, new facts, ideas, and concepts must be connected to old ones.[52] As this body of knowledge increases, the demand for teachers who can apply it to the learning process of individual students will increase as well.

Working with Special-Needs Students

Looking at current trends, the Institute for the Future[53] projects a steady increase in students who come to school from backgrounds of poverty, as second language learners, or those with special learning needs. To be successful in the decades to come, teachers in the new millennium must be both pedagogically and culturally competent to meet the particular needs of these diverse learners.

Our TLN colleague Kathie Marshall has served as both a teacher and a literacy coach in inner-city Los Angeles for more than 3 decades. She understands the challenges:

When I returned to teach in 1996 in Los Angeles I was struck by the diversity of my students—70% Latino, 10% African American, 15% White (most Russian immigrants), and the rest Asian. Most all were on free or reduced lunch. There was a story behind each of my students—but my greatest concern was Dalila, who came into class each day, placed her head in her arms on the desk, and remained pretty much out of touch throughout her 2 hours with me.

At first I couldn't tell if she was tired, depressed, or just demonstrating her disdain. Her grades were awful. Slowly I began to try making contact with her before, during, and after class. I began one of my favorite practices—assigning "Letters to Mrs. Marshall" as homework once a month. Eventually Dalila began to share with me some of her challenges: an abusive dad, an alcoholic mother, and an older brother in trouble with the law. I responded at length anytime she shared herself with me.

One day I realized with a shock that Dalila was actually sitting up! She began to care about pleasing me, I think. She wrote in one of her homework letters, "I like the way you teach. I like the way you treat us. I wish all of my teachers taught like you." Her grades began to improve: D's and F's became C's and then B's. Soon, Dalila and two other girls began hanging out with me after the nutrition bells so persistently that I nicknamed them the "Barnacles."

How did I reach Dalila? Through my own persistence and my efforts to learn about her and her family. Slowly she began to trust me, I guess. Slowly she began to notice that I really cared about her well-being. One of my favorite moments was one day when I told the class I would be absent the next day because I had to go to a PD meeting. All of a sudden, Dalila's body stiffened; she looked me in the eye and cried, "You're going to be absent tomorrow? But you're the only reason I come to school!!"

I have often thought about that comment from Dalila and wondered how many students have *no* reason to come to school—and how we could prepare teachers to better understand and respond effectively to students like Dalila. How can we help more teachers learn to work with students whose families have lost their homes? Who come to school hungry but are embarrassed to eat the free meals offered because it's not cool? Whose brother was killed 2 years ago by a gangbanger? Whose dad is in prison? This part of teacher education is most often missing and it's critically important in our most challenged schools.

Jose Vilson tells the story of "Henry," a Haitian immigrant.

"Henry" walks to middle school alone on his first day. He's a late registrant, entering his first day weeks into the fall semester. He looks at the crowd outside the school and follows the girls and boys who trickle in left and right, a subtle din made by the whispers, giggles, and quiet conversations about Pokemon, last night's football game, and who's dating whom. He can't understand it, so he continues following the administrator's hand signals.

When it comes time to walk to class, he follows the students who look most like his age, smiling along the way but nervous throughout. The school aide, although curious, tells him something he can't understand, then points him in the right direction. "That way," he thinks. He sits in the back of the class. The teacher has his back to the students, writing on the SmartBoard to get the class started. The other students look at Henry strangely and some murmuring begins. The teacher turns around to see what started the commotion. He's startled by Henry, who never showed up on his attendance roster and whose appearance comes without any warning.

The teacher puts up his "Problem of the Day" and waves Henry over. The teacher asks him, "What's your name?" Henry recognizes the word "name" so he says, "Hen . . . Henry."

"Are you new?"

He nods.

"When did you get here?"

He shrugs.

"Do you speak English?"

Henry puts his thumb and index finger really close to each other, indicating that he really doesn't know much English at all. The teacher asks Henry to sit down in class again while the teacher teaches his lesson. The class is reading books Henry can't read. The class is writing essays Henry can't write. They're answering questions Henry can't respond to. He recognizes the pictures on the board and around the classroom, but he can only partially name them in his native language. He whispers to himself the name of each picture he knows, in his native language, and then goes around the room pointing to things, even while everyone else is reading.

After class, the teacher takes Henry to his administrator, who reveals to the teacher that his name isn't Henry but Hennrick, a 12-year-old Haitian boy who, only a month before, lived in a little town near Port-au-Prince. After settling in to an apartment with an aunt and uncle, Hennrick's mother inquired and brought him to the nearest school. He gets dressed in the most proper clothes possible, a white-collared shirt, a vest, and polyester slacks like he wore in his native school. He eats some cornmeal and hurries on his way with his mom to his new school.

When he enters into the school, he notices faces similar to the ones in his former school, except with different customs: different dress code, different way of acknowledging each other, and more importantly, more acclimated to their surroundings. Fortunately for Hennrick and his mother, someone in the main office spoke Creole.

They know little about him. The school doesn't have a good way to communicate with his former school. Hardly any of the teachers in his new school have any training in working with students like Hennrick and little perspective about his cultural background. As a result most already have low academic expectations for him.

By sheer circumstance, there are two teachers who are prepared to work with Hennrick—one who actually had an ESL credential as part of her university teacher education. The other was myself—and while I did not get a lot of formal training at all through my alternative credentialing program, I am of Hennrick's culture; my family is from Haiti.

When we went to the principal and described Hennrick's situation we got quiet acknowledgment, but not much help or guidance in how to serve this very bright, caring young student well. "Okay, we'll just make you two the ones in charge of this student, and if you need anything, let me know." We soon connected Hennrick's love for the arts to his aptitude for math. We developed a program of study that could use instruction in the arts and math to help him learn English. Knowing children is a prerequisite for teaching them. Hennrick was lucky—but the millions of children who come into our schools with similar obstacles shouldn't have to depend on luck.

We look to a future when our preparatory and support systems, not luck or providence, ensure teachers are ready to teach students like Hennrick.

Teachers Working with Each Other

Our TLN colleague Marsha Ratzel, a Kansas middle school science teacher, entered teaching after a "first" career in hospital administration. Professional collaboration was commonplace in the corporate environment in which she worked—it was a primary means of gaining and sharpening professional skills and knowledge. She found a very different situation when she began her second career in education 2 decades ago. Teachers, for the most part, worked in isolation. Professional training, when it was offered, came from the top down, with little or no attention given to the valuable synergistic effects of collegial collaboration. In recent years, Marsha says, that has begun to change, but the outlook on professional development for teachers "is still more about what can be done *to* us than what we can do together."

> I hope that part of what the future holds is teachers learning to
> learn for ourselves. The world changes so quickly and we have
> to stop leaning on outsiders to train us. We have to cast our
> own vision for what we want for our teaching careers, what we
> need to learn and how, and figure out how to go out and get
> it. I cannot wait for someone else to take care of what we need
> to know and do—that is the problem. Every teacher needs to
> be in charge of his or her own professional development—and
> important pieces of that PD will come from other teachers who
> have a deep understanding of the work we do.

Collaboration among us is a must. A large-scale research study, reported in 2009, concluded what we have always known. Teachers learn most from each other. The researchers, using 11 years of matched teacher and student achievement data, found that peer learning among small groups of experienced and qualified teachers seemed to be the most powerful predictor of student achievement over time.[54] A close reading of the study reveals that a lion's share of an individual teacher's value-added gain to student learning, as measured by standardized test scores, was attributable to *shared* expertise. In reporting on this groundbreaking study, *Education Week* concluded, "Teachers raise their games when the quality of their colleagues improves."[55]

Consider this scenario written by our coauthor Ariel Sacks, a Bank Street College graduate and 6th-year middle grades teacher in New York City, as she imagines her own professional practice in the year 2030:

> I have been teaching for almost 30 years now. I am a teacher
> leader in the Lightyears Network, which includes two schools in
> New York, one in Louisiana, another in Japan.
>   7 a.m.—Drink coffee, open Palmnet to the Lightyears online
> platform and the Web. Every teacher, student, and parent in the

NYC public schools has such a device, but each one is connected to its respective school's platform. I project it on the kitchen wall in front of me. A message from Mrs. Hendricks. Her son was robbed by teenagers while walking home from school yesterday. Her message includes a map of her son's walking route. I access his schedule. Band practice today until 5 p.m. I search his route for Safety Lookouts, which include parents, high school students, and storefront owners. Bingo! Three indicate availability weekdays at 5 p.m. I send out an automated message to both the teachers on my team locally as well as community support providers and neighborhood volunteers, who are accustomed to these alerts, telling them exactly what time to look out. The problem is solved in 2 minutes and requires less than 10 minutes of each of their time. I designed this program with two teachers and a technology volunteer last year because of an uptick in neighborhood violence. We received a school-based teacherpreneurship grant to create it.

8 a.m.—Analytic time where I conduct reviews of student blogs and performance assessments on my Palmnet on my subway ride to school.

9 a.m.—Eighth grade English. I share the room with Mr. Yau, a second-year English teacher for whom I serve as master mentor. I am the head teacher for one 90-minute class daily, during which he assists part-time. He is the head teacher for the other 90-minute class, while I observe and assist part-time. Students enter and busily begin checking each other's literature blogs from the night before on their Palmnets, which I've programmed to become available for viewing and commenting at exactly 9 a.m. The blogs include responses to yesterday's discussion of a novel. We've partnered with a class in Japan, reading the same novel; their blogs are available for viewing and commenting. I circulate, checking in with a few students who had not finished the book for yesterday's discussion. They open their electronic margin notes from last night. I okay them to enter today's discussion.

9:15 a.m.—Students assemble around a seminar table to continue face-to-face discussions of the novel. A computer screen helps me moderate. Students press a button when they want to comment; their name appears on the screen. There is also a digital tally showing how many times each student has spoken. Mid-discussion, the computer screen highlights names of students who have not spoken yet; I ask them to comment.

My Palmnet, a G35 smartphone, records and transcribes our conversation into written words, which will be available on our class literature blog. Tomorrow we will videoconference with the school in Japan for final discussions of the novel. In the evening, I'll do a virtual lesson study with my colleagues locally, in San Francisco and in Tokyo.

10 a.m.—Break. Students may talk, walk, or use their Palmnets.

10:10 a.m.—Writing time. Students to reflect in their journals on how our observations of the novelist's craft in discussion today might be useful in their own writing. Then students work on their stories. Each student has a writing partner from our schools in Japan or California. Students are writing stories that are set in their partner's region. Their partners post videos and photos of their neighborhoods and answer questions about their settings.

10:45 a.m.—Meeting with Mr. Yau. We debrief my facilitation of today's discussion. I ask him which points he thinks I might follow up on tomorrow and how I might do it. We look at his class's fiction writing through our Palmnets, and determine that half of the students need more work on subject-verb agreement (something he'd taught a few months ago). We send evidence of this need to his portfolio and brainstorm a few ideas for reinforcing this skill with those students. Mr. Yau is seeking to improve his students' knowledge of grammar and culture (with a focus on both English and Chinese) and will have a chance, with my help, of earning performance points and a pay raise if we meet his goals.

11:30 a.m.—Lunch . . . eat in garden café with colleagues; informal professional discussions intermingle with personal conversation and video chat with my international network of teacher leaders.

12:30 p.m.—Meeting at NYC partner middle school. The school has a number of recent immigrants from Yemen, who need ESL instruction that includes teaching our alphabet and phonics system. I meet with English teachers to plan a way to address these students' literacy needs immediately, without boring them developmentally or isolating them from other students socially.

2 p.m.—A period dedicated to pursuing an area of professional growth of my choosing. I decide to return to my school, to a workspace with a view of the garden. A group of

students is working there with neighborhood retirees. I smile thinking of two of my students who have decided to turn their stories, set in rural Louisiana and Japan, into sim-game plots. They are working with a professional game designer who is donating his time right now. I want to duck down to the study hall where they are meeting, but I can't. I've received a national teacherpreneur fellowship and work virtually with a group of accomplished teachers from around the country. We are funded by the federal government, writing a book about the future of education. My professional guild has helped broker the deal for me. Things are changing quickly and we want to start creating the schools our children's children will need in 2050, now.

7 p.m.—I log on with colleagues locally and internationally and use a G35 version of Quantified Self[56] to document and share, both internally and publicly, what our students are learning, how well we are serving their needs, and what we will be doing next to advance their academic achievement and citizenship skills. The tools allow us to provide evidence of our achievement as teachers and leaders. Our expertise and data are used as part of the Urban Teacher 2050 residency program—an effort to develop a new generation of teacher-leaders for 2050.

For current teachers, one element that might resonate most in this scenario is opportunity for frequent engagement for Ariel in embedded professional development—as an individual, as a team teacher, as a community facilitator, and as a member of a research team of colleagues from around the country and the world. Such school-day opportunities are precious and rare for teachers today. But we are adamant that if today's teachers ever hope to be fully supported as lifelong learners, they must create and embrace opportunities to model this kind of continuous professional growth. Which brings us to the next major force that we believe will shape the future of education—the seamless connection between critically important brick-and-mortar schools and the ever-expanding opportunities for students to learn in cyberspace.

CHAPTER 4

Emergent Reality #2:
Seamless Connections
In and Out of Cyberspace

A Radically Different World

If you think our future will require better schools, you're wrong. The future of education calls for entirely new kinds of learning environments.

If you think we will need better teachers, you're wrong. Tomorrow's learners will need guides who take on fundamentally different roles.

As every dimension of our world evolves so rapidly, the education challenges of tomorrow will require solutions that go far beyond today's answers.

Source: 2020 Forecast: Creating the Future of Learning, KnowledgeWorks Foundation

---

Emily Vickery sets the scene for us:

> Now we have evolved from the Network Age to the Hyper-Connected Age, a period characterized by the unprecedented use of rapidly changing technologies. From mobile devices and smart technologies, to video publishing and the use of Twitter, the merger of mobile technologies and social media to publish and connect with others has skyrocketed.

Let's face it: Major advancements in new technologies and bio-engineering are reshaping our everyday lives and challenging policymakers, practitioners, and parents to rethink what the public schools look like and *what counts for learning*. In the first decade of the 21st century, mobile-platform solutions, educational gaming, and virtual courses are becoming more and more omnipresent. New interactive digital media is evolving, and even in lower-income communities, students are becoming more wired for learning with the rise of mobile technologies. In fact, online learning for K–12 students increased from 45,000 enrollments in 2000 to roughly 1 million in 2007, serving not only those who want to accelerate their accumulation of course credits but tweens and teens who are struggling academically or socially, young mothers who need to care for their infants, and special students with restrictive medical conditions.[1] Although more students are engaged in online learning in the United States, these numbers are still relatively small.

Clay Christensen and his colleagues who coauthored the 2008 book on human capital trends, *Disrupting Class*, look to online learning as "an exciting disruption," because it allows anyone—anytime and anywhere—to access a consistent learning experience.[2] They note that in Georgia—a state where there are about 440 high schools—there are only 88 well-qualified physics teachers. For Christensen and his colleagues, one solution to the shortage is to "increase student access to the very best teaching through online offerings that transcend the limitations of geography."[3]

In addition, customized online learning can provide students instant feedback about their progress and tailor extra assistance and tutoring around the material they don't yet understand. Best of all, say its advocates, students can work at their own pace and according to their own schedules. Recent studies have also shown that online learning can yield higher student achievement than traditional classroom delivery. Over a 12-year period examining 99 studies, researchers at SRI International compared online and traditional classroom performance for the same courses and found that students learned more virtually. (They reported modest but statistically meaningful differences, with the important caveat that most of those studied were of traditional college age or older.)[4]

As Dylan Tweney, senior editor of *Wired* magazine, noted:

> There's no doubt that the Internet is (and evermore becoming) an extension of human intelligence, both individual and collective. But the extent to which it's able to augment intelligence depends on how much people are able to make it conform to their needs. Being able to look up who starred in the second season of the Tracey Ullman show on Wikipedia is the lowest form of intelligence augmentation; being able to build social networks and interactive software that helps you answer specific questions or enrich your intellectual life is much more powerful.[5]

Learning in cyberspace must frame efforts to transform the teaching profession that serves students and families. While the flexibility and self-directedness of online learning is appealing, Renee Moore reminds us that it is not a panacea or cheap outsourcing strategy. Good teaching matters in every learning situation:

One of the first things I learned about teaching online is that it's not just about putting a bunch of notes on the Web for students to read, then giving a test. That's bad in a classroom and deadly online. I had to learn to think about my teaching in multisensory ways, which took a little while. Fortunately, others had gone before me from whom I could learn.

Our co-author Susie Highley, a school media specialist in Indiana, sees online learning as a powerful and affordable means of extending access to excellent teaching:

While some might think that tremendous costs will be involved, especially for technology, there can be tremendous savings by foregoing today's traditional textbooks in favor of credible Web resources—and reducing the need for vast physical spaces by relying more on virtual space. School systems can also save great sums of money by sharing more resources among themselves through consortia, via the Internet. The costs for "netbooks" and "smartphones" continue to plummet as their functionality increases; in the near future it is reasonable to expect that many (and likely most) students will have constant access to powerful electronic devices that fulfill many different needs—some of them educational.

Admittedly, changing the roles and/or reducing the tight grip of entrenched educational publishers will not be simple. But the potential exists that by 2030, students and teachers, rather than corporations, will be identifying and assembling much of the content to be studied. Online learning got its start, not as a way to displace teachers, but to fill in learning gaps. Why not expand the reach of a master physics teacher now serving isolated students in rural Iowa to students in urban areas? Why not cultivate a network of physics teachers who effectively teach online?

The expansion and effective organization of virtual and mirror worlds (such as Second Life and Google Earth, respectively) will have a dramatic effect on human interaction and learning. Students will also be logging into their own unique "metaverse"; once they do, they will likely find a descendent of today's Netvibes or Pageflakes software, aggregating the components of their educational experience with guidance from a team of educators who know a great deal about each student's particular learning needs and interests.

Today's mainstream models of online learning are still transitioning from a more traditional classroom metaphor to something closer to 21st-century entertainment media. Multiplayer, role-playing games are nothing new to most savvy computer users under the age of 35, but the latest Internet-server-based MUVEs are reaching a level of sophistication that will soon force online educators to prove to their K–12 students that they've "got game." The technologies behind massively played Web games like World of Warcraft and EverQuest, and the understanding of the link between virtual gaming and real world social relationships growing out of Web phenomena like Facebook's FarmVille[6]—coupled with rapid advances in the neuroscience of learning—will be irresistible to trailblazing educators and, very likely, ubiquitous in the years ahead.

Why do we believe that? MUVEs allow for multiple participants to access virtual contexts, work with digital artifacts, communicate with each other, represent themselves through "avatars" (graphical and text-based), and model problem solving in situations that simulate the real world. MUVEs have the potential to offer students "cognitive apprenticeships" and can take them to places heretofore inaccessible due to disconnects with geography, time, and expertise—where they can explore ideas and possibilities through many windows and contexts.[7] The most advanced examples of these technologies are also incredibly engaging. By March 2010, 9 months after the MUVE-like FarmVille appeared within the Facebook social network, there were 85 million active users involved in the game and 25 million observers—all total, about 1% of the Earth's population. And FarmVille was not a "shooter" game; in fact, it had many of the characteristics of a higher-order educational experience. Wikipedia offered this simple summary: "The game allows members of Facebook to manage a virtual farm by planting, growing and harvesting virtual crops, trees, and raising livestock."[8]

Cognitive scientists have come to demonstrate how humans learn best in situations that are authentic and distributed, calling upon information sources that are both internal and external to the learner. Early efforts like River City, developed as a proof of concept by researcher Chris Dede and others at Harvard and George Mason universities, confirm the usefulness of MUVE environments in accomplishing this kind of learning experience.[9]

Emily Vickery confirms that the shift we see toward digital forms of learning is not just a change of venue:

Today, being truly "wired" means more than simply having
access to infrastructure, hardware, software, and online courses.
It also means having access to and mastery of the latest digital

River City is a MUVE for teaching scientific inquiry and 21st-century skills in middle school science classes. Drawn from the National Science Standards, River City is designed around topics that are central to biological and epidemiological subject matter. As visitors to River City, students travel back in time, bringing their 21st-century knowledge and technology to address 19th-century problems. River City is a town besieged with health problems, and students work together in small research teams to help the town understand why residents are becoming ill. The River City MUVE features an underlying simulation that allows students to manipulate variables to help determine the cause of the epidemic. Students collect data, form hypotheses, develop controlled experiments to test their hypotheses, and make recommendations based on their findings to other members of their research community.

By design, the phenomena students investigate in River City are too complex for any one student to master within the time allotted for the project. Central to the River City experience is the social distribution of perception, learning, and reasoning through the affordances of the simulation and within various group activities.

Source: excerpted from Dieterle, E., & Clarke, J. (2010). Multi-user virtual environments for teaching and learning. In M. Pagani (Ed.), *Encyclopedia of multimedia technology and networking* (2nd ed), http://muve.gse.harvard.edu/rivercityproject/documents/MUVE=for=TandL=Dieterle=Clarke.pdf

tools that define what is today termed the Web 2.0 world—tools that empower us to create, produce, collaborate, and participate in shared learning and citizenship in local-to-global contexts.

Our TLN colleague Marsha Ratzel, a middle grades science teacher in suburban Kansas, offers a concrete example from her own classroom:

I want my instruction to fit what real world folks do outside an educational setting. This year we've been following a ship, called the *JR*, from which real scientists are drilling up core samples of the earth's crust. From those samples, they are able to track (with micropaleontology) how that particular crust was formed. There are geoscientists, biochemists, oceanographers, and so on, involved. This research ship maintains an online, onboard teacher-in-residence who communicates with kids. They get the onboard teacher to ask the scientists questions for them, video different kinds of scientific processes and just give a sense of life onboard a scientific research vessel. It has totally engaged some of my kids . . . they are fascinated by how a drilling rig can go down through a hole in a ship and not capsize the whole ship. This is real science, and students get the sense that they are involved in the work of real scientists. Why cannot more students have this experience?

Marsha's story well illustrates Emily's conclusion: "I cannot emphasize enough that the mastery of today's Web 2.0 tools and those of the future—the tools of innovation—is key to the success of learning in the 21st century." And Web 3.0 is already upon us, where semantic tagging of content connects different applications to find and remix information for an individualized experience far beyond anything we've yet experienced. Web 3.0 is bringing intelligent searching, extreme personalization, and, yes, behavioral advertising.[10]

As the Web morphs and grows, we are also paying attention to the rapid development of mobile platforms that allow students to be connected to a world of learning from just about anywhere via a handheld device. Emily Vickery explains:

> An example of multisensory innovation is the collaboration between Wonderfactory and Time, Inc. to produce the interactive *Sports Illustrated*, an explosive mash-up of text, video, hyperlinked information, and social networking, all delivered in a handheld device which will, undoubtedly, influence the future design of interactive learning environments. The U.S. Department of Education has noted the onslaught of handhelds used in mobile learning by earmarking $5 billion in competitive grants focusing on the use of multisensor, tough computing, including their use in preschool and elementary grades.[11]
>
> One innovation in mobile learning has been quick-response codes, which support the move away from school-based learning to place-based learning. According to Educause, "QR codes are two-dimensional bar codes that can contain any alphanumeric text and often feature URLs that connect users to sites where they can learn about an object or place (known as "mobile tagging"). Decoding software, on tools such as camera phones, interpret the codes, which are increasingly found in places such as product labels, billboards, and buildings, inviting passers-by to pull out their mobile phones and uncover the coded information. QR codes link the physical world with the virtual by providing on the spot access to descriptive language and online resources for objects and locations. In this way, the codes support experiential learning, bring scholarship out of the classroom and into the physical experience. The greatest importance of QR codes could lie, not in their specific use, but

in the opportunities they offer for moving away from keyboards as input devices in learning environments."[12] QR codes redefine the "field trip" and the learner's experience. Learners may walk along Boston's Freedom Trail or wander a woodland path accessing QR codes that unleash history lessons and biological explorations, from tree identification to animal habitat.

Another place-based piece of learning innovation weaning teachers and learners from the keyboard is Google Goggles. Instead of typing in search terms on the Web to find information, learners can take a photo. Called visual searches, this capacity will add to the experiential learning toolbox.

Mobile devices could do far more than allow students to communicate with teachers or begin an assignment at any time. They enable students to stay engaged in a perpetual state of learning on the way to or from work or their physical classrooms. Emily points to global positions system (GPS) capability in phones as another important innovation that will make its mark—for interactive learning modeled on geocaching, as well as for monitoring student safety.

We do not know for certain where we will be in 2030. What we do know for certain is that children and teens will need—as they always have—wise and effective teachers to guide them. And to think that there are policymakers and others influential in the media who claim we do not need teacher preparation.

Melding the Virtual and Physical Worlds

It is tempting to view the future through a utopian lens—imagining a learning environment in which the use of memory-enhancing drugs and IQ-boosting neurostimulants helps all students focus on high achievement and productivity—in which genetic engineering reduces or eliminates learning disabilities, and innovations in bio-engineering expand the opportunities of individuals who are physically challenged to engage with others in school and work. A future in which all children are learning all the time.

But we know that scientific advancement doesn't take place in a social vacuum. Powerful societal trends are already in play that will shape American life over the next 20 years in somewhat predictable ways. Our own thinking about education's future has been influenced by the important work of the KnowledgeWorks Foundation (KWF) and the Institute for the Future—a partnership that first produced *The Map of Future Forces Affecting Education* in 2006 and more recently the *2020 Forecast: Creating the Future of Learning*.[13] Rather than extrapolate the future from the promises of science or other research, this body of work looks at past and current trends to suggest what we might logically anticipate for the years ahead. While KWF's construct of the future is sobering, the purpose is not to depress us, but to help us "make better decisions in the present" that will help ensure a viable and responsive learning environment for students tomorrow.[14]

The pragmatic futurists working with KWF forecast a nation and world with increasing problems of bio-distress and pandemic illness that could wreak havoc on students' health. What KWF calls "the sick herd"— individuals coping with bio-distress and chronic illnesses—will continue to expand, resulting in more inconsistent attendance during the "regular" school day in brick-and-mortar buildings.[15] In mapping out this likely future, the researchers point to current trends like the increase in childhood obesity, escalating incidences of student mental illness, and the growing frequency of asthma, diabetes, and other chronic conditions attributable to the environment of decaying cities. Pandemics, they believe, will become more common, as new strands of avian flu and other infectious diseases surface—exploiting "vulnerabilities in the human population that bring about massive impacts to cities, institutions, and economies."[16] While the Obama administration's hard-fought health care reforms of 2010 hold promise that fewer Americans will find themselves uninsured in the coming years, at this point the reforms are incomplete and politically fragile. The KWF trends-map predicts that unless the United States achieves and

FIGURE 4.1. Sick Herd

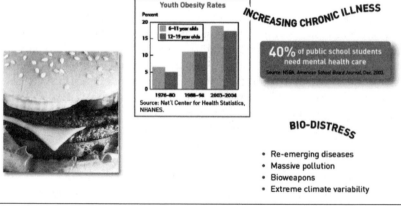

Source: Reprinted by permission of KnowledgeWorks Foundation and Institute for the Future.

sustains a true universal health care system, we will still see multiple generations of family members without reliable and affordable medical and preventative care. As a consequence, schools will be confronted with educating more and more students to higher academic standards, while recurring illness (and predicted economic downturns) undermine their efforts.

In this likely version of the future, we can also anticipate that, despite the promise of online learning, the turbulent economy will force increasing numbers of parents to rely even more on schools to serve in their age-old custodial role—taking care of children in physical settings while adults stitch together a patchwork of part-time jobs to make financial ends meet. The economic recession that began late in the last decade is instructive: In 2009, well over 40% of the nation's families had a member who lost a job or took a cut in pay—leading to a new job-scarce era with an impact predicted to last for many years.[17] In fact, in March 2010, pink slips were handed out to about 22,000 California teachers, representing approximately 9% of the state's entire teaching workforce[18]—creating more instability in the teaching profession and more economic chaos in the nation's largest state. Don Peck, writing in the *Atlantic* of March 2010, observed that chronic unemployment "is a pestilence that slowly eats away at people, families, and, if it spreads widely enough, the fabric of society."

> The worst effects of pervasive joblessness—on family, politics, society—take time to incubate, and they show themselves only slowly. But ultimately, they leave deep marks that endure long after boom times have returned. Some of these marks are just now becoming visible, and even if the economy magically and fully recovers tomorrow, new ones will continue to appear. If it persists much longer, this era of high joblessness will likely change the life course and character of a generation of young adults—and quite possibly those of the children behind them as well. . . . It may already be plunging many inner cities into a kind of despair and dysfunction not seen for decades. Ultimately, it is likely to warp our politics, our culture, and the character of our society for years.[19]

In such a scenario, our future schools will be called upon to prepare students academically for good jobs in a post-industrial economy and tomorrow's educators (many of whom are already teaching today) will need to help students develop the social, psychological, and physical capacities to survive and make their way in the world, especially in what the KnowledgeWorks Foundation describes as VUCA communities—those marked by volatility, uncertainty, complexity, and ambiguity. "Economic instability, lack of shared norms, and weakening infrastructures (will) challenge urban communities to redefine sustainability [and look for] ways to pioneer security, safety and sustainability," predicts the KWF map of future forces.

As a result, brick-and-mortar schools will be critical in achieving this sustainability. Well before 2030, educators working daily with children face-to-face will need the resources and political support to expand their in loco parentis responsibilities. School buildings that once opened from 7 to 3 for 180 days a year will need to become year-round, 24/7 community centers of learning. We like the idea put forth by KWF that schools can become "hubs of design knowledge"—providing a venue for students to engage in project-based learning that contributes to their local communities.[20] They also must be safe places, where teachers and other professionals know children and their families well. We talk about our own vision of the new community school later in this chapter.

Much is said today about the promise of technology and cyberspace education to "liberate" students and their parents from the tyranny of archaic school district bureaucracies and recalcitrant teacher unions.[21] In some situations, the virtual school is being marketed as a cost-cutting solution for embattled elected officials. The use of online simulations, video on demand, and virtual helpers will get education out of the red, argue public school critics like Terry Moe and John Chubb, because "tech is cheap and labor [i.e., teachers] is extraordinarily expensive."[22]

Putting aside for the moment the spurious notion that we can somehow rely heavily on computer programs, a handful of teachers, and outsourced low-wage workers to educate America's next generations—we believe the evidence is overwhelming that our best public education solution in the future will be a model that seamlessly blends virtual and face-to-face learning and ensures that all students will grow into healthy, knowledgeable, and resourceful citizens of a globalized world, well prepared to cope with both the promise and perils of coming scientific and social transformations.

The story of the future we want to communicate is, not just about how—in 2030—technology will fuel new conceptions of teaching and learning, but also how essential human relationships in brick-and-mortar school buildings will continue to be. In the next chapter we describe a highly differentiated teaching workforce prepared to serve students and their families in many kinds of settings—including in challenged urban and rural communities that demand wrap-around educational, social, and health services. The teaching profession must look very different and carve out new roles for teachers to play—some who very well may continue to teach in the typical 6.5 hour time slot between early morning to mid-afternoon, but many others who will be teaching during the late afternoons and evenings. And their teaching will be far more than the 3Rs. We imagine that many more teachers, especially the most accomplished and well compensated, will serve in essential leadership roles entwined with the community—teaching children and their parents, as well as collaborating with key social and health care agencies and programs—and fulfilling these roles in *both* brick-and-mortar and virtual settings.

The Diverse Needs of Students Today and the Schools Tomorrow

There are policy mavens in both the progressive and conservative education reform camps who imagine that while physical schools may continue to exist as cyberspace evolves, these facilities will mostly serve as places for young people to socialize face-to-face while a small workforce manages and supervises student interactions with technology. As we've said, this is a naïve perspective, given what we know about the challenges that teachers already face in many schools and the preponderance of evidence suggesting that those challenges will increase—not decrease—in the near future. Our TLN colleague Kathie Marshall, who has taught and coached for more than 30 years in inner-city Los Angeles, describes just a *few* of the students she teaches today:

> First there is Aly, who expresses her interest in being more popular by being bad in front of her peers. Then there is Johnny, who's SO hyperactive and has yet to be diagnosed and treated for ADHD. He is angry and defiant and can instantly steer the class off course and shatter the concentration of those around him. Then there is Tony, whose learning difficulties so mask his real ability. My own teaching is undermined by other teachers who lack the pedagogical know-how to give him enough time to complete tasks. In my professional opinion, when it comes to academics, Tony's ability is at the top. But anyone who is going to help him learn needs to realize how much processing time he requires and how much he still misses his brother.
>
> There's Leo, whose immaturity and impulsivity interfere with his exceptional abilities; and Ady, who was just transferred to my class because she threatened her previous English teacher, who was not very adept at handling her. I also work with Isaiah, who fluctuates between being a top-notch student and a top-notch smart aleck whose favorite response is, "I have anger issues!" Then there are Samantha, who's proficient but whose home problems (domestic violence) have caused her to become one of the most frequent visitors to the deans' office. And Robert, who hides his hearing difficulties from his peers and who has an older brother undergoing chemotherapy for cancer.
>
> More than anything these students need teachers who take the time to know them well and have the skills and knowledge

to translate that understanding into teaching strategies that [ensure that] they will learn English and math and many other life skills.

Our TLN colleague Susan Graham, a seasoned NBCT of 25 years teaching experience, describes her work with Kymra, "one tough cookie" who was self-contained because of a history of violence—except in her Family and Consumer Science class.

> Kymra ran away at 14 and she was smart enough to have survived living "around" and picking up some courier work for some drug dealers in Richmond for 6 months before she wound up in the juvenile justice system. She was mad as a caged wildcat most days and, needless to say, Kymra and I spent a lot of time out in the hall together. She told me in no uncertain terms that she didn't need a fat ol' white woman telling her what to do because I wasn't the boss of her. I told her I understood that, but due to circumstances that neither of us could control we were going to be together an hour a day and that she did have a choice: some degree of compliance with and tolerance of me "and the other stupid teachers" (as I laugh—trying to make her smile) so she could retain what little freedom she had—or we both knew she'd have to go back to "juvie" and have no control at all. She rolled her eyes, made that middle school disgusted sound, and pouted. And went to work.
>
> She didn't like me and she didn't like school, but I saw I could engage her over time by teaching math and other skills through cooking. Of course, Kymra informed me she didn't intend to make biscuits my way. She knew how to cook and didn't need me to tell her what to do. But as she described her grandmother's biscuits, she began to open up and tell me of her granddaddy who died. Her father had a drinking buddy who would mess around with her (beginning at age 12), and her daddy didn't do anything about it—but her granddaddy did. He was no longer around to protect her. That was why she fled and is still on the run. But we are making progress in school, and Kymra is now leading some of our math lessons with some of her grandmother's recipes.

Most members of our writing team are teaching or have taught in schools that are not adequately staffed to serve a high-needs student pop-ulation. We regularly witness new teachers with little training in classroom management struggling to handle student disengagement, apathy, and violence. The context may be different for Jose Vilson and Ariel Sacks in New York City's depressed neighborhoods than for Jennifer Barnett and Renee Moore in the South's rural impoverished communities, but the message is the same. Students bring the volatility and challenges of the outside world into the schools where they are expected to sit still and learn—often as a single, isolated teacher attempts to reach 35 or more children at once.

How, we wonder, will computer programs and poorly trained teaching assistants help children like those that Kathie, Susan, and so many of us teach become successful learners? While it is true, as Kathie points out, that we have teachers in our school systems today who are not prepared to serve these children well, clearly the solution lies not simply in software (however promising and engaging) but in making sure we have more—not fewer—Kathie Marshalls and Susan Grahams in the stress-filled years to come.

The Community-Centered School

If we are not careful, only some students will enjoy the flexibility and independence of cyberspace learning and "unbundled" educational options. We can predict that more privileged students—bolstered by support systems of knowledgeable adults and ready access to technology—will have the structure, access, and freedom to pursue personalized and largely virtual courses of study. But what of the many other students who will not have ready access to these resources? Their families will still need to rely on school buildings where children are taught and supervised by committed adults looking out for their interests while also receiving two meals a day. Once they leave school, of course, these young people will enter the same hyper-connected world as their plugged-in peers, so it will not be enough to simply provide them a safe harbor—we also need to prepare them to enter that world on equal footing.

Emily Vickery describes the idea of a school based in the community, an idea she notes is not new:

> The push for community-based schools is not new. The Coalition for Community Schools,[23] established in 1997, calls for the school to be the center of community life beyond the school day and opening up to multiple uses, from offerings in the visual and performing arts, athletics, academic tutoring, and credit recovery to neighborhood dinners, parenting classes, child care, and medical outreach.

We have not seen these ideas become widespread, but we do see promising examples. Our co-author Carrie J. Kamm works with the Academy of Urban School Leadership (AUSL), which oversees several turnaround schools in Chicago and serves as a laboratory tasked with fully preparing teacher-leaders who will commit to careers teaching in high-needs communities. She calls for more schools that offer services by these community-based schools, including mobile health clinics and facilitation with the city's social-support service providers. But, importantly, these schools don't stop at meeting students' and families' most basic needs. They also draw on the rich culture of Chicago to enhance student learning by supporting programs like artists-in-residence and interactions with diverse experts and individuals who are community assets.

Carrie writes:

> Whether students receive the majority of their education in a brick-and-mortar setting or if they split their time between brick-and-mortar schools and online learning options, students will need learning environments that are safe, promote discipline and expect and insist on high levels of engagement. . . . By 2030, the ways in which students receive education may look quite different, but human-to-human interaction will still in some way be a part of that experience. Teachers will need to advocate for students living in the inner cities, many of whom will require a full-service brick-and-mortar school to gain the knowledge, skills and self-efficacy needed.

Community-centered urban and rural schools of the future could build upon the precedent being set by AUSL and several other visionary programs today. By supporting a full range of educational and support services under a single roof or within an easily accessible perimeter, they could create seamless environments for students and families to take advantage of opportunities while also leveraging the cost efficiencies of shared space. On-site services and facilities could include fully equipped gyms, health clinics, job centers, local university offices, local businesses dedicated to working with students as interns, performing and graphic arts centers, and, yes, technology hubs, where students and families could take full advantage of virtual learning technologies and opportunities to connect to communities outside their own locales.

These thriving community-centered schools call to mind the KnowledgeWorks Foundation's concept of a "Hub":

The fundamental purpose of a Hub is to create a fully aligned P–20 education system, from early childhood education through college and workforce development, along with lifelong learning opportunities for everyone in the community. The design includes universal health care and early childhood education, family-friendly workplaces, service learning opportunities, and parent engagement in their children's education. In this scenario, the walls between school and community break down, and old-fashioned learning mechanisms such as apprenticeships are renewed. Most learning takes place in real-world settings, where its relevance is readily apparent. The Hub serves the community as a whole by providing economic growth and anti-poverty initiatives through coordinated economic, workforce, and community development programs.[24]

The Hub, as defined by the KWF, is framed in large part by the distinctiveness, early success, and expansion of the Harlem Children's Zone (HCZ) project, "a unique, holistic approach to rebuilding a community so that its children can stay on track through college and go on to the job market."[25] HCZ works to "reweave the social fabric of Harlem, which has been torn apart by crime, drugs and decades of poverty" by creating integrated in-school, after-school, social-service, health and community-building programs. HCZ includes both the Baby College, a series of workshops for parents of children ages 0 to 3, and a K–12 education program through its specially designed Promise Academy charter schools.

HCZ's transformative goal, says founder Geoffrey Canada, is to make it possible for children from high-needs communities to:

Get what middle-class and upper-middle-class kids get. They get safety. They get structure. They get academic enrichment. They get cultural activity. They get adults who love them and are prepared to do anything. (We are) prepared to do anything to keep these kids on the right track.[26]

In the Promise Academy schools, classes have a ratio of one adult for every six students, and with growing philanthropic support, there are state-of-the-art science labs, a first-rate gym, and a restaurant-style cafeteria that serves to feed hungry children well but, also, fight obesity. And in these charter schools, class size and teacher quality are not part of the usual zero-sum game played out in the debates over the teaching profession.

The first Promise school opened in 2004. It may be a decade or more before a fair assessment can be made of HCZ's success in meeting Canada's dream of true equity. But what both the Hub and HCZ community approaches recognize is that schools can—and have—helped students overcome some of the impact of social and economic disadvantage. They acknowledge that while teaching quality is paramount in closing the equity and achievement gaps, the actions of teachers and administrators, taking place in a traditional school paradigm, cannot completely neutralize those impacts.

We see an urgency to both explode the strictures of learning imposed by the traditional brick-and-mortar school while also preserving and expanding some of its essential functions for those who need them. One critical step in this transformation will be to tear down the traditional barriers that make too many schools appear detached from their distressed communities. Adults inside and outside these schools need opportunities to discover that many solutions to entrenched problems will only be found by working together.

We recently learned of an elementary school called Sopori, located in the poor border town of Amado, Arizona. By opening its doors to the larger community, the school has found a way to leverage local property taxes to offer state-of-the-art facilities and services, including a swimming pool, breakfast for all the students, a data tracking system, and a preschool. The preschool is free to families, so long as the majority Spanish-speaking parents attend English classes while their children are learning.

Our TLN colleague, Dan Brown, teaches at the SEED Charter School of Washington, D.C., which he says "has a mouthful for a mission statement." SEED is much needed—and much of what the wide variety of teachers and counselors do on a daily basis cannot be done online. Dan writes,

> SEED is an urban, public, nonselective, college-prep boarding school, located within the community it serves. The mission is complicated by the reality that this college-prep community is taking root in a perennially struggling swath of the city (wards 7 and 8) that contains about 140,000 residents and only one sit-down restaurant, a Denny's. More than three-quarters of children born in Ward 8 enter the world in single-parent homes. The SEED school sits on the site of what used to be a shuttered elementary school that was torched two dozen times and saw a little girl shot to death in an act of senseless violence. The road is uphill, but since its founding in 1998, and especially since a new principal took over in 2007, SEED D.C. is proving that a community school with the right model can transform lives for the better. This is where I teach English to 11th- and 12th-graders.

The students, selected by lottery as they enter 6th grade, live in dorms on a small, 5-acre gated campus in southeast D.C. Sunday night to Friday afternoon. Two overlapping staffs—the academic faculty for the school day and the student life staff for evenings and overnight—collaborate to provide round-the-clock support. This costs 2.7 times the local per pupil allotment. Each of the approximately 320 SEED students receives three meals daily, an extended school day, small class sizes (rarely more than 15), a rigorous college-prep curriculum, exhaustive college counseling, a dorm environment including membership to a college-named "house," and a phalanx of support services and off-campus exposure opportunities.

On a typical day at SEED, students awaken by 7 a.m. and head to breakfast in the cafeteria. From 8 a.m. to 4 p.m., the dorms are off limits as students attend four 100-minute blocks of classes and a lunch period. When the academic day ends, students are in the care of "life skills counselors" [LSCs] who lead the students through HALLS [habits for achieving lifelong success] classes, study hall, extracurricular activities, and dinner. The LSCs go home at midnight and a smaller staff of resident advisors [RAs] supervises the students overnight and, then, gets them up in time for breakfast.

These efforts are producing promising results. In wards 7 and 8 of Washington [D.C.]—where SEED is located and a majority of its student population lives—a mere 5% of high school freshmen graduate from college within 5 years of enrollment. (The national average is 23%.) SEED now sends 97% of its graduates to college. The school is too new to have meaningful college graduation data, but SEED's first cohort of high school graduates (class of 2004) earned bachelor's degrees at higher rates than the national average. Most SEED students are the first in their families to enroll in college.

The work on the ground is intense and unending. Most students enter with below-grade-level skills and many contend with a relentless litany of tragedy and stress that accompanies urban poverty. Recently, my infinitely patient wife told me, "SEED is consuming you." Yet despite my need to seek a healthier work-family balance, SEED is certainly the best teaching opportunity I've ever had. My colleagues are smart and dedicated, and my administrators are supportive and receptive to teachers' ideas. I teach intimate classes and craft my own curriculum based on state standards. Unlike other public school environments in which I've worked, there is little bureaucracy preventing me from pursuing special projects, like publishing a paperback literary anthology (*Truth Be Told: Diamonds in the Rough by the Class of 2009*) or partnering with the National Shakespeare Theatre to bring in a teaching artist to direct my students in a performance of Henry V. This autonomy energizes the staff.

The 21st-century community-centered schools we envision will not attempt to shelter high-needs students from the neighborhood that surrounds them but partner with their neighbors to create a dynamic resource that invigorates both the community and the school.[27] And it is schools like SEED and teachers like Dan that make us hopeful as well as impatient for the changes that must come.

We're Wasting Time Arguing About 20th-Century Schools

As teachers thinking about change and the future, we're struck by how much energy is spent debating the problems of the public education system as it existed in the days of *A Nation at Risk*.[28] The 1983 landmark report from the federal government focused primarily on the failures of American schools and on students spending more time in school and getting more rigorous doses of content while their teachers would be subjected to greater scrutiny and evaluations based on how well their students performed on standardized tests. In 2010, President Obama's R2T competition among states and plans for the reauthorization of the Elementary and Secondary Education Act, while clearly taking several steps forward, focus on many of the same 20th-century educational issues.

We have not yet come to grips with the digital revolution and the truth that schools today exist in a radically different social, economic, and educational paradigm. Until we do, policymakers, practitioners, and the public will continue to be distracted from the key issues and actions at hand. By concentrating on the future, rather than fighting the battles of the past, we can create a public school system that is focused on the results that matter in a post-Internet, 21st-century economy and society.

Stephen Steele, of the Institute for the Future, has suggested that by 2020, we have entered into the post-literacy era, "with everything 'smart' and information constantly available," and, as a result, "reading and writing [takes] on new dimensions in [the sphere] of human skills."[29] As Steele asserts,

Problem solving and reasoning [have] became more important. Reading and writing, more largely replaced by voice in–voice out types of inter-actions. Instantaneous language translation at higher levels of accuracy than could be attained by human beings replaced the need for translators and written word as we currently know it.[30]

After winning national awards for her "brick-and-mortar" education career, our co-author Shannon C'de Baca became an online science teacher in a state-supported virtual high school. She reminds us that while physical school settings will continue to be important for many students, for the reasons outlined here, we cannot afford to cling to antiquated notions of schooling growing out of ignorance, nostalgia, or fear of the future.

Public education is cluttered with the detritus of past traditions that are outmoded or—at worst—were not very good ideas to start with. We have in the past adapted much and let go of little or nothing. This leads to an overload of work for the keystone of education—the classroom teacher. An analysis of any teacher's day would show [that] much of it is filled with repetitive tasks that could be automated with existing technology or eliminated as redundant or no longer relevant.

There should be no sacred cows. All aspects of brick-and-mortar schools should be on the block: schedules, school day, classroom structure, administration, counseling, parent involvement, co-curricular activities, school year, teacher compensation, tenure, community connections, curriculum, standards, assessment, and even lunch.

Our knowledge of how people learn continues to expand exponentially. We have some significant data and instruments that can help us determine individual learning preferences. And yet we adhere to a system of assembly-line education delivery that requires all students to reset their thinking every 50 minutes, all the while expecting them to master increasingly complex content that does not chunk easily into small boxes of time. It just doesn't work. And most of us who have lived in this system know it doesn't work.

New technologies are offering us an unprecedented opportunity to re-imagine School. We have to rethink the commodity of time, resources, and learning for both teachers and students. Any path in the future will see a blend of face-to-face and online education. However, always at the core will be the students and their connection to good teachers.

FIGURE 4.2. Teachers' Use of Technology

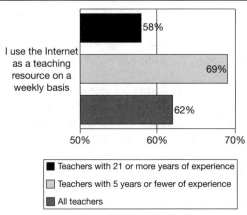

Source: MetLife survey of the American teacher: Past, present and future. (2008). New York: Author. Reprinted by permission of MetLife.

Contrast Shannon's insights with the facts revealed in the 2009 national *MetLife Survey of the American Teacher*, which found that barely two-thirds of the teachers surveyed use technology on a weekly basis in their classrooms. Our TLN colleague Kenneth Bernstein offers some insight into the problem:

> I acknowledge that I do not use technology as well as I should, even though I spent 20+ years as a certified data processor in the private sector before I became a high school teacher. I would love to use it more, but the school system approach to technology is archaic. The computers are so loaded down with levels of security and pieces of irrelevant software that the first time a student signs on to a particular computer it takes at least 10 minutes before s/he can do anything constructive.

A 2007 study by the National School Boards Association found that more than six in ten American school districts have rules against participating in bulletin boards or blogs; six in ten also prohibit sending and receiving email in schools; more than eight in ten districts have rules against online chatting and instant messaging in school; and more than half of all districts specifically prohibit any use of social networking sites in school, however secure and for whatever educational purpose.[31] And, as our colleagues in under-financed school systems frequently reminded us, the problem is, not always about the interface between school technology and the larger digital world, but about sheer access to such tools. Kathie Marshall, who teaches in Los Angeles Unified, relates this story:

I don't use enough technology either, but it's not for lack of wanting. Last year I sort of threatened the tech guy because I mentioned I had no computers but had a special ed student whose IEP said "must have access to technology." So I got four totally worthless computers: old, slow, and with no useful software. When another teacher offered me four of hers, I eventually gave up asking for the switch after six requests ended without action. Later I was offered a laptop cart for a week. When we tried to use them, we discovered ten of 25 would not turn on, and none of those that would turn on had wireless Internet access. Kids disappointed. Teacher frustrated.

Access to technology is still a huge issue—for students as well as teachers.

The KnowledgeWorks Foundation forecasts that today's stark distinction between virtual and physical learning environments will begin to vanish by the year 2020. This view assumes that school system firewalls will necessarily become more sophisticated and flexible and that teachers and students will find the use of technology more fluid and user-friendly. Whether or not that happens, our co-author Renee Moore believes that the advent of digital tools and connectivity represents new opportunities for students whose lives do not fit into the traditional 8:30 to 3 school day. She offered this snapshot of how networked virtual learning might support her close, attentive work with students, in and out of traditional school settings:

FIGURE 4.3. The End of Cyberspace

The End of Cyberspace:
from physical versus digital
to seamless physical and digital

URBAN COMPUTING

- Ubiquitous wireless
- Displays everywhere
- Global positioning
- Global information systems

FIRST-PERSON VIEW OF GEOGRAPHY

Targeted information, embedded in place, turns each location into a personal space. Watch for schools, malls, and neighborhoods, to become digitally tagged for learning.

Context-specific information becomes visible in place

CHEAP MOBILE DEVICES

Lower priced laptops, PDAs, cell phones, and iPods create a new, customizable platform for learning content and interactive curriculum.

Source: Reprinted by permission of KnowledgeWorks Foundation and Institute for the Future.

Poor rural and urban students would no longer have to receive
their education locked [literally] inside unhealthy, unappealing,
outdated buildings. While we might have an adequate physical
space to serve as our "hub," even if we did not, my students
could access me and I could reach them from anywhere. We could
turn a marketplace, library, park, backyard, or rooftop into a
learning site. I could virtually engage them in conversations that
mattered with people, including experts, from around the globe.

Using her school ID card as a projector, Makiaya could
watch a 3-D image of her virtual classmate, Tyrone, reading
aloud his latest piece of writing on the side of the refrigerator
while she fixes dinner for her siblings whom she keeps until
her mother gets home from work. Tia could record what would
become the draft of her next piece as she's riding home from her
job on the night shift at the restaurant. I could do an individual
writing conference with Jason from his cell at the state-of-the-art
juvenile detention center while, simultaneously, sitting at my
portable teacher center noting the progress of several students
whose name and progress charts are coming up on my lesson-
management pad.

Our TLN colleague Bill Ferriter, who writes regularly about effective
teaching with technology for *Educational Leadership*, imagines a future
where students and families can choose how much interaction they have
with other students and adults in physical schools:

What I'd like to see in 2030 is rich diversity in the kinds of
schools that we offer to students. Why can't districts have
brick-and-mortar buildings for the parents and students who
value the intimacy that human relationships lend to education,
blended classrooms for parents and students who want some
measure of interaction with others alongside the opportunities
for differentiation and individualization that online courses offer
and complete online courses of study for students who are driven
by ideas instead of individuals?

And why shouldn't districts experiment with dozens of
different school structures all the time? Couldn't schools that
are designed to promote global interactions between peers
in classrooms on different continents stand next to schools
designed to teach a classic curriculum and schools designed to
offer real-world learning opportunities through internships in
the local community?

Diversifying schools this way, Bill says, will provide the opportunity for innovation—and the potential for districts to create a range of unique learning environments that parents and students could choose from based on their own interests and abilities.

Connectivity for All

Education futurist Howard Rheingold describes the convergence of mobile technology, peer-to-peer networks, increased connectivity, and other technologies that will make smart networks, not only possible, but common by the year 2030:

> When you piece together these different technological, economic, and social components, the result is an infrastructure that makes certain kinds of human actions possible that were never possible before: The killer "apps" of tomorrow's mobile info-com industry won't be hardware devices or software programs but social practices. The most far-reaching changes will come, as they often do, from the kinds of relationships, enterprises, communities and markets that the infrastructure makes possible.[32]

The ability of adults to participate proficiently in such networks will determine their capacity to, not only enjoy prosperity in tomorrow's economy, but to engage in shaping the society in which they live. We know from our own teaching experience that not all of our students today are the texting, blogging, tweeting types depicted in mobile phone commercials. In fact, much of our ambivalence about the right balance between virtual and face-to-face learning opportunities grows out of our desire to ensure that these currently "unplugged" students do not continue to be left behind, as they have been so many times before when the currents of educational advancement swept past inequitably funded schools and classrooms.

Connectivism should not be the proprietary domain of the affluent. Where technology access lags, teachers will still do all they can to serve as the facilitators of connections. In the mid-1990s, high-speed Internet connections in the Mississippi delta (where Renee Moore teaches in one of the nation's poorest communities) were unthinkable. This did not stop Renee from connecting her students with a sister class in South Africa for a year of correspondence and knowledge sharing. Our colleague Jennifer Barnett led her high school juniors in rural Alabama in creating a simulation of the Ellis Island immigrant experience through research of primary sources and period photographs, shuffling them among the inadequate and outdated computers in her K–12 school. These are the lengths to which teachers will go to improve the odds for the students they serve. Think what they might do with more support and more faith in their ability to lead our nation into new ways of learning.

We believe that as basic needs are more universally met and opportunities for enrichment broaden, the walls between virtual and brick-and-mortar worlds will continue eroding. Whether students enter into the world after creating and pursuing an independent course of study that brought the world's resources to their fingertips, *or* after they've experienced the full riches of a community unified in its goal of educating its youth, *or*, ideally, some combination of the two, these high-achieving young adults can move forward with their potential for lifelong learning realized.

In Chapter 3, Jose Vilson spoke of Hennrick, a 12-year-old Haitian boy who found his new American public school poorly informed about his past education and poorly prepared to welcome him and attend to his individual needs. Here Jose offers a more hopeful scenario "in the not-distant future":

> As Hennrick and his mom register, he receives a handheld personal computer (HPC) no bigger than a deck of cards, which powers up when he puts his fingerprint onto the start button. Instantly, the device connects to the state central database and displays all of his pertinent information (including his passport information and immunization card). It checks for his past performance records via a global student information system and arranges for academic progress assessments, as needed. Within a few minutes, the system downloads his personal profile, his personal schedule, homeroom teacher, student handbook, and other pertinent information to his virtual hard drive. For Hennrick, the school is also able to upload language packages and multilanguage visual dictionaries (namely, Creole and French).
>
> When Hennrick has a question that his teachers can't quite make out, or he just needs a cultural connection with someone, he can be quickly directed to a trained individual in the building who knows French Creole. Even if the building doesn't have such a language speaker, he can instantly begin to communicate using his HPC.
>
> On the first day, his teacher doesn't wonder who the new kid is. With help from his HPC, Hennrick already knows and repeats classroom rituals and routines. His teachers assign him a student

to buddy with, someone who shares some of his variables. His teacher has been reading Hennrick's assessment data, and he's already assigned him a seat with all these criteria in mind. As Hennrick looks to his right he sees a smiling girl, who nods and says in a big, friendly voice, "Bonjou konpè-m."[33]

CHAPTER 5

Emergent Reality #3:
Differentiated Pathways and
Careers for a 21st-Century Profession

Outgrowing a One-Size-Fits-All Profession

Teaching is emerging from the shadows of its past history as a semi-profession. Undermined by a public that has not fully understood the complexity of the job and also by decision makers who have enacted a hodge-podge of conflicting teacher recruitment, preparation, evaluation, and retention policies, teaching has been the career that just can't seem to get enough respect. On one hand, policymakers have insisted that teachers should be better prepared. On the other, they have promoted alternative certification programs that require only a month or two of summer training before new recruits are expected to teach in some of the nation's highest-needs schools. Over the past 30 years and more, teaching has in a sense suffered the effects of an organizational bipolar disorder.

Read this slice of teaching reality from our coauthor Kilian Betlach, who left his job teaching in a high-poverty California school after 6 years:

> You're a new teacher, learning your job, working at it, trying to get better. It's hard, a rough slog, but you're trying those best practices, listening to smart people, and doing your best to learn and reflect. Things are bad, and worse before they get better, but if you stay long enough, after some time, you may start to figure things out. If you get the right help you do get better, and that's when things get—for you—much worse.
>
> Your quality as a teacher has changed dramatically, but your title, position, responsibilities, and compensation have remained stagnant. You are so much better than you used to be, but nothing, nothing in the structure of your profession reflects this.

You know you need to learn more. The strategies you took from your credentialing program are running dry, and district-run professional development is either non-existent or dramatically disconnected from promoting student achievement. At best, you teach in a place where the best teachers teach the most vulnerable students. But probably not. You probably teach in a place where the best teachers "earn the right" to teach higher-performing students who more readily acquiesce to your wishes.

You look around and realize the energy and effort spent on developing better instruction and better assessments, the energy and effort poured into creating dynamic environments and learning experiences, the energy and effort directed toward making yourself that turnaround teacher who motivates, inspires, and ultimately closes gaps—all that grit and grind has no bearing on your professional standing whatsoever. None.

If you follow the education policy debate, you know the new teacher attrition drill: Almost 25% of novice teachers leave within the first 3 years, and most of them in their first year.[1] The turnover rate is much higher in high-needs schools; some estimates say up to 50% are gone after 3 years.[2] But perhaps most importantly, 57% of all outward mobility occurs within the first 10 years of a teacher's career. Those who survive the first half-decade and then leave teaching are likely being drawn to different careers that offer more intellectual challenge, professional prestige, and opportunities to make decisions about how they accomplish their work.[3] When it comes to teacher attrition, preparation and working conditions really matter.[4]

Public education was lucky to have Kilian for 6 years as a teacher. He came to teaching through Teach for America, staying on at his high-needs California middle school beyond the program's required 2-year commitment. In his widely read blog Teaching in the 408, he wrote extensively about how his abbreviated training program did not prepare him for high-needs schools—and neither did the education program that eventually credentialed him while he learned on the job.[5] Like too many new teachers, he had to learn by the seat of his pants, often at the expense of his students.

Kilian was given his most difficult possible assignment on the front end of his career—and just as he began to master some of the art and science of teaching, he reached his absolute frustration point and made the decision to leave the classroom. Kilian was not a statistical anomaly.

Careful researchers have found a relationship between the amount of experience a teacher has accumulated and the achievement of his or her students.[6] TLN member Mark Clemente entered teaching after serving in the U.S. Navy. He says it took him 6 years to begin to fully realize his effectiveness as a teacher:

> The first marker for my career came at the end of my third year. I felt that I actually had a handle not only on content delivery, lesson planning, and classroom management but also on seeing the themes that connected the topics with the content. The second marker in my career came at my 6th year of teaching when I chaired my high school science department and was selected as district teacher of the year. The award wasn't the marker though. The marker was the credibility I gained with my principal and my colleagues who began to see evidence of the effects of my teaching. The third marker was going through National Board certification, where the process made me reflect on my teaching more deliberately and look as hard at what was working and why as I did at what was not working.

Some early-career teachers, like Mark, get the support and recognition they need to become effective and committed professionals and eventually grow into true experts. Others who are just as eager to make a difference give up the fight because they find themselves unsupported while they search for effective ways to meet their students' learning needs—or because they are denied substantive opportunities to mature professionally by exercising leadership. Kilian Betlach poignantly puts it this way:

> First we ask new teachers to do too much with too little preparation, and then we ask too little of them in what should be the second stage of a teaching career.

Historically speaking, teaching has edged slowly toward a more results-oriented profession. But for the most part, America's public schools still rely on a relatively dysfunctional system of teacher development. Policy analyst Rick Hess has suggested that in many ways the human capital pipeline that supplies our public schools is "the result of more than a century of compromises, incremental adjustments, and calculated moves designed in response to the exigencies of another era."[7]

In recent years, policymakers, policy experts, and reform-minded philanthropists have emphasized the need to ramp up public education to meet the demands of a global economy, turning their attention to the strategic management of human capital, or "the acquisition, development, performance management and retention of top talent in the nation's schools."[8] A wide array of initiatives have been launched to attract nontraditional recruits to education, to measure effective teaching, and to fashion a conceptualization of "highly qualified" teacher that goes beyond the purely input-oriented definitions framed by No Child Left Behind.

These attempts at change are resisted by a strong tide of tradition. In the early 21st century our nation's teacher development system still seems to be built on the premise that talented females, as a captive labor pool, are willing to work for below-market wages. School district recruitment and hiring practices rest on increasingly outdated mid-20th-century organizational assumptions about teaching and learning, as well as the industrial-era career mobility patterns of baby boomers—not those of generations X and Y. To make matters even more unstable, school systems will soon be hiring their first teachers from the emerging iGeneration—born between the mid 1990s and late 2000s—the first humans to grow up completely immersed in the participatory culture of Web 2.0, social networking, and wireless mobile technologies.

Many of the nation's 1,200 university-based–teacher-education programs are attracting more academically able candidates than in the past; but too many still do not focus on preparation for high-needs teaching in urban and rural communities.[9] And while there are outstanding universities that do this exceptionally well, there is no system to spread their know-how to other institutions. More school districts are getting into the teacher preparation and credentialing game, but hardly any of them are organized to train new teachers effectively on the job, and even fewer of them are very good at growing their own talent—especially from the pool of community members who might begin their education careers as teaching assistants, mentors for students, or content experts from the private sector.

School district and union collective-bargaining agreements continue to focus primarily on seniority and security. Stark divisions of labor and contentious relationships between administrators and teachers hinder creative reforms and further bifurcate those who lead and those who teach. Unions increasingly are ridiculed for tenure rules that were originally designed to protect teachers from administrative abuses, but are now often cited as convenient cover for ineffective teachers.[10] A closer examination of the "tenure problem" uncovers an almost worthless system of teacher evaluation dependent on administrators who do not have the time—and often lack the skill or training—to distinguish effective from ineffective teaching. A hard look at the evidence suggests that poor teaching is less a problem of inherently "bad" teachers than of a dysfunctional system that routinely assigns individuals to teach out of field and expects them to succeed with students (e.g., second language learners) they have not been trained to teach.[11]

More problems prevail. Lockstep teacher compensation systems ensure uniformity and predictability for teachers and the school boards who pay them. But the price of predictability (and in the case of school boards, defensibility) is unacceptably high. These archaic systems stifle teacher creativity, ignore market realities, and isolate teaching expertise. Few, if any, focus on what matters most—student learning. School funding schemes that rely on local tax capacity dictate low teacher salaries in urban and rural districts—almost guaranteeing that local boards and administrators do not have the financial resources to compete in the teacher labor market for the most accomplished professionals.

At the same time, state school boards and legislators routinely lower hiring standards to expediently address teacher shortages—especially for schools serving our nation's most vulnerable students. New teachers tend to be assigned the most challenging classes without comprehensive mentoring from trained experts who have time to support them. Even those teachers who are well prepared and well qualified often find they cannot teach effectively in schools where poor working conditions—understaffing, inadequate or unsupportive administrators, limited time to learn, too few opportunities to lead and collaborate—define their professional environment.

Early 21st-century investigations of school districts thought to be exemplary have surfaced only limited evidence of progress toward a new framework for staffing schools.[12] Modest gains are being made on some fronts, including more successful recruiting of talented teacher-candidates[13] and streamlining of district hiring practices. From the viewpoint of developing a stronger teaching profession, however, most of the innovation still seems to be on the margins, with little attention being paid to developing teacher-leaders who can promote buildingwide and districtwide student learning that will meet the demands of the new economy and a democracy that is increasingly threatened by growing socioeconomic divides.

Even when effective teachers are selected to help lead schools, most end up working without any coherent career development system that includes regular opportunities to accept new challenges and spread their growing expertise. School principals are still asked to do too much—managing the three Bs of "buses, books, and bottoms" (i.e., transportation, distributing resources, and student discipline) while they are also expected to become adept leaders of their school's instructional program, no matter the content area or specialty involved. While more principals have been trained to examine student data and organize school schedules and resources to increase standardized test scores, few are prepared to develop and utilize teacher expertise and leadership for more-ambitious student outcomes. And too many school-leadership-development programs of today pit principals against teachers (and the school administration against the teachers' union), instead of figuring out how to elevate the potential of both and establish strategies for working together toward 21st century, results-oriented schools.

The (very) conventional wisdom for rethinking the teaching profession continues to be: *Undermine unions, get rid of industrial-style bargaining, and place more control over teaching in the hands of "management."* While some progressive principals and superintendents have seized upon the powerful potential that lies in establishing partnerships with teachers to develop, elevate, and spread teaching expertise, these school leaders are still in the minority and their successes have yet to influence the teaching-policy mainstream. We hear increasing policy talk about creating "differentiated pathways" into teaching, but the proposals, by and large, are spruced-up versions of old ideas being sold as if they were something entirely new in the world. Typically, these policy schemes make it easier for individuals to enter and exit teaching quickly while "solving" the teacher quality problem by judging and firing bad teachers and paying more to those who can demonstrate their ability to raise standardized test scores.[14] Few, if any, focus on a comprehensive strategy to deepen and spread teaching expertise or offer *differentiated roles* for teams of teachers and other supporting professionals to work with each other over time in the best interest of students and their families.

We don't have to guess about the outcomes of such recycled policy approaches—their progenitors are everywhere in our most challenged schools and districts today. Just as many rookie teachers begin to reach their pedagogical stride, they will either leave the profession or give in to the isolation of the classroom. They and their more experienced teacher colleagues who survive the judging-and-firing process will reshape their work around the narrow expectations of a standardized-testing regime. Students—as our TLN colleague David B. Cohen described in a satiric essay published at the Accomplished California Teachers blog—will become high-skilled takers of tests. David used the device of a former student writing a letter to his favorite teacher:

> By providing me with chances to read anthologized literary excerpts and random workplace documents, all followed by multiple choice assessments, you showed a commitment to my learning, and my test scores that spring really proved how far I had come. I was totally comfortable dealing with any readings

chosen for me, and comfortable choosing the answers to other people's questions. I also remember that you showed us how to answer the questions without even doing most of the reading, and that sure did help on the test!

. . . I tried [college] for a year, but none of the instructors cared as much as you did, so it was hard to connect. A lot of times they assigned us really long readings and didn't even give us any points for doing all that homework. Then, we had to write essays on these ridiculously hard questions where you couldn't even find the answer in the books. I did my best and put together my five paragraphs and everything, and I still got low grades. When they don't tell you how to find the answers and don't even give you the motivation, well . . . it just wasn't for me. It's just too bad that all those skills we practiced in your class don't even seem to matter in college.[15]

Redefining the Profession for Results-Oriented Teaching

Recruiting, preparing, and retaining effective teachers for high-needs schools and for the 21st century, says former NCATE president Arthur Wise, will require a "new paradigm [that is] based on how professionals work"—a breaking away from "the egg-carton organization" of schools that "expects that every teacher will replicate the appropriate curriculum and instruction for 25 students each year, every year, from the beginning to the end of a teaching career."[16]

In fact, in the early 21st century, opportunities for teacher career growth *that remains rooted in the classroom* are exceedingly rare. Among those of us working in the TeacherSolutions 2030 project, this is perhaps the most urgent issue to address if American public schools expect to attract and prepare talented, committed, and highly intelligent teachers who grew up in the post-industrial age and have career expectations very different from the postwar baby boomers now reaching retirement age.

After a year spent as a policy associate for the Education Trust, our co-author Kilian Betlach returned to the front lines, this time as an assistant principal at another high-needs school in northern California. Certainly, students will benefit from his teaching expertise and deep commitment to their learning. However, Kilian sees his new position as more of a career change than a promotion. "Administrative roles are to teaching what hospital administration is to doctoring," he observes. The primary lesson to be learned here is not about professional frustration but about a maddeningly flat career trajectory that is increasingly unappealing to talented members of generation Y.

"We need a vehicle for un-flattening the profession that allows teachers an opportunity for advancement without needing to leave the profession or assume leadership positions as a second job," 30-year-old Kilian writes. "We need teaching promotions that don't force you to stop teaching. Why did I have to leave the classroom to lead?"

Looking to the year 2030, we imagine and seek a much more flexible career path for teachers that provides many opportunities for leadership and entrepreneurship while preserving a deep-down, everyday connection to students.

To reengineer teaching from the ground up, we need to begin with preparation. How should we prepare our future generations of teachers for their chosen profession? Why not take the best of both university-based and alternative approaches, recruiting from a large pool of talented teacher-education students, recent college graduates in other fields, and midcareer job-switchers? Then prepare a carefully selected cadre of new teachers for the most challenging assignments through extended internships under the supervision of expert teachers—who may also be partnering with researchers to document best teaching practices. Rigorous performance assessments would not only determine who will teach but set high standards of practice. The most expert teachers would teach students as well as serve in hybrid roles as mentors, coaches, and teacher educators. These proposals are not new. But turning these ideas into reality is another matter. Doing so will require policymakers and practitioners to redefine the work of teaching and *seriously* embrace the role of teacher leaders.

It must start with how new teachers enter the profession. All novices would have a reduced teaching load in their first 2 years. Their progress would be assessed using objective measures of their performance and their roles and responsibilities adjusted accordingly. Some would teach under more supervision than others. Early opportunities beyond the classroom would give novice educators the chance to demonstrate and sharpen their leadership skills.

Then take it a step further. Consider how a team of six to eight teachers of varying expertise and experience (and with different career intentions) might work with 150 to 175 students over a number of years. Among the team might be several highly accomplished teachers who will supervise and work with a selection of novice teachers and be supported by teaching assistants, content specialists (or adjunct faculty), virtual mentors, community experts, master networkers, and other capable volunteers. Instead of continuing to pursue the impossible dream of finding a single seasoned teacher expert for every classroom in every school, district-college-community compacts would focus on cultivating these close-knit teacher-teams.

Let's dig a little deeper and consider categories of teachers that might be included in an optimized staffing model—one that is resilient to change as it constantly prepares new individuals to assume key roles in the future:

- *Master teachers* are recruited, developed, and paid at levels that will encourage them to stay in the community for 20 years or more. These teachers serve in hybrid roles that include teaching students, working with colleagues, and serving as liaisons with the community. They may devote 40% of their time to teaching and lead outside the classroom the other 60%. They support and supervise teachers with less preparation and experience, including novices who are preparing for solo teaching. Master teachers are judged and rewarded on how effective they are in spreading their expertise. They are recruited from other locales and also developed from within. Many are identified through the National Board certification process, which has been made more rigorous and relevant. As appropriate, they are provided with specific training to be successful in low-performing schools. They acquire the adult leadership skills necessary to create a culture for improvement. They are also provided with training in coaching and instructional practices so they are well prepared to support the professional development of other teachers.
- *Professional teachers* are career teachers who see teaching as their long-term profession. Most will have preservice preparation from a top-ranking college of education; some will become master teachers as they gain experience and additional professional development. Professional teachers will underpin the work of master teachers, providing excellent instruction for students and support for colleagues—and important continuity within the school.
- *Resident teachers* view themselves as teaching for at least 5 to 10 years and are seriously prepared, most notably through intensive residencies where they learn to teach in high-needs schools under the tutelage of master and professional teachers, with guidance and support from university researchers (who help bring empirical evidence to best teaching practices) and community organizers and social-service support providers (who help bring connections from home and neighborhood to school). Resident teachers

are specially recruited with the idea in mind that they
may eventually assume roles as master teachers, change
agents, and teacherpreneurs outside the traditional school
structure—in other learning systems, nonprofits, education-
related businesses, and so on.

- *Apprentice teachers* will typically be recent college graduates
  prepared to begin teaching after an intensive summer
  program. They will be teamed with master teachers for
  continuous support during their teaching years. Some will
  teach for at least 3 years as part of their service commitment,
  and the district's human development (not capital)
  system will be designed to optimize their success while
  acknowledging that they may not stay in teaching for very
  long. Of course, while many Apprentice I teachers may view
  teaching as a temporary service to the nation or the first in
  a series of career "callings," others may develop into master
  teachers over time.

- *Adjunct teachers* bring specific, needed content expertise
  and will work part-time. These may be people working in
  the private sector, retired teachers, or other individuals,
  as well as adults who can bring important community
  knowledge into the school. Some may be considering
  midcareer transitions to teaching. Most will receive training
  comparable to the short-term teachers but designed for
  individuals from the community.

- *Individualized instruction specialists* include teachers with
  preparation to work with students who have special needs,
  students who are English language learners, students from
  different linguistic and cultural backgrounds, and students
  with atypical learning styles. These individuals work in
  partnership with the other teachers, focused on inclusion
  models and building upon individual students' capabilities
  (as opposed to pull-out, deficit-based models of instruction).
  They will be equivalent to professional teachers and some
  will become masters.

- *Virtual teachers* may come from any of the above categories
  but have received special training in how to teach effectively
  via a blend of online technologies, ranging from MUVEs to
  video-streamed seminars to web-embedded student learning
  communities. Master virtual teachers may be teamed with
  short-term teachers or adjunct teachers to create composite
  learning experiences for students. With special preparation,

they have the know-how to blend in-class and online activities, drawing on the expertise of multiple teachers, while also offering powerful approaches to professional development. Through their facilitation, teachers can connect to other teachers—anytime and anywhere—and students have access to teaching expertise they would not have otherwise.

- *Community leaders* may come from local nonprofits who serve students and their families in any number of settings, including after-school and summer programs. Many of these local experts are natives of the community. They will be critical in preparing "outsiders" who are recruited to teach in local schools (including those in more-isolated rural communities) and need to know local context and culture to be effective.

These different types of teachers and educational support persons would be combined differently in different schools. A structure would be in place that promotes the best use of these human resources and ensures strong collaboration among teachers in the different tiers. The system needs to embrace the best of what all educators have to offer and how they can be strategically organized and utilized. It would be flexible enough to accommodate individuals who change their career goals as they mature.

A caveat is in order. Our vision may, at first glance, look like another career ladder for a few teachers to climb. Not at all. As co-author Shannon C'de Baca notes:

The work of 21st-century teaching is too much to fall on the backs of any one teacher. We need a fluid profession that allows different types of teachers, all well prepared, in scaffolding a career lattice to focus collectively on the needs of students.

Our vision is *not*, as free-enterprise advocate Rick Hess would suggest, a way to "substitute cheaper instructional aides for more expensive teachers," but a way to create a stable, interlocking group of expert teachers, generalists, and specialists who work together to serve students and their families. In his writings about the prospects for a 21st-century teaching profession, Hess points to some powerful ideas, but most of his solutions remain organizationally gridlocked in 20th-century conceptions of professional practice. For example, he imagines that a few content experts would "give variations of the same lectures on the Civil War, right triangles, the digestive system, and countless other discrete topics" to groups of students sorted by ability. Others would "use a Palm [computer] to conduct the diagnostics traditionally done on paper to assess early reading," and still others would "supervise homeroom" and "patrol the cafeteria." In an effort to create a more hierarchical profession, Hess calls for an elite leadership team of highly paid specialists who draw on an inexpensive army of generalists and an array of computer technologies to help students master content. What is missing is the core group of expert teachers who know each child and his or her family well and understand how to design instruction based on that knowledge.

Hess's view of human-capital management in education, while helpful in promoting a much needed alternative framework, largely ignores brain development and the social, emotional, and intellectual characteristics of children. The nature of pre-adult learning sets a minimum standard for all individuals in teaching roles that is far above what Hess imagines for "cheaper instructional aides." Within our framework, there is room for smart specialization like that described by Julianna Dauble, a 5th-grade teacher from Washington State, who participated in one of our online brainstorming sessions about the future of teaching. Julianna explains how multidimensional teaching roles could fulfill a clear need that would enable her to teach more effectively and work with a wide variety of high-value colleagues:

> Teachers in 2010 fulfill countless roles, most of which are not defined but embedded in daily practice. We are, in so many ways, spread too thin. I envision that true education reform will come back to the concept of integration of content areas through collaboratively designed projects, with a host of my colleagues involved, incorporating the highest academic standards within them. In 20 years I hope that the workload teachers face is aligned to their skills and areas of interest. We no longer would be teaching grade levels but my interdisciplinary team would be working with small groups of students over time. I would no longer have to cover a wide range of standards and topics for a discrete set of 11-years-olds who rotate in and out of my classroom each year. I would specialize in teaching certain major concepts over several years—helping my students deepen their understanding. And then I could also develop as either a virtual mentor so I could have more workplace flexibility or, later, maybe serve as a family educator who would focus on connecting both parent and child education.

Our view suggests that, in 2030, education generalists may be the most valued and well-paid members of teaching teams. In fact, the concept of team teaching we have described here will help guard against the downsides of too much specialization, which our TLN colleague Jon Hanbury warns against:

> The current medical profession revolves around specialists. The premise behind this shift appears to be that we need experts on each vital organ of the body. To some extent this is true. But with the specialties come the pitfalls. My mother, age 92, experienced a setback with her health last year because her oncologist was suggesting treatment that her urologist would have rejected had he known. And her radiologist only intensified the situation to the point where she almost died. It's a case of the right hand not knowing the whereabouts of its counterpart!
>
> The same is true for our schools. Working in an at-risk setting, I advocate for teaching the total child. Nearly 20% of my student population is homeless; thus, I see the need for a classroom teacher to advocate for these students at risk. If an instructor's focus is narrowed to only one aspect of the child's education, then he or she sees only a snapshot of that child's potential. And yet I see value in having a team approach that supports all of our teaching and helps improve our performance. That's one reason I became a math coach. I view myself as a resource for the teacher, which in turn is a resource for the students.

Marti Schwartz echoes Jon's concerns that the last thing many students today need is a string of detached specialists who never get to know them well:

> So many kids today, and not just those from low-income communities, come from home environments that do not support their academic and emotional growth. And those two are related. If we add a whirlwind of specialists, we may very well undermine efforts to get all students college and career ready. . . . In the high-needs high school charter where I teach, every kid is in a twelve-person advisory with one adult—a subject teacher, resource teacher, support person, whatever. They meet twice a day and, sometimes, to just "check in."

One of the new roles possible in our vision of a 21st-century profession might very well be that of a teacher who has some of the skills and

responsibilities of a guidance counselor and serves as a home base or locus on a team of teachers, working with students and teachers to make
sure the focus is always on the whole child. Bill Ivey describes the role of
advisors in his school:

> In my school, we require all teachers to be advisors. While it is a
> job that can be to some extent learned, not all teachers have the
> dispositions for it. We need to make sure teachers are ready for
> this role and are trained. It is so needed.

What is truly needed is a larger array of experts, both specialists and
generalists, who are organized horizontally and vertically. They will have
lots of room to move in and out of different roles, take on more or less
responsibility, focus on more or fewer students, and serve in and out of cyberspace, as well as in and out of their school buildings. Our vision is built
more on the concept of a career *lattice* (not ladder). We do agree with Rick
Hess that many of today's teachers are asked to do too much (e.g., "help
diagnose and coach a troubled reader, tutor an advanced science student,
explain key math concepts, field a parental complaint, observe a peer, and
work with children with special needs"). But we do not agree that the
solution is a more steeply sloped hierarchy of "higher-ups." Instead, we
believe the answer can be found in a distributed work model. Each of the
tasks Hess enumerates above is one that requires professional expertise;
the solution is to share these professional responsibilities through team-
work, not to declare some of them less than professional work.

A 21st-century, results-oriented profession will need to empower
more (not fewer) teachers and other service providers to take on leadership roles. Doing so will require an intricate, well-constructed menu of opportunities and options. For example, in crafting its vision for teaching in
2020, the KnowledgeWorks Foundation has looked at current trends and
suggested a number of new jobs that teachers might need to fill in the near
future. They include a number of roles that could emerge with advances in
science and technology—or as a result of increasingly stressed communities. Most encompass responsibilities that many of today's policy analysts
have yet to consider. They can help all of us push our thinking about the
future of teaching beyond the firewalls that enforce status quo thinking:

- *Learning Fitness Instructors* who will help learners build and
  strengthen the basic cognitive, emotional, and social abilities
  essential to learning by using simulations, biofeedback, and
  hands-on activities to reduce stress, hone mental capabilities,
  and learn brain-friendly nutrition

- *Personal Education Advisors* who are assigned by certified local education agencies (such as schools, resource centers, and libraries), or selected and contracted by families, to help families create, nurture, and maintain personal learning ecologies
- *Community Intelligence Cartographers* who will tap the collective intelligence of their local communities. They will leverage social networking strategies to develop "swarms" and "smart mobs" in order to identify emerging learning opportunities in the community, organize community members, and locate community resources
- *Education "Sousveyors"* who will keep the learning process transparent and will stimulate public discussion through blog posts, pictures, podcasts, and videos as they keep learning on the forefront of stakeholders' minds
- *Social Capital Platform Developers* who will provide an accounting of people's contributions to teaching and learning practices and outcomes—electronically tracking program outcomes to resources and collaborative processes
- *Learning Journey Mentors* who will work with personal education advisors, learning fitness instructors, community intelligence cartographers, and assessment designers to co-create and navigate learning itineraries with small groups of students
- *Assessment Designers* who will create appropriate methods for evaluating media literacy, learning discovery journeys, and other innovative forms of instruction[17]

Through a new national network established by the Center for Teaching Quality (CTQ), we are learning from teachers who began their careers in the new millennium. They tell us that they eagerly anticipate the possibilities raised by hybrid jobs—teaching students but also performing a wide variety of support roles in their communities and in cyberspace. One thing is clear: Many young teachers today, who will be in their late 40s in 2030, will not remain in teaching if the job description each day for the next 20 years will be only to teach five 50-minute classes.

The possibilities for hybrid teaching roles will certainly expand as the future unfolds. Emily Vickery, a TeacherSolutions 2030 team member with a particularly long view of education trends, cites this list of possible 2030 jobs suggested by the author of *The Networked Student*, Wendy Drexler, a high school teacher in Florida:

- Learning Architect
- Multi-User Virtual Environment [MUVE] Guide
- Network Sherpa
- Modeler
- Gaming Expert
- Learning Concierge
- Synthesizer
- Connected Learning Incubator
- Change Agent

"This new lexicon may or may not come about in just this way," Emily says, "but it captures the essence of the changing role of *teacher*."

High school teacher Mark Clemente sees a job list like Drexler proposes as an isolation-breaker—creating cross-curricular responsibilities that would promote much deeper collaboration among secondary teachers who would share ownership of all student learning:

> Why couldn't the roles like those highlighted by Emily become the primary jobs of teachers, with specialization coming at the content level? This is the kind of change we need. Right now as a high school science teacher, I only interact with other teachers in my content area. It takes a real effort to work across department boundaries. Totally redefining roles would certainly remove these boundaries. It would allow more teachers to collaborate and innovate and be more reflective of the direction the rest of our highly technologized society is moving in.

No matter which new and (from today's perspective) exotic roles may ultimately emerge in the coming years of rapid technological and social change, teachers will need to be prepared to take them on. What must that preparation look like? How can we create differentiated career pathways that lead us away from hierarchical models and toward a 21st-century–results-oriented teaching profession? We begin by transforming our increasingly obsolete systems of teacher education and compensation, and in doing so transcend the current debates over traditional versus alternative certification and teacher pay based on experience/credentials versus test-measured performance.

Teacher Education for a Differentiated, Results-Oriented Profession

"The achievement gap can only be closed by professionalizing teaching and eliminating the educator achievement gap—that distance between the teachers we are, and the teachers our students need us to be," writes Kilian Betlach. The effort to close these gaps must begin *at the beginning*, by exerting more control over recruitment, training, and assignment of teachers.

In our vision of the future, American schools are far more selective about who enters teaching by the year 2030. But the focus is not just on recruiting future teachers who can claim high grade point ratios from competitive colleges. While higher pay will make it possible to attract individuals with top-notch academic records into teacher education—a not unimportant building block for developing a results-oriented profession—the "right people" will bring much more. Our co-author John M. Holland comments:

> I think we assume that we can learn how to be a teacher by
> being a student. I think this is likely a false assumption. I think
> the biggest difference is that, as learners, we do not have to step
> outside of ourselves. As a teacher we must step outside ourselves
> and assume the dual perspective of both teacher and learner.
> There is a lot of talk about recruiting more relentless and gritty
> teachers. These qualities are important. But they are not enough.
> We need to recruit those who have dispositions that allow them
> to understand what it is like for someone else to learn. And then
> we need to prepare them with the skills they need to teach each
> child differently, drawing on that understanding.

The early 21st-century evidence is clear: Not enough teachers—whether they enter teaching through university-based programs or shortcut approaches—experience the quality of training they need to serve students well. In fact, a 2008 survey of traditionally prepared novices and "prominent" alternative certification recruits revealed that many new teachers feel less than fully prepared to individualize instruction, especially for students who are struggling. While university recruits, compared to their alternative counterparts, were more positive about their training, this and other studies make it clear that many novices enter the classroom feeling uncertain about their readiness to tailor instruction to each student.[18]

Carrie J. Kamm, one of our co-authors, lamented the weaknesses of her own formal training as a teacher.

> During those first months of teaching, the vision I had for myself
> was challenged daily. None of my preservice experience taught
> me how to walk students from our classroom to the cafeteria

FIGURE 5.1. Impact of Alternative vs. Traditional Preparation on Readiness and Retention of Teachers

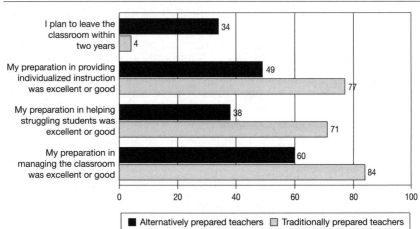

Source: Public Agenda. (2007). *Lessons learned: New teachers talk about their jobs, challenges, and long range plans.* Washington, DC: Author. Reprinted by permission of Public Agenda.

without the whole floor knowing we were in the hallway. None of my preservice experience prepared me to teach reading to students who read from a pre-primer level to an 8th-grade level, using a district-mandated 5th-grade basal text. None of my preservice experience prepared me for working with my so-called mentor teacher who accused me of "stealing" ideas for classroom posters from her walls.

I never expected my preservice preparation program to teach me everything that I would need to know and be able to do as a new teacher working in a high-needs, urban context. But the fact of the matter is, I did not have the practical skills I needed to manage a classroom from the first day, and that made me less than effective. Preparing teachers to work in high-needs schools can be and must be better if we are to stop the "revolving door" of teachers entering and exiting these schools each year.

Co-author Kilian Betlach, citing both his truncated pre-service training and the discordant master's degree in education he earned later, notes that:

Teacher preparation is trapped in a dichotomy of insufficiency. Traditional-route programs train teachers on generic skill-sets insufficient for the incredible language, ethnic, and socioeconomic diversity found within urban classrooms. Yet, alternative-route programs require prohibitive amounts of on-the-job learning that is impractical and frequently ineffective. Neither approach effectively prepares career teachers for the rigors of high-needs urban classrooms.[19]

Our TLN colleague Taylor Ross, a young primary grades teacher at high-poverty Brighton Elementary School in Jefferson County, Alabama, serves on the Governor's Teacher Quality Commission in her state. "I have yet to meet a new teacher who really believed that their undergraduate (or even graduate) studies fully prepared them for the classroom," she observes. "Many of us walked into one of the most challenging careers feeling overwhelmed and in over our heads."

Taylor's own pedagogical training at Samford University in Birmingham has received the National Award for Effective Teacher Preparation, awarded by the U.S. Department of Education. The program allowed her to observe and practice-teach in many diverse classrooms, something she found vital:

> Even though I was uncomfortable in some of the schools I
> taught in (because I knew it wasn't my niche), I also feel very
> fortunate that I was able to experience so many different kinds of
> schools, grade levels, and so on. The actual classroom experience
> shaped my own beliefs about the kind of teacher I would be.
> In my preparation program the assignments I was given and
> the workload I experienced helped reaffirm my desire to work
> in low-performing schools with at-risk students. I learned how
> difficult teaching is and, while I have miles to go in my own
> teaching practice, I am thankful for a teacher education program
> that prepared me for the challenges I face on a regular basis.

As Samford demonstrates, not all colleges of education are "notoriously troubled," as suggested in a March 2010 editorial in the *New York Times*.[20] Across the continent, another university with a similar name has demonstrated how even a prestigious research institution can develop highly effective teachers while supporting innovative (including charter) schools. At Stanford University in Palo Alto, California, teacher candidates matriculate through the 15-month Stanford Teacher Education Program (STEP). The intensive course of study includes 45 units of graduate coursework that tightly weaves together theory and practice, requiring students to perform a wide variety of work for up to 20 hours per week at a nearby partner school. The program hones in on five major areas: social and psychological foundations of education; content-specific curriculum and instruction; language, literacy, and culture; general teaching strategies; and the student teaching practicum. Most important, the program's year-long clinical experiences are "completely wrapped" around coursework and are vital to Stanford's efforts to create change agents who can help transform schools. Practicing master-teachers work hand-in-glove with university professors to jointly prepare these new recruits for today's schools as well as the schools of tomorrow. A 2006 report indicated that the vast majority of STEP graduates seek positions in high-needs schools, remain in teaching at much higher rates than graduates from other teacher education programs, and highly rate their preparation on almost every dimension.[21] Recent evidence shows that STEP graduates produced higher value-added achievement gains for their K–12 students than those of the other university-based programs as well as those who entered teaching from alternative routes.[22]

One STEP graduate told us:

> How did I learn to teach? My cooperating teacher was always finding ways to solve problems with me. She gave me a chance to try new things and fail. She experimented with me. She even read the text I was reading in my college courses and helped me make the connections between theories of learning and how to use specific instructional practices. She also was a magnet for underperforming and even troubled kids—and she modeled for me how to respond differently to kids with diverse needs.

The opportunity to observe many teachers and to learn from them how to implement high leverage instructional practices seems to be the common denominator that successful educators point to when they describe the qualities of good preparation programs. Our TLN colleague Gail Ritchie, a veteran elementary teacher, NBCT, researcher, and instructional coach, offers further testimony about the critical importance of blending theory and practice in preparing new teachers well:

> I was fortunate to work for 3 years as a kindergarten assistant while I was getting my masters in education and initial licensure to teach in Virginia. I believe that my day job served as the real-life apprenticeship that made the theory and information of my night coursework make sense. The coursework was good. As a result I felt very prepared, pedagogically and content-wise, for my first year of teaching. But that is not all.
>
> For 3 years, as I observed and learned from my mentor, I had seen the importance of forming positive relationships with my students and how to unfold curriculum in a way that made sense for specific students. She also taught me, through her example,

to make room for what students are interested in learning. It is quite possible to incorporate the required curriculum within a unit of study that the students ask to pursue. I saw, in living color, how to blend "natural" teaching ability with "learned" teaching ability.

Another TLN colleague, Marsha Ratzel, entered teaching through an alternative-certification program after a "first career" in hospital administration and went on to earn national board certification. As she sought to deepen her grasp of content-specific pedagogy in math and science, she found that "you have to be in a classroom and working with kids in order to have some context." The preparatory needs of different teachers will vary according to their background and experience. There's no one-size-fits-all preparation program—or, more precisely, there shouldn't be. Mark Clemente, who entered teaching through the Troops to Teachers alternative-certification program, speaks to his experience and the importance of substantial and substantive "student teaching" before flying solo in a classroom:

My military training really helped me a lot. Not many alternative-certification candidates have had the experiences with training young people that we in the military have. But I did learn a lot in my preparation program, especially in courses taught by experienced teachers. But the drawback was that my program required only 6 weeks of student teaching. I think this is really where teacher preparation in general needs to change. I still remember starting my first year. I had lesson plans ready but I really did not know what to do on the first day of school. We must have deliberate and specific clinical training, at least a year in duration, so serious recruits can learn to do serious teaching.

Co-author Carrie J. Kamm survived her early experiences as an underprepared teacher in a high-needs urban school and went on to earn national board certification and acclaim for her classroom prowess. Today she is a lead mentor in a Chicago urban teacher-residency program that prepares promising recruits in a yearlong, hands-on program, under the tight supervision of seasoned experts. She describes her vision for the future of teacher education in a world that won't be neatly divided between brick-and-mortar schools and cyberspace:

By 2030, the ways in which students receive education will look quite different, but the human-to-human interaction will still in some way be a part of that experience. As changes in learning systems take place, teachers will need to insist upon and create learning environments that support student risk taking, develop academic habits of mind, and support students in meeting high standards. More and more, teachers will also need to be prepared to advocate for students living in the high-needs communities, many of whom will require a full-service, brick-and-mortar "school" to gain the knowledge, skills, and self-efficacy to succeed.

Today's urban residency programs are beginning to develop such teachers who have deep pedagogical expertise and knowledge of their students. And I know from my own experience that there will always be a need for teachers who also have the skills to advocate for inherent policy changes. As residencies evolve, they will likely need to expand their mission to include the development of "hybrid" teachers and other educators who have the additional skills and expertise to sustain full-service schools for those children who need them. Currently, we train residents to be highly skilled teachers of record in traditional grade-specific and content-specific classrooms. In the future, we must do more.

Our TLN colleague Heather Wolpert-Gawron entered teaching in her late 20s after working in several jobs in the Hollywood entertainment industry. A winner of regional teacher of the year honors and the author of several how-to books for teachers (as well as the popular edublog Tween-Teacher), Heather's vision for the future of teacher education begins with the expectation that a wide array of teachers will be recruited from different walks of life and experience different training regimes based on their backgrounds and their prospective roles and responsibilities. Unlike today, she says, no individual will take on major responsibilities for students, especially the most vulnerable, without extensive preparation and evidence that they are up to the task. She begins her imagining this way:

The year is 2030 and teacher recruitment and preparation look a lot different. No, we are not flying around on a jetpack like George Jetson—but we *are* experiencing a variety of clinical placements for a profession that demands varied roles.

The teacher credentialing programs of the future will demand a more honest introduction to the challenges and rewards of teaching, while also more accurately predicting a candidate's future ability to teach. While today's programs are all about counting courses, the teacher recruitment and preparation programs of the future are all about finding and preparing teachers who possess the Three Cs: content, communication, and character and then testing them through performance assessments (not multiple choice tests) to see who should teach what—and under what conditions.

By 2030, teacher credentialing programs have become differentiated—clearly focused not only on quality but on matching the teachers they produce to the verified needs of the marketplace. They lure folks from every profession to share their knowledge with students of all levels. And while there is flexibility about the paths candidates can travel to achieve a credential, the programs have become more rigorous gatekeepers for the profession as a whole—so much so that individuals who achieve a credential no longer hear "oh, just a teacher" at parties, but appropriate awe. Hey, it's my fantasy, right?

What would a course of study look like in Heather's 2030-styled teacher education program? She imagines "classes" and apprenticeships that are seamlessly connected, through a series of modules that involve candidates in both online study and in work in school and community settings. In many ways her vision is not all that far afield from current teacher-residency programs like the one Carrie helps lead in Chicago. She offers this description of the thinking process that teachers are trained to develop through their residency work. What she describes is much more substantive than the training offered in many traditional- and most alternative-preparation programs.

Placing new recruits in high-needs schools' classrooms as residents—with carefully vetted and trained mentor teachers—addresses the problem of inappropriate preservice placements often encountered in traditional teacher education programs that focus on universal requirements and generic processes. I like teacher educator Marty Haberman's analogy that one cannot prepare to swim the English Channel by doing laps in the university pool. Our approach to residencies contends that, if our new teachers are going to swim the English Channel, they need to learn their craft in similar waters with an expert coach who can model for them how to swim fast and strong. But modeling does not mean just watching and doing.

In residencies we offer cognitive apprenticeships, which differ from traditional student teaching in three important ways.

First, in traditional apprenticeships the process of learning how to carry out a task is easily observable. In a cognitive apprenticeship, one needs to deliberately make the thinking visible. For example, we expect our mentor teachers to be transparent in their thinking about their pedagogical decisions— like how and why fractions are taught this way and why students learned a concept or not. Mentors must be able to assess the resident teacher's level of understanding of why particular teaching decisions are made and what impact they have on student learning.

Second, in a traditional apprenticeship [often called "practice teaching"] the teacher learning is completely situated in the workplace. However, in a cognitive apprenticeship, learning is situated both in the workplace and in some other educational context. And here this needs to be, not just in a typical academic context, but also the community in which the student lives, both before and after school. The mentor teacher plays an integral role in guiding the resident teacher to make these connections.

Finally, in a traditional apprenticeship, skills to be learned are applied to the task at hand and are not necessarily applied in other situations. In contrast, the tasks in our teaching program require teachers to apply the knowledge and skills they are acquiring in multiple situations, under the guidance and coaching of a variety of mentors, not just one.

Today, it is rare for teachers not in immediate physical proximity to learn from each other in any deep way. In many locales new recruits seldom have the opportunity to learn from expert teachers, like those who are National Board–certified. Nor do we see preservice teachers in one school of education sharing experiences and insights with their counterparts in another. New technologies will change all that.

Bank Street College, based in New York City, is one of the nation's most respected teacher preparation institutions. Bank Street understands the importance of cross-institutional partnerships and routinely works with Hunter College and Columbia University to recruit and develop effective social workers for high-needs urban schools. "Teaching requires such a constellation of multiple disciplinary and professional ways of thinking and acting," Bank Street provost Jon Snyder told us. "No single department within an institution, or for that matter, no single institution itself can completely meet what the growth and development of our children require. The only way we can have what we want—high quality teachers for all our children—is to share what we have."

Snyder defines the "we" as those who share the responsibility for the development of teachers. It is a group, he says, "that includes, at least, institutions of higher education, districts and schools, and unions/professional organizations, as well as resource-rich institutions like the Exploratorium in San Francisco or the Natural History Museum in New York City. Those of us who share this responsibility need to stop seeing each other as competition (or sometimes even enemies) and start seeing each other as allies with a common cause."[23]

Cross-institutional partnerships in higher education are rare today. In our vision of the future, they won't be. Through worldwide networks, we imagine that teacher recruits from Anywhere, USA, will be conferring with other preservice teachers and their mentors whenever a need exists. Imagine, for example, residency teachers in Oakland, California, or Cleveland, Mississippi, in routine discussions about second language learners with colleagues in Singapore.

Singapore, indeed, would be a good choice. The small Asian nation has one of the most sophisticated systems of teacher development in the world. Teachers are highly recruited, well prepared, and well paid. In a country where teaching is among the most respected professions, the concept of "alternative certification" would sound very odd indeed. Most important, in Singapore there is a clear relationship between who is expected to teach, how they are trained, what they do, and how they are compensated.

Professional Compensation for a Differentiated Profession

Public education has been long criticized for paying teachers for "seat time," as our co-author Renee Moore puts it. Since 1921, when the cities of Denver and Des Moines began to offer "single salary schedules," most teachers have come to be paid for the number of years they have taught and the number of workshop hours and formal academic credits they have accrued. As issues of racial and gender equity gained traction in the 1940s, the single-salary schedule became an accepted way of assuring at least a semblance of "fair pay" for women and teachers of color. School reformers who lament the continuing allegiance of teacher unions to this lockstep compensation system often forget the long history of teachers being paid on the basis of social prejudice, administrative whim, or political ideology.

Today, many school reformers (and a large majority of the public) support the idea that teachers should be paid, at least in part, for the effectiveness of their performance. But it's not as easy as it sounds. Scholars have clearly documented the many failed merit-pay schemes in years past—including those in the 1920s, 1950s, and 1980s.[24] These compensation-reform initiatives floundered, in large part, due to unre-solved technical and political issues. In the early 21st century, merit-pay programs are still on shaky ground—in part because of unstable metrics but, also, because reward structures have been built on the assumption that most teachers need to be paid more to work harder and raise stu-dent test scores. Research continues to prove otherwise, but stubborn policy leaders plow ahead.[25]

A recent report by the Aspen Institute shows how Singapore has cre-ated a system of teacher education and performance pay that motivates academically able recruits to learn to teach and then work collaboratively as they travel down three distinct career paths—all designed to continu-ously improve their skills, spread their teaching expertise, and keep the best of them in the classroom. The Singapore teacher-pay system is really a teacher-development system. Better-prepared teachers and those in high-demand fields have higher starting salaries. Teachers are specially trained to work with challenging students and new curriculum and are paid $10,000 retention bonuses as early as their 5th year in teaching. Schools are judged primarily by national exams, but teachers are judged primarily by external review panels that assess them on how well they support parents and community groups and advance student learning, while also "con-tributing to the character development and well-being of their pupils." Career Level-2 teachers can be paid as much as vice principals and some master teachers can earn as much as a local superintendent.[26]

If there is a caveat, it's that—unlike the United States—Singapore's public education system equitably funds its schools, and well-prepared teachers have the resources and technology needed to help their students reach world-class standards. The bottom line is that Singapore students far outperform their American counterparts on every international com-parison of academic achievement. As our co-author Cindi Rigsbee, a fi-nalist for the 2009 National Teacher of the Year, noted after studying the Singapore system:

> Policymakers and business leaders frequently challenge us to
> educate our students as well as those from Singapore. Perhaps
> they need to help us develop a performance-pay and teacher-
> development plan similar to Singapore's.

We rarely see proposals to reward teachers in ways that inspire inno-vative practices and spread teaching expertise. We're impressed with the thinking and writing of Daniel Pink, who draws on the science of motiva-tion to demonstrate clearly how current performance-pay schemes, which focus on a "narrow band of circumstances" and "if-then rewards," typi-cally undermine or even destroy creativity.[27] Pink has pointed out that the key to high performance is not rewards and punishments—it is "unseen intrinsic drive" and "the drive to do things because they matter."[28]

Co-author John M. Holland writes:

> There is untapped power in the passion of teachers that seems to be systemically squeezed out of them through the seniority pay system. But there is also the stultifying impact of paying teachers for raising test scores and other narrow measures. The more we uncork the "love" teachers have for helping students learn more, the faster the engine of school change will move.

Co-author Renee Moore describes how performance pay *could* work to improve public schools:

> In the future, our pay systems must build on more rigorous and comprehensive evaluation measures of student and teacher performance, so that the right indicators can create true accountability for teachers and administrators. It must draw on accomplished teachers as full partners in designing and implementing such measures, so the resulting accountability systems will be transparent and useful to policymakers, practitioners, and the public. It must rest on a nuanced approach to paying teachers differently, so that our public school systems are more flexible in adapting to future changes, including the many forces and events we cannot yet delineate.

In fact, Edward J. Lawler, a current guru in the strategic management of human capital, writes that most companies reinvent performance-pay systems every 4 years or so in response to shifting priorities and metrics.[29]

Renee asks us to imagine the shift in momentum for change likely to occur today if the following were true:

1. Base pay for all teachers across the country ranged from $45,000 to $70,000 (in 2011 dollars);
2. All teachers were eligible to earn performance-based supplements to the base pay for helping their students make significant (and authentic) academic gains;
3. Local school districts had flexibility to distribute incentive funds for teachers based on specific community needs or shortages;
4. Teachers received incentive bonuses for working together with their colleagues to produce better results for students over time;

5. Teachers who chose to teach in high-needs, low-performing schools and demonstrate proficiency in doing so received significant incentive bonuses;

6. Teachers were rewarded for leadership rather than seniority; and

7. Teachers who had proven themselves accomplished at helping students achieve were given opportunities to shape policy, curriculum, scheduling, and other key decisions at the school, district, state, and national levels.

Several years ago, Renee served on another TeacherSolutions project that specifically studied performance pay and designed an early 21st-century incentives system with the elements she describes above.[30] Now she takes those ideas one large and provocative step further, as she imagines teachers negotiating their own working conditions and compensation (individually or in small teams). She notes:

> Unlike other comparably prepared professionals, teachers are seldom able to negotiate their own individual hours, calendars, or compensation or, even, to determine their own "deliverables" of teaching and learning. This lack of clear goals and opportunities for teacher entrepreneurship and empowerment can lead to mediocre outcomes for students and schools.
>
> We have only begun to experiment with some of these options in a very few places, but the possible impact of large-scale implementation of these changes would truly alter the future of education in the United States. To be sure, changing the compensation system for teachers is only one crucial part of a multifaceted reformation of public education that must involve parents, students, educators, entrepreneurs, researchers, and policymakers. Nevertheless, if we begin now to shift how our society compensates teachers for professional services, we can accelerate student achievement—especially for those who have been historically left behind or left out in public education—while generating a critical mass of highly effective teachers for the mid-21st century.
>
> Changing the way we pay teachers would have an immediate effect on the working conditions of teachers, which has been demonstrated directly to influence student behavior and performance. By changing the pay structure, we would establish new expectations for teachers' professional performance. This new pay structure would then necessitate a

concurrent, and desperately needed, change in how teachers are evaluated, including how administrators are trained to do those evaluations—if administrators in the future evaluated teachers at all.

Our co-author Ariel Sacks, who recently turned 30, is candid in discussing salary as one consideration (among others) in her career goals, as it is for all professionals:

> I have often been asked what it will take to keep me in the classroom until 2030. My general answer is threefold: (1) freedom to develop, try out, and share my ideas; (2) leadership opportunities that extend beyond my classroom but don't require me to leave teaching altogether; and (3) formal recognition (including salary) for the skills I acquire and contributions I make to my students, school, and profession as I progress in my career. These three conditions are also crucial to the creation of smart schools, starting today.

As our TeacherSolutions 2030 team brainstormed different teaching roles and job configurations, our thinking began to suggest a new framework for compensation—transcending the marginal changes promoted by early 21st-century performance-pay systems.

The first iteration of this framework recognizes that failed merit-pay systems have not tied compensation tightly to meaningful measures of student and teacher productivity and have therefore done little to spur on creative pedagogical practices and spread effective teaching practices (see Figure 5.2).

In 2030, our most expert teachers will need to share what they know, not just nationally, but internationally, and earn more for doing so. But like other reformers have suggested, base pay must be fair and sufficient to attract and equitably reward teachers for the challenges of teaching. Teachers should be able to negotiate their base compensation, much like university professors currently do, based on their experiences and past performances, in and outside of the classroom. A newly minted graduate of a well-respected teacher-education program who has passed a rigorous performance assessment and is specifically trained to work with high-needs students should be able to demand a higher starting salary than another teacher education graduate with no special training and no interest in working in a high-poverty neighborhood. If the well-prepared recruit is willing to commit to teaching for at least 5 years, then he or she should be paid even more.

FIGURE 5.2. Base Salary

	Student Learning Impact*	Knowledge and Skills Impact	Market Demand	Community Impact	Teacherpreneurial Activity	Base and Differentiated Pay
Resident teachers (Promising recruits who enter teaching after specialized training or residencies)	$45,000 base; grants and interest-free loans for professionals supporting families, single parents, etc., to aid transition to teaching	Resident teachers are expected to concentrate on the curriculum and clinical teaching of their residency but may earn grants to participate in or develop teacherpreneurial projects and/or research with the guidance of a master teacher.				$45,000+
Apprentice teachers (Promising recruits who enter teaching after limited training, but teach under more supervision)	$35,000 base	Portfolios, peer assessments, student assessments demonstrate above average growth for moving into independent teaching	Apprentice teachers may earn additional compensation for collaborating with peers on projects that lead to a demonstrated impact on learning, the community, etc.			$45,000 (upon passing performance assessment, likely to increase)
Adjunct Teacher	Part-time salary based on market salary in the field and/or supplemented with tax and other incentives	May earn additional compensation for spreading content area skills to peers, developing subject-specific pedagogy	While adjunct teachers are limited by their subject-specific training and part-time roles, they are able to partner with professional and master teachers and receive compensation for special research and projects on a case-by-case basis. Adjunct teachers may also transition into an abbreviated residency if they choose to enter further into the teaching profession.			

		Student Learning Impact*	Knowledge and Skills Impact	Market Demand	Community Impact	Teacherpreneurial Activity	Base and Differentiated Pay
Virtual Teacher	$50,000 novice base to $70,000	Virtual portfolios and assessments demonstrate fostering growth in student learning	Continued learning and mastery of new tools/resources; development of virtual lessons and assessments into resources for peers	Developing methods for impacting high-needs students through the virtual medium	Development of digital resources for the community that promote public engagement and learning	Release time to develop new virtual models, curriculum, etc., or serve as individual contractors and offer classes/seats/individualized instruction by contract to different communities	$ 120,000
Individualized Instruction Specialist Teacher	$50,000 novice base to $70,000	Specialized instruction and support of peers contributes to increased gains in student learning as measured in portfolios and assessments	Demonstrated development and spreading of skills that improve learning in specialized area	Carrying and spreading expertise into high-needs contexts	Advocacy for diverse student populations, etc.	May apply for 20% project development time to develop ideas with the support of a master teacher; may contract with non-profits, government, etc. Sabbaticals and free-market work periods available	$120,000

FIGURE 5.2. Base Salary (continued)

	Student Learning Impact*	Knowledge and Skills Impact	Market Demand	Community Impact	Teacherpreneurial Activity	Base and Differentiated Pay
Professional Teacher	$50,000 novice base to $80,000	Meet goals for student learning; track progress through assessments and portfolio; offer interventions that transform barriers to student learning	Development of skills that enhance student learning; spreading of expertise to peers	Demonstrated skills to effectively teach high-needs students or subjects and be assigned accordingly	Developing programs or resources or building new relationships within the community	May apply for 20% project development time to develop ideas with the support of a master teacher; may contract with nonprofits, government, etc. Sabbaticals and free-market work periods available	$150,000
Master Teachers (including those in hybrid teaching roles)	$60,000 base after teachers identified with "master path" after 3- to 5-years teaching, up to $100,000 base	Demonstration of highest achievement gains through assessments and portfolios; helping peers to achieve their goals	Continued acquisition of new skills and knowledge making a measurable impact on peers' performance and school culture	Demonstrated impact in high-needs schools/subjects; increasing peers' efficacy in these areas	Developing programs, resources, and new relationships in community; leveraging change that directly impacts students' lives and learning	Shifting cycle of sabbaticals and project development time; access to development funds; great flexibility to contract within the educational market and draw base salary from different sources while maintaining strong connections to the home community	$200,000

In 2010 non-inflation-adjusted dollars (Based on the fact that average teacher salary in 2010 was around $51,000, but actual salaries varied

Teachers could earn considerable additional pay for a host of performances and roles. These pay supplements would be designed to encourage and reward best teaching practices—bolstering and accelerating the achievement of local, state, national, and international school improvement goals. They would reward the hybrid roles we have described elsewhere in this book—roles that new millennium teachers tell us they are seeking—as teachers in these roles negotiate contracts, individually and collectively, not only with school districts but with nonprofits and user networks.

Student learning metrics would be built from a range of assessments, all validated, with many created by expert teachers themselves. Novices would be judged on their efforts to help their students make gains on local assessments, while experts would be expected to do so on international benchmarks. Ever-evolving handheld computers and data management software are allowing teachers to keep track of student learning in once unimaginable ways—and would become tools to easily assemble reports for teachers' own performance-pay reviews.

Our TLN colleague Heather Wolpert-Gawron imagines that by the year 2030, the relationship between compensation and credentialing might look like this:

> Not everyone earns the same credential. Some will demonstrate much higher levels of competency and performance, and those with a meritorious credential would be eligible for teaching jobs with more responsibility and pay. Based on the evidence, some new teachers will be recruited and prepared to serve in more specialized roles; others will serve more as generalists. Both roles will be valued, but placed differently in schools and within teacher teams. Data from their preparation program will provide lots of information for those who will decide who should teach what and to and with whom.
>
> Depending on what candidates have proven they can do, they will be granted different levels of autonomy as they begin their careers. Some new teachers will be able to take things on quickly, others will need more scaffolding and time. Some new teachers will climb quickly up the salary scale and be offered tenure—not as job protection but in recognition of accomplishment and the fact that the school system does not want them to leave the profession.
>
> We will have more evidence to help identify those who are most ready to serve in familiar-sounding roles like teacher educator and community organizer, as well as the very 21st-

century roles of Learning Architect, Synthesize or MUVE Guide—or even the highly prized Change Agent. In fact, the teacher-residency programs of tomorrow, with support from the federal government, will present a Chiron Award[31] to graduating candidates of great potential who are expected to serve as change agents. Schools staffed with Chiron Award recipients are rare, but the winners are sought after as some of the best and brightest new teachers in our country.

While novices, if well trained, could be paid more for teaching a high-needs subject, advanced teachers would be rewarded when they teach in a high-needs assignment (e.g., more challenging students in high-needs subjects and schools). Experts would be paid more when they supervise novices (and teaching assistants and adjuncts) in high-needs schools—and they would vet advanced teachers before those teachers are allowed to mentor and coach.

Teachers should also be paid more for a range of leadership opportunities—local, state, national, and international. For some, this means serving as local spokespersons for the district or developing and running a community outreach program that connects home and school and user networks. Other expert teachers, many of whom will serve in hybrid roles, will lead policy and research projects (in concert with university and think tank partners). Some will serve as chaired university professors of teacher education. Others will lead their unions—now more accurately labeled as professional guilds. Some expert teachers will be the highest paid anybodies in a school district. Some will become teacherpreneurs.

CHAPTER 6

Emergent Reality #4: Teacherpreneurism and a Future of Innovation

Scaling and Spreading Teacher Expertise

Over the last decade, growing numbers of school reformers have identified educational entrepreneurship as a means to ramp up the process of transformational change. For some, the energy that comes from innovation is a much-needed catalyst in school districts beset by an "asphyxiating bureaucracy" with a "culture of timidity and risk aversion."[1]

Real change, they argue, requires individuals whom researchers describe as "relentless" problem solvers.[2] Some reformers speak of visionary thinkers who create brand new for-profit or nonprofit organizations that can entice nontraditional recruits into teaching and mobilize them to have a large-scale impact on the entire public school system.[3] The new recruits, they say, must possess what some psychologists call "learned optimism," through which their effectiveness begins and ends with an "internal locus of control"—a relentlessness in the face of bureaucratic barriers and the longstanding organizational inertia so characteristic of America's public schools.[4]

The conventional wisdom appears to be that most current teachers are not selected for their "propensity to conceive radical new ideas and build organizations to realize their visions." According to this construct, current teachers—especially those who matriculated through education schools for their training—are just not capable of entrepreneurial thinking and action. Therefore, the argument goes, those working outside of education, or an entirely new generation of recruits with the right dispositions, must be "induced" to work in the public schools if meaningful reform is to take hold.[5]

There is no question that many of the more than 3.5 million teachers in our public education system became educators because they liked school as students and are quite satisfied with its current organizational structures and rhythms. They are not all that interested in teachers play-ing roles outside of their classrooms or schools. But our own collective experience suggests that there are also many teachers who want dramatic changes in their profession—and those that do are not just from the cur-rent crop of generation Y recruits. At the same time, we have learned that younger teachers, in order to remain in teaching, are far more likely to *expect and demand* more-differentiated and entrepreneurial roles. As Chris Dede recently claimed, "the many affordances of modern technology can now support both a broader suite of roles involving 'teaching' and a range of educational delivery systems beyond the walls of the school."[6]

Unfortunately, many of the foundations and non-profits now promot-ing dramatic changes in public education do not put a high priority on deeply preparing teachers to teach and keeping them in the profession. Some alternative certification providers are often touted for recruiting tal-ented young people into teaching—and forgiven for only modestly train-ing them because they are not expected to teach more than 2 years. Folks with this attitude seem to be saying, "Why on earth would talented gen-eration Y recruits want to remain in the classroom, when they can do their service to America and then seek out more lucrative and interesting jobs?" And those jobs are not always outside of the educational sphere. More and more, new recruits to teaching are not expected to teach for very long before they move on to become educational entrepreneurs. After taking a quick look through the classroom window, they're now eager to get into the business of fixing schools.[7]

While we are all for entrepreneurism in public schools, we have a dif-ferent view of what it takes to be a successful and enterprising change agent in education. Our co-author Ariel Sacks used the term *teacherpreneur* during one of our team writing sessions. She predicted that the schools of 2030 will need growing numbers of teacherpreneurs, which she described as teacher-leaders of proven accomplishment who have a deep knowl-edge of how to teach, a clear understanding of what strategies must be in play to make schools highly successful, and the skills and commitment to spread their expertise to others—all the while keeping at least one foot firmly in the classroom.

> And we need to begin to cultivate such teachers now, she says.
> Many teachers like myself could play any number of
> teacherpreneurial roles depending on the needs of my school
> and the funding source—community organization, think tank,
> or university. Right now many of us are developing curriculum
> materials, mentoring teachers, or creating partnerships between
> our schools and other organizations. And I can imagine more: I

could do policy work outside my school and/or be a freelance writer, with perhaps only half of my salary paid by the school itself.

The beauty of hybrid, teacherpreneurial role is that I would always maintain a classroom teaching practice. Teaching is the soul of my work in education. If I lose that, I think I'd feel disconnected from my purpose and passion—and my colleagues. At least in my own mind, my work would lose relevance and, understandably, I would lose credibility with my teaching peers.

Too many reformers have romanticized the marketplace, relying on choice and financial incentives to drive changes in the teaching profession. We believe in risk-taking teachers who are recognized and rewarded for innovative practices. But as our collaborator John M. Holland makes very clear, it's not really about the money.

We are talking about teacherpreneurs as an aspect of teachers' "ownership" of their profession. An evolution. Many of us aren't selling anything but a vision for a better educational future for children. We aren't necessarily asking to be compensated for this future so much as to be incorporated into the marketplace of ideas.

There is no need, says our co-author Ariel Sacks, for the false dichotomy of teachers either teaching for the love of children or to earn a professional income:

Our principal motivation isn't money, but to make education better. Nonetheless, our ideas need to be valued financially even though our "clients" (students) don't pay us. It's easy for other professionals to work not "just for the money" because there is so much money to be made in their field. Teachers should not shy away from the money issues—because it can make us more visible to our colleagues and the public.

Not only do these differentiated, entrepreneurial roles increase the "stickiness" of the teaching career by creating fresh challenges and opportunities as well as rewards, they preserve and enhance the body of knowledge and expertise that defines a profession. Our co-author Kilian Betlach offered his own ideas of teacherpreneurism and the hybrid opportunities that would have kept him in a teaching (rather than a purely administrative) role:

These new teacherpreneurial roles would replace the old
notions of mentor, master teacher, or department chair, which
insufficiently diversify professional standing and function as
poor replacements for promotions that are part of a recognized
and organized professional system. These new roles would
ground the profession in the work of teaching, while recognizing
that teacher leadership has a place and a value and a function
beyond honorific titles and extracurricular duties. Leadership
would no longer be a thing you ascribed to "after" teaching, or
when you were "done" teaching. Nor would teaching need to be
seen as something to master and move on from.

There are nearly endless combinations of endeavors that
could compose a hybrid teaching position that promotes
teacherpreneurism. . . . What remains central is the repudiation
of the dichotomous nature of the profession: You either teach or
principal, mentor or follow. The "or" in the equation represents
an inauthentic choice, and one that limits the effectiveness of
both individuals and the system as a whole. The removal of this
"either-or" barrier would bring a far greater array of skills and
strengths to bear on student achievement, improving academic
performance exponentially.

In our conception, the teacherpreneur is always engaged with students, while also investing know-how and energy into important projects,
including those supported by the district, the state, or a partnering organization. Early examples of teacherpreneurs aren't hard to find. Our co-
author Shannon C'de Baca is a trailblazing online educator who, not only
brings her science knowledge (and student management skills) to Iowa's
virtual high school classrooms, but also trains new teachers via distance
and face-to-face mentoring in Asia and the Mideast. Our TLN colleague
Lori Nazareno is co-leading a new Denver public school that's entirely
run by teachers. In Rhode Island, Marti Schwartz, another TLN member,
mentors new teachers for Brown University, contracts privately to provide
professional development in several community school systems, and is
also a literacy teacher and coach at an inner-city high school.

Many other colleagues are providing professional development and
training to peers who are gaining expertise in teaching children with different learning needs—or helping build effective professional learning
communities in high-needs schools. As TLN member Sarah Henchey
says, "This shift, at least instructionally, has already begun. More districts
and schools have developed literacy and math coaches to support teachers. AIG and ESL specialists provide pull-out, push-in, and professional

development." As we imagine it, teacherpreneurism will build out from these teacher-leader-coach beginnings. As entrepreneurial roles evolve, it will become more and more commonplace to select a cadre of the most highly effective and creative classroom educators and give them the independence and financial incentives to innovate in ways that—in Phillip Schlechty's memorable phrase—"shake up the schoolhouse."

After a dozen years teaching in a suburban Birmingham, Alabama, high school, our co-author Jennifer Barnett returned home to rural Talladega County to teach English and social studies at a small K–12 school. Her use of digital tools and the Internet and her commitment to project-based learning (PBL) soon attracted the attention of district administrators, who were considering an ambitious plan to make PBL a mainstay in all schools in the countywide district. Today Jennifer is beginning to serve as a teacherpreneur, leading major innovations at Winterboro High—the first Talladega school to transition to project-driven instruction. It's her job to support both the integration of 21st-century skills and teaching strategies and to promote collegial collaboration. Her report, 1 year into the initiative, illustrates both the powerful effect of a change agent and the important quality of collaborative leadership that will be essential in the teacherpreneur role:

> Winterboro School has become a very rich school. It would seem more likely for an extremely rural school with over 90% free/reduced lunch status to become part of a Top 10 list of at-risk schools, but this is not the case. A 21st-century transformation is happening.
>
> After searching for a curriculum redesign and settling on schoolwide adoption of a project-based learning experience for all students in every course, we can see that this school's students are changing. Only the "old thinkers" of the nearly 400 visitors we've welcomed this year have asked about our students' test scores. (I'm so humored by their impatience in trying to prove our work invalid.) Most see what I see. Our students present themselves as confident young professionals placing value on what they are doing and why they are doing it. They believe they are relevant.
>
> How do I know? Macy, an 8th-grader who didn't like the change at first, surprised me with her evaluation of school a few weeks ago. Macy and I were discussing favorite books. She and her friends began to tell me about all the books that would have been great to read alongside *The Odyssey*, which their class had been studying. I asked Macy when she read. She told

me that she read in the afternoons, preferably outside under a tree. When I told her how surprising it was to hear that she preferred to read after school, she quickly explained why. Macy said when she gets home from school she doesn't turn on the TV or the computer. She doesn't want her phone to ring or to send or receive texts. She said that she is always tired and needs to unwind and reading seems to help. Her friends agreed. They said they needed to "chill out" for a while. School is tough.

Much can be said about what our students are doing now, but I'm most interested in why it is working. It may be a worn-out concept in the second decade of the 21st century, but collaboration is the key. It is happening everywhere. Teachers are working with each other. It has become our addictive drug and not one of them is ready to let go. Students see it and follow the model. Why? Students want to be confident, valuable, and relevant. They realize that social friction can create amazing energy.

This collaboration is not happening by chance or because of fantastic technological advancements. Collaboration is happening by design. Before they could model collaboration, the teachers have had to learn how to work in concert with one another. One thing most people don't realize is this: Most of us don't know how, as a group, to exchange ideas, create plans, and distinguish between what's good and what's great. Embracing ambiguity is the key to successful collaboration and many teachers struggle with that. We want a decision, a plan, and we want it immediately. Unfortunately, successful collaboration takes time, patience, and a great deal of knowledge and skill.

Here's the rub. Our Winterboro staff is very young and inexperienced. They have very little time and even less patience with themselves. Yet, the sessions are carefully designed to bring the right mix of knowledge and expertise to the collaboration table. The teacher-leader in the hybrid role can make this happen in every school in America. I want every "poor" school in this country to offer its students the opportunity to become rich in confidence, value, and relevancy. We haven't reached the mountaintop yet, but we can see the sun shining on the other side.

There is good evidence of Winterboro's early progress: The isolated high school, which shares building space with students in grades K–8, was selected by *U.S. News & World Report* as one of the "Best High Schools in Alabama" for 2010. The magazine's selection methods, developed by School Evaluation Services, a K–12 education data research business run by Standard & Poor's, are "based on the key principles that a great high school must serve all its students well, not just those who are college-bound, and that it must be able to produce measurable academic outcomes to show the school is successfully educating its student body across a range of performance indicators."

The Making of Teacherpreneurs

In the early 21st century, thousands of teachers—pursuing the possibilities offered by Craigslist and eBay—began to "cash in" on their teaching, "selling lesson plans online for exercises as simple as M&M sorting and as sophisticated as Shakespeare."[8] Early efforts like Teachers Pay Teachers and We Are Teachers have provided unprecedented venues for classroom practitioners to be rewarded for good ideas and plans.[9] For the teacher-founders of Teachers Pay Teachers, creating "an empowering place where teachers buy and sell original and used teaching materials and make teaching an even more rewarding experience"[10] is a critical initial step. We Are Teachers combines social networking and e-commerce to offer a first generation of "tangible business opportunities" for teachers "to productize what they do, to be paid for their expert advice, and to have a stake in the knowledge marketplace."[11]

While we agree that selling good pedagogical ideas online can elevate the status and visibility of effective teachers, we also worry that teachers acting as individual vendors in an already crowded marketplace may ultimately tamp down the spread of best practices from one teacher to another, anytime and anywhere. We have something bigger in mind. We see teacherpreneurs, not primarily as marketers, but as expert practitioners who are paid to spread their ideas and approaches as virtual mentors, teacher educators, community organizers, and policy as well as action researchers. The purpose in creating teacherpreneurs is, not to identify "super teachers" who will make a lot more money, but to empower expert teachers who can elevate the entire profession by making sure that colleagues, policymakers and the public know what works best for students.

Our TLN colleague Heather Wolpert-Gawron offers a good description of the role we see for teacherpreneurs in the future:

> I and others who are excited by this concept imagine
> teacherpreneurs to be a subset of accomplished teachers who
> act as change agents within their own schools, finding creative
> solutions and mobilizing the resources to accomplish those

solutions. We imagine teacherpreneurs to have the freedom and power to interact in the global education marketplace, developing—and selling—their talents and ideas. We imagine teacherpreneurs will become the go-to experts in our profession and no longer will we be beset by peddlers of canned professional development who troll the nation giving workshops and presentations that are too generic or out of touch with today's classrooms—intentionally or unintentionally undermining efforts for teachers known to be successful with today's kids to spread their expertise to one another.

Spreading pedagogical expertise through deeply knowledgeable teachers is a venture with great potential. And it can happen virtually. Our co-author John M. Holland talked about how and why the Internet paves the way for a brand of teacherpreneurism that transcends the hierarchy of the single school and district.

Smart networks, as Clay Shirky has described in his book *Here Comes Everybody*, have changed the world by making it easy for individuals to organize. Shirky describes how the Internet and mobile technologies have changed the social nature of our society by making communication between and among groups simpler and more instantaneous than ever before. Now that more people are online than offline, the way people define what is worth knowing and who is worth learning from has changed. This is what the profession will be like for teachers in 2030—we can choose to learn from the best—from teacherpreneurs who are highly rated by our colleagues in professional online networks, teachers who really know children and really know how to teach.

In the future, an effective teacherpreneur will not only know how to use codified skills and knowledge but will also incorporate the creativity associated with artists, inventors, poets, and others who see connections where many do not. John describes it this way:

First, they must fully embrace the scientific and research-based aspects of the profession. They must be able to see through cracks in their practice, analyze data to make appropriate decisions about how best to teach their students, and understand complex content in a deep enough way to communicate its most important and tested aspects to their students. Ultimately, I believe teaching must be reconceptualized as a creative profession. Creative individuals see what others do not; they consider what's before them and make new meaning. For teachers, meaning equals learning. Another way to look at it: In the competitive world of design, the artist or designer is expected to take a product and create an ad or representation of the product that makes consumers want to buy it. If we change the word *"buy"* to *"learn"* and the word *"product"* to *"content,"* then we are basically describing what teachers do in the classroom or in virtual settings with students—and what they can do outside of the classroom as they spread what they know to other teachers or researchers or policymakers or community members.

With advances in communications hardware and software, by 2030, teacherpreneurs will be engaged in a worldwide teaching marketplace, where they lead colleagues and their students through increasingly individualized learning experiences. The value they bring is not a series of prepackaged multimedia or online-delivered products, but teachers' special abilities to identify the needs of their particular students and facilitate learning in physical or virtual environments. Those who seek these teacherpreneurs out for their special skills will not be looking for marginal gains on a 20th-century standardized test, but for a professional who can help another teacher increase his or her mastery, or help highly fractionated families keep their children engaged in learning and performing well on multidimensional 21st-century assessments.

John describes how pedagogical entrepreneurs have already begun to emerge:

> When publishing became "free" to almost anybody, and the Internet's potential audience became the entire world, the line between expert and amateur began to blur. The big idea here is that there will always be teacher-experts, but those seeking teaching expertise (including teachers, parents, and students themselves) will be the ones to decide who is an expert. The combination of self-publishing and the use of the Internet as a platform for communication has already given rise to "communities of practice" around topics ranging from lessons in how to teach fractions to using brain research to perform the teaching act at the highest levels. Teacherpreneurs will increasingly be leaders in these communities, which will stretch far beyond the confines of their school or district—a virtual domain where they are able to impact the profession on a large scale.

At the start of the 21st century, accomplished teachers see a growing need to connect and learn from their peers. Our co-author Susie Highley offers an example of powerful professional development that illustrates how teachers can develop into instructional experts and then guide their colleagues in teaching more effectively:

> The most valuable, lasting, and inspirational professional development I have ever experienced was through the Teacher Leadership Academy (TLA)—actually run by a state agency. My cohort group included over 30 teachers from other systems and nine teachers from my district (elementary, middle, and high school). It was through this program that I first received in-depth instruction in Understanding by Design, problem-based learning, classroom applications of brain research, distance learning, differentiated instruction and more. Most important, I gained the knowledge and skill needed to teach other adults successfully—something quite different from teaching children and adolescents. Because the program lasted for 2 years, we had ample time to apply what we had learned in our own classrooms, and share our knowledge in faculty meetings, district trainings and coaching opportunities—and also by creating videos and participating in online cohort discussions.

Emerging technologies also make it possible for expert teachers who are physically distant from one another to be "cherry-picked" and organized into entrepreneurial groups to meet specific purposes. At the Center for Teaching Quality, the Return on Investment Initiative began in 2008 using a virtual mentoring model to connect teachers in high-needs schools to a cadre of specially trained virtual coaches who were also National Board–certified teachers. The NBCT coaches work with colleagues in live webinars and asynchronous discussions in an online learning community. Supported teachers have included both novices and those seeking national certification themselves. Webinars cover specific topics, such as classroom management or analyzing the success of an assignment. Through informal virtual conversation, isolated or underresourced teachers have access to just-in-time support from their expert peers. Similar strategies can be used to strengthen the skills of content-area teachers (e.g., science, history, or teachers in schools with a sudden influx of second language learners). The teachers offering the support may be hundreds—even thousands—of miles away.

Teacherpreneurism for Connected Learning

Co-author Emily Vickery points out that our increasing understanding of how students learn, and the rise of a Web-enhanced learning ecology, create a demand that teachers know more and teach differently—transforming teacher-education by extension:

> As online learning communities continue to grow and more and more people interact with synthetic Web-based environments, the skills that teachers need to master may sound more like something from the script of an interstellar sci-fi thriller than from traditional teacher workshops and preservice courses.
>
> Instead of reviewing lecture notes for Introduction to Education Psychology, teachers may need to cultivate expertise in the Psychology of Avatar Development; instead of Classroom Management, perhaps Orchestrating Learning in Synthetic Environments will be more useful. Teachers will, in fact, be orchestrators of learning—a concept we talk about today, while seldom doing much to accomplish it, but one that will force itself upon most everyone who expects to be a teacher in 2030.
>
> As part of this transformation, colleges and university professors and school district administrators and consultants will no longer be the center of all teacher learning. Instead, like users of Wikipedia, teachers will play a key role in defining the curriculum and debating what is important to know and what the future of teacher education should be. Teacherpreneurs will be driving the learning of their colleagues.

Imagine that in 2030, about 15% of the nation's four million teachers are serving in teacherpreneur roles. No longer are school districts relying on canned curriculum and one- or two-shot workshops delivered to general teacher audiences by a consultant who has not taught students for more than a decade. Instead, 600,000 classroom teachers are in the "consulting" business as well, working in the public sector and perhaps also for themselves, not only teaching children regularly, but providing the highest quality professional development via the connectivity of the wired world. As public support for this phenomenon grows, more teachers become participants in creative educational enterprises, consulting with game makers to produce Web-based and personal "edutainment" products built on a framework of scientifically based learning—or serving as knowledge brokers between academic scholars and researchers and both youth and adult learners. Because they remain grounded in classroom practice and realities, they are more likely to be far more credible with their full-time teaching colleagues and more likely to spread teaching expertise to them.

But what may set teacherpreneurs apart from educational entrepreneurs is the focus on students as partners—not only in learning but in reform as well. Andy Hargreaves' stimulating discussion of "Fourth Way" educational reform argues that long-term school improvements cannot be sustained without a number of pillars in place, including *students as partners in change*.[12] For Hargreaves, student involvement in change begins with teachers who can conduct assessments for learning that create student ownership and responsibility. The profession needs more teachers who have the skills to teach students how to teach themselves and their peers, both inside and outside of brick-and-mortar classrooms.[13]

For students to be prepared for the mid-21st century global economy, teachers will need to be highly skilled at helping students screen and synthesize, sort, vet, and categorize vast amounts of information. Imagine teachers being prepared for and skilled as mavens of discriminating or "astute" learning—helping students gain the knowledge and skills to decide what is worthwhile of an ever-growing amount of online content and what is most valuable to their own personal learning plan. Those teachers who do it best will get paid more for it—not because their students do it better than other students, but because they help other teachers learn to do it well and, thereby, benefit many other students.

Our colleague Ariel Sacks imagines that expert teacherpreneurs will, not only establish cottage industries in their own communities and regions, but join together in powerful teaching collectives, using their sharply honed 21st-century pedagogical skills to create innovative learning systems funded by governments and philanthropies and to promote ideas for social good on a large scale.

John M. Holland picks up on the concept and moves it further:

> Grassroots economics is usually defined as local solutions to
> local problems. But just as the Internet has changed the meaning
> of local from geographic groups to affinity groups, the idea of a
> grassroots education economy takes on entirely new meaning.
> Long-tail and niche markets will become more viable areas
> for teacherpreneurs, as learning becomes more entwined in
> the virtual environment. For the first time, teachers are being
> presented with the opportunity to act creatively to design and
> guide lessons and the acquisition of content based on their

understanding of learning. The ability to create individual pathways for student learning will be a marketable skill—one that teacher leaders can also translate into adult learning in online professional communities.

And Emily Vickery takes these ideas even further:

The world's best teachers will learn of the other expert teachers through their own networking. Just as students will have choices, so will teachers. They will have a range of options in hanging out their real and virtual shingles; advertising their talent, knowledge, and abilities. They may offer their services as a solo venture or band together with others, forming collectives, to provide learning opportunities. Some collectives will have loose affiliations, while others will be sustained for the long term.

Teacherpreneurs for Research

Stephanie Van Horn, a young Colorado teacher leader and member of the CTQ New Millennium Initiative, talked to us about how action research informs her teaching and the need for more teacherpreneurs who spend a portion of their time in the role of action researcher, looking at a range of evidence on student learning.

I work best when I can talk through an idea with an expert—a literacy specialist, our special education teacher, my teammate. I also work best if I can [look at evidence] and see it in action, try it, tweak it, try it again, and weigh the options. We are only going to get better at teaching and help others in the profession improve when we spend more time looking at what works and what does not. I love the aspect of teacher research/action research in my classroom. I just wish there was more time built into my day to collaborate with other teachers—in and out of my school—and to engage in meaningful analyses of our practice. As a relatively new teacher in 2010, I feel I'm doing "drive-by collaboration" when I see my teammates at lunch or in the hall, maybe before and after school, and try to talk through an idea. But what if we had time set aside to carry out well-organized action research, the results of which were spread and valued not just in my building but in all schools in my district and across the nation?

Our TLN colleague Jon Hanbury, a math coach with 37 years of elementary level teaching under her belt, describes how she has learned to research and reflect:

> With experience, I have found a greater need to engage in teacher research. Not only have I grown professionally through this inquiry into my teaching practice, I've enjoyed the intrinsic rewards of sharing with my colleagues and administrators. It's such a rush when something I have unearthed is considered for schoolwide implementation. I cannot imagine what it would feel like if the state took on some of the good ideas we have cultivated. Maybe that's why I enjoy teaching more now than I did years ago.
>
> What if teacherpreneurs worked side-by-side with researchers to study teaching effectiveness? What if opportunities to do action research became a tool to recruit and retain individuals who were not only good at teaching kids but had that scientific bent that makes you want to experiment and document what works best? Wouldn't that help us keep more motivated and inquisitive teachers in the career? Wouldn't that help connect research to practice and vice versa?

And what if Jon and others actually got paid more for doing and spreading successful research about teaching? It's not preposterous—professors get paid more when they conduct worthwhile research and bring in grant money to their universities.

Generation Y teacher Kristoffer Kohl, a former TFA corps member, has successfully carved out a teacherpreneur-like role in his school as a part-time classroom teacher and part-time researcher. In doing so, he's fulfilled both a school need and a personal need to grow professionally:

> I had the idea of a schoolwide position that would make useful sense of the overwhelming amount of student "data" that schools have, but rarely use wisely, to inform and improve instruction. There are too many tests and too little time for teachers to decipher all the information. With the time afforded in my role as part-time teacher and part-time data strategist, students' assessment results are now used less as a summative judgment of classroom instruction, and more as information for teachers to use to understand the effects of their teaching and justify, with evidence, the approach they take with individual students.

Having joined the teaching profession through TFA, my approach to the classroom was founded on the value of data to guide my instruction. One of the organization's primary principles is the use of data to inform teaching. Additionally, as a business economics major in college, I went into the classroom comfortable with numbers and figures. Rather than pushing the value of data on others at my school site, my aptitude as a data strategist was discovered by colleagues that witnessed how I was using the information to shape individual lessons, student groupings, and long-range plans.

I honed my data analysis skills in my first 2 years in the classroom. Beginning with a basic understanding of Microsoft Excel, I was able to use a number of functions to dig deeper into student assessment results. What I found more useful than the numbers, however, was the presentation of those values. A series of numbers on a spreadsheet is meaningless if you are unable to actually see what the numbers mean. After using data to guide classroom instruction (first year), then grade-level instruction (years 2 and 3), the administration thought it would be valuable for me to spend time looking at schoolwide data. We have used the information to guide schoolwide intervention efforts, as well as our school improvement process.

I think teachers need to understand why data are valuable, how they can positively impact the classroom, as well as the ability to discern valuable data from useless data, which may actually be a question of valuable assessment versus useless assessment. Helping [teachers] gain that understanding is part of my job now. This kind of role is absolutely essential for me remaining engaged with the profession.

Teacherpreneurship can be cultivated by maintaining creative mindsets about schools, students, and learning. Such creative processes and discussions are intellectually stimulating and make educational innovation possible. It is such thinking, theorizing, philosophizing, and experimenting that allows our schools to move forward. If we do not dream bigger and better, then we are bound to remain stagnant.

Teacherpreneurs for Best Practice and Policy

Teacherpreneurism is also about the marketing of ideas. All of the bloggers mentioned in this section began blogging because they were passionate about teaching and learning. They gained audience and began to realize that their voice had power, not the power of dollars but the power of ideas. The "passion seed" is an important aspect of this form of teacherpreneurism and it helps to contradict the argument that teachers just want to be paid more. Most bloggers don't get paid to blog. Those who are paid (rarely for more than their time, if that) are being rewarded both for their expertise and for their creativity. The concept of "Strong Opinions-Creatively Expressed" is what makes this brand of teacherpreneurism work. Put another way: "Passion + Creativity + Expertise = Power." Without the passion it wouldn't get done. Without creativity, no one would listen. Without expertise, it wouldn't matter.

Trailblazing "teacherpreneurs" are popping up in schools and districts as never before. They are known by the spread of their ideas, which is accelerated by their entrepreneurial tendency to create networks and continually seek out new audiences to which they can not only spread their expertise but find or cultivate like-minded colleagues.

Our co-author Cindi Rigsbee, a school literacy coach and new-teacher mentor, witnessed the power of a "raised profile" when she became North Carolina's 2009 Teacher of the Year and then went on to become one of four finalists for National Teacher of the Year. Cindi spread her experiences and pedagogical insights as she spoke to teachers, university education departments, and civic organizations in literally hundreds of workshops and meetings across her state. But she has reached her widest audience thanks to the connectivism of the Internet. Her popular blog the Dream Teacher raises critical issues affecting effective teaching practice and successful schools. Here's a sample from her entries:

> In working with administrators I shared the story of my 1st year teaching—1979—and how in that high school every classroom door was closed. Every teacher taught in isolation—there was no sharing of plans or resources, no discussions of student needs, no back and forth on what was working or wasn't. [Today] we are spending more time meeting with other teachers, but we aren't observing other teachers. When we do we pick up ideas for what works with certain students (students we may teach as well), we could also be more informed about what others are teaching so that we can plan collaboratively.

One of Cindi's posts at the Dream Teacher caught the attention of producers at ABC's *Good Morning America* when she wrote of the qualities of effective, inspirational teachers and her own search for the elementary teacher who had influenced her career choice. Ultimately, she was reunited with that teacher on the national morning TV show, which led to the 2010 book from Jossey-Bass—*Finding Mrs. Warnecke*—which not only recounts the story of her search but shares insights from her teaching practice.

TLN member Bill Ferriter, a middle school English and social studies teacher, has built a wide national audience through his blog, the Tempered Radical. A true teacherpreneur, Bill's status as an expert in seamless technology integration grows out of his willingness to freely share resources from his own teaching—and led to an offer from *Educational Leadership* magazine to write a monthly column on digital learning. Bill was also a leader in establishing professional learning communities (PLC) at a newly opened school in Wake County, North Carolina—an experience that translated into work as a consultant and author for the education publisher Solution Tree. His first (bestselling) book, *Building a Professional Learning Community at Work: A Guide to the First Year*, includes a foreword by PLC experts Rick and Becky DuFour. His second book, *Teaching the iGeneration*, helps teachers and principals think through the implications for learning of a generation growing up with wireless technologies and the interactive Web.

Bill describes how he emerged as a teacherpreneur while still remaining firmly anchored in his classroom:

> What's really interesting is that building an audience has been easier than I ever imagined. As a teacher, I stand at the forefront of every major policy initiative in education. I'm living our shift from an isolated profession to one focused on collaboration. I've struggled with making data a more important part of my practice. I've worked diligently to find ways to incorporate new digital tools into my instruction. I've been punished by standardized testing and coercive accountability.
>
> And I write honestly about all of these topics. Through my bits, readers—regardless of what role they fill in education—can see the impact of their actions. They can rethink policies. They can redesign their instruction. They can restructure their schools and/or districts. I offer a looking glass into the hearts and minds of classroom teachers—and that's a looking glass that concerned professionals everywhere are dying to peek into.
>
> Early on, the Center for Teaching Quality spotted potential in the thoughts that I was posting in the online Teacher Leaders Network conversation and asked me if I'd be interested in spending a summer as a teacher-in-residence studying the results of CTQ's teacher working conditions survey.

Editors from both NSDC and ASCD spotted my writing online and asked me to write full-length articles and regular columns for their magazines. Publishers from nearly every major publishing house have contacted me to gauge my interest in writing books for them after seeing something that I'd written posted online.

I've never gone looking for opportunities, simply because I haven't needed to! Making the choice to be visible and being committed to freely sharing what I know about teaching and learning—recognizing that my knowledge and experience have value—has brought others to me. The connectivity of the Web offers teachers a chance like never before to make their voices heard.

Like dozens of other TLN members, Cindi and Bill have also taken advantage of an entrepreneurial partnership between TLN and a number of media outlets, including *Teacher*, an online magazine published by *Education Week*, where TLN members post weekly articles about policy and expert practice that often reach an audience in the hundreds of thousands. Cindi's essay "Teaching Secrets: Five Tips for the New Teacher" has been among the most popular. Her pithy advice, "if you make them the enemy, you will lose," was exactly the straight talk novice teachers were seeking. The magazine compensated Cindi for her time and expertise, and any new teacher with access to Google can easily find her advice and benefit from it.

Cindi balances her writing with a hybrid role that's really three jobs in one—acting as a districtwide new-teacher mentor, a school-based literacy coach, and a reading specialist working directly with students each morning. To accomplish all that, she does what most teacher-leaders do. She pushes more areas of her life into the corners and valiantly manages the circus act of being as effective as she can in at least two "100% jobs" while not letting any of the balls she is juggling drop. But creating more hybrid roles for teacherpreneurs is not about creating more superhero teachers expected to do more and more, cutting into a much-needed life outside of school and students. Too many reforms of today and yesterday have taken the "caped crusader" approach—relying on teachers to take endless, extraordinary measures in order to close the achievement gap. All too often these extraordinary teachers burn out early, compromising the gains they have made individually in their classrooms, and sometimes in their teams and schools. Hybrid roles should be structured so that effective teachers have the time and support to work successfully in teams, getting extraordinary results together—results that transcend the outcomes that can be measured by standardized tests.

Hybrid roles open the door to teacherpreneurism by promoting the flexibility and atmosphere of innovation necessary for a creative profession to flourish. In turn, teacherpreneurism capitalizes on the collective talents and ingenuity of hundreds of thousands of teachers who seek to solve problems as well as spread their expertise in and out of cyberspace and in and out of their schools. Bill describes how teacherpreneurism is good for both teachers and for education as a whole:

> At the simplest level, being professionally compensated for my talents beyond the classroom has enabled me to stay in the classroom full time for far longer than I ever dreamed possible. As the primary breadwinner for my family, making ends meet on the ten paychecks that I get as a classroom teacher each year is simply impossible. Writing and presenting beyond the classroom is my way of working full-time. Without the extra pay that I make, I would have moved on—into administration, into full-time consulting work, into the policy arena—a long time ago.
>
> But I see benefits for teacherpreneurism that stretch far beyond my own wallet. Every time I create a new resource for classroom teachers who are working as part of professional learning teams or trying to integrate technology into their classrooms—decisions that I make based on my desire to be compensated for my ideas—I know that my peers will have access to quality tools built from the experiences of another full-time practitioner instead of the professional dreamers that haven't set foot in a classroom in decades.
>
> I also share my views on policy, through the classroom teacher's lens. That's not something that puts much bread on my family table, but to me it's an essential part of teacher leadership. Every education policy gets beta-tested in our classrooms and by sharing my feedback in very public ways I'm not only letting policymakers know what I think but encouraging other classroom teachers to do the same. To me that's teacherpreneurism too—rallying our profession to come out of the classroom closet and speak up.

Our co-authors John M. Holland and Jose Vilson couldn't agree more. Both are outspoken advocates for policy reform, using the vehicle of their highly visible blogs to make their views heard. Jose is a respected policy voice in the national community of urban and Latino educators, whose credibility comes from his daily work as a middle-grades math teacher and coach in New York City's Inwood/Washington Heights neighbor-hood. John, an NBCT in early childhood education, is a national leader in the preschool education community and lead blogger at Inside Pre-K, a group blog supported by the public education organization Pre-K Now, which advocates for high-quality, voluntary pre-kindergarten programs for all 3- and 4-year-olds.

TLN members Heather Wolpert Gawron and Elena Aguilar blog at the popular Edutopia website. Heather also attracts a large audience to her TweenTeacher blog, where she adopts a light, sometimes irreverent tone to discuss both classroom practice and the implications of current policy and research. Heather draws insight and authority to discuss policy *from* her classroom. Her audience trusts her as a teacher. This trust will be powerful as teacherpreneurs begin to advocate for the policies they understand are best for students. TLN member Ken Bernstein, an AP government teacher in Virginia, blogs at the popular political website DailyKos and has also written for the Lesson Plans blog of the *New York Times*. Describing the opening days of school in one Lesson Plans post, Ken wrote:

> For me to be a successful teacher, I have to build relationships. I am demanding. I insist that my students take intellectual risks. Otherwise how will they grow, and develop more skills? Those relationships take time and energy.[14]

Providing insights into the craft of teaching like this is important for teachers advocating for change. Dan Brown, who writes about his school, SEED Charter, in Chapter 4, is author of the 2008 book *The Great Expectations School*, and blogs for the Teacher Leaders Network and also for the *Huffington Post*. He is able to link to hot education news and debates and share his viewpoint with a huge cross-section of readers. He wrote recently in response to a *New York Times* editorial that reprimanded teachers for balking at the use of standardized tests for teacher evaluation:

> A teachers' job is complex (to put it lightly), and does not begin and end with test scores. The scores should count toward teachers' and students' evaluations, but our country has boarded a runaway train of overvaluing these tests. The directive in the *Times* editorial to force teachers to further emphasize the Big Test damages hope for genuine strides toward fair accountability and supportive education.
>
> There are a lot of reasons that high-stakes testing has become so entrenched in our school system. The test results are easy to

tabulate, reductive and malleable for political purposes, meet the short-order demands of condensed news- and election-cycles, and keep publishing companies raking in cash.

If you don't know students personally and know nothing about classroom life, it's a lot easier to advocate the Times' simplistic strategy: Cut all teachers out and let self-proclaimed "reformers" impose testing regimes designed to churn out stats, not to support children's diverse needs.

Dan's tone is sharp, but he creates an effective contrast between test data for political ends and the real learning-needs of students. As teachers gain a public audience for their voices, they will be able to leverage public attention to their ideas and concerns.

Indeed, some teacherpreneurs are going a step further and using the Web's capacity for viral networking to mobilize educators and the public around important education policy issues. Anthony Cody, an Oakland, California, science coach who keeps the blog Living in Dialogue at *Teacher Magazine*, was one of many teachers who watched the fledgling Obama administration's education initiatives unfold during 2009 with a mix of hope and strong reservation. When Anthony concluded that the administration was not listening carefully enough to classroom teachers on important subjects like implementing national standards and assessing student learning and teacher performance, he independently launched a Facebook page for a project he tagged "Teachers' Letters to Obama."

Anthony's first goal was simple if time-consuming: Gather letters from teachers that shared a classroom-eye view of the plans put forth by Obama and Education Secretary Arne Duncan. More than 100 teachers from across the country submitted letters (or posted them on their own blogs) sharing their hopes, questions, and concerns about education policy and their students' futures. Anthony submitted the letters to Secretary Duncan and elevated the project's profile by sharing samples of the letters on his widely read blog. *Education Week* agreed to publish an op-ed column by Anthony that included letter excerpts and a download link to the complete set. The Facebook group quickly grew to more than 2,000 teachers across the nation. A letter-writing campaign to senators was planned next. Anthony posted guides and resources that made it easy for teachers to get in touch with their elected officials. Teachers began sharing bits of policy-related news and their own rallying cries through wall posts on the Teachers' Letters to Obama group page. Other Facebook groups supported by teaching advocates linked up with Anthony's page.

In an early April 2010 reflection at his Living in Dialogue blog, Anthony wrote:

Teachers are finally learning how to organize. It took some intense provocation, because we do not rile easily. But from Florida to Fremont High School in Los Angeles, teachers are doing what it takes to be heard. And this is not your mother's protest movement. Teacher protest is alive in the digital age, and we are using the latest tools of the times . . .

Facebook has emerged as a tremendously powerful vehicle for organizing. . . . Facebook membership has more than doubled in the past year, and more than 100 million Americans are registered users. Facebook allows you to set up a group, host discussions, and share links and videos. . . . But the best thing about it is that since this is a social platform, posts can permeate into our everyday social scene, so amidst the flurry of news from friends like "I just popped some popcorn and am going to watch *Casablanca*" we can get posts with the latest news about teachers protesting in Florida or an invitation to write our congressperson about [the reauthorization of the Elementary and Secondary Education Act]. And since so many people belong, it is possible for important news to spread virally outward.[15]

Anthony went on to describe the complementary effects of tools like blogs and video-sharing sites, where teachers, students, and parents can communicate their messages using multimedia, share coverage of local political actions and other events, and link everything back into the central social network.

Anthony and his "TLO" efforts may not advance a results-oriented profession. But he has shown that an independent group of teachers can capitalize on the growing blogosphere and cyberspace in advancing policy ideas.

Understanding and analyzing policy is a skill to be developed just like any other. Effectively communicating with policymakers is another. The virtual communities housed at the Teacher Leaders Network seek to cultivate those skills in teachers by sharing resources and research for discussion and debate—and following up with both thoughtful criticism and well-grounded solutions. To be effective teacherpreneurs in the policy arena, expert teachers find that they must learn to widen their focus and think *beyond* their classrooms, and learn to tell compelling stories that connect powerful evidence to their teaching and students' learning.

TLN's TeacherSolutions teams offer one effective model to help meet this need. Each team consists of a diverse cross-section of 10 to 18 teachers who develop a response to a specific education policy issue, such as how best to pay teachers for performance, or how teacher working conditions impact student learning. With support from the staff of the Center for Teaching Quality, teams draw on their own understanding of schools while surveying and analyzing important research. Most important, they engage directly in live discussions *with* researchers and policymakers using virtual tools. The teacher teams are paid—modestly—for the time they spend deepening their understanding of issues and related research, discussing the merits of different ideas with one another and then drafting a final report and creating multimedia pieces to share their insights.

It is expected that TeacherSolutions team members will become experts. They are early prototypes of policy entrepreneurs, and their work is important because they are connecting classroom practice to policy. A team of teachers well versed in current research and arguments around an issue can cut through rhetoric with grounded insights. For example, the 2007 TeacherSolutions team on pay for performance, instrumental in our own thinking, developed a framework for professional compensation that unflattens the career ladder and rewards teachers, not just for raising student achievement (as measured by one test), but for constantly improving their own practice and spreading the impact of their effective teaching to peers.

We've found that teachers who care passionately about policy are also teachers who want to lead positive change from within their classrooms. Hybrid teaching roles would make that possible. Ben Jackson is a high school English teacher from Denver in his early 20s. He loves teaching, coaches the basketball team, and led the charge to develop an autonomy agreement at his school. Ben also acts as a local virtual community organizer for the New Millennium Initiative, a national effort to develop the next generation of teacher and union leaders. As you can see, Ben is piecing together numerous opportunities outside his normal teaching responsibilities that keep him fully vested in a teaching career. Inside the current employment-structure of schools, he pays a high personal price for all this involvement. But Ben has his own hybrid-teaching job description in mind that would allow him—as part of his regular job—to connect his work in the classroom to the work of policymakers and the making of more effective teaching policies:

> As a hybrid teacher I would spend half of my time teaching
> AP English to low-income, minority students who otherwise
> would not be exposed to such material or rigor. The other half
> of my day would consist of various activities related to policy
> research, analysis and development. Some days I might study

the effectiveness of policies within my own school, gathering information about student achievement as it relates to teacher experience or preparation programs. Other days I may be examining district-level data on similar issues and generating recommendations about effective teacher preparation and mentoring, which would be disseminated through a formal white paper.

Some days I would spend time meeting with school board members or state legislators, sharing my findings or analysis related to relevant policy discussions. When a new bill is introduced into the legislature, I might testify to its potential effect on the classrooms in our district, state, and nation. Some time might also be spent meeting with other hybrid teachers, planning, executing, and analyzing independent research studies or discussing areas in need of reform and building a list of who should be approached in order to begin conversations about the issue. As a hybrid teacher, I would be the reasonable, knowledgeable voice of teachers in policy debates not because I am representing classroom teachers but because I am a classroom teacher.

Opportunities like this are what will keep generation Y teachers like Ben in the classroom. While teaching may not change fast enough to keep all of today's young teachers on board, we do know that to build the out-standing teaching force needed by the year 2030, mechanisms to cultivate the leadership of and create opportunities for teachers like Ben will need to be built into recruitment and development mechanisms. They need to be part of the regular job. Ben describes what teachers have to know to teach as well as engage with policymakers:

Oddly enough, a teacher's job is almost identical to that of an effective policymaker. In short, a teacher's job is to identify needs or diagnose problems, intervene effectively, assess the intervention and reflect on the process. For example, a teacher might administer a pre-test and realize that a student needs to learn what a simile is. It is up to the teacher to determine if a student needs help identifying a simile, defining a simile, using a simile or is it that the student is having trouble in the writing but can actually explain a simile orally? Then, the teacher creates a lesson to teach the skill(s) and assesses the effectiveness of that instruction via formative or summative assessment. The assessment is graded and the teacher must make decisions about the effectiveness of his or her instruction on that student—What should be done differently? What should be replicated?

The same process is used to develop effective policies. Policymakers identify problems or issues of concern and must first diagnose the true cause of the problem. (Think teacher evaluation systems—is the issue the rules and tools used to evaluate teachers or the humans using the tools?) Often, this is where a teacher's knowledge, skill and experience would be most useful but is rarely solicited. This is also a place where teachers provide a very honest perspective—we are very clear about what is possible and what is unrealistic. The assessment of education policies is historically the first place (much too late) where educators' input is received. Without a comprehensive understanding of the problem being addressed or the process used to arrive at a particular diagnosis, teachers are left in the dark as to why an assessment is being done in the first place. This then carries over into the reflection. Teachers are asked about the effectiveness of policies without a clear understanding of what the policy is intended to address. Someone outside of the classroom has boiled down a complex policy decision into a concise summary and asked for input without an understanding of how a teacher might interpret such information. Effective teachers excel at the entire process from start to finish, but most teachers are only involved in the latter half.

Teachers often see the complexities in education policies well before anyone else. While some might view these nuances as nothing more than isolated experiences or exceptions ("Well, what about the art teacher who has been teaching for X years but has moved to another district and is now at a school where the principal does Y but the union says Z . . ."), they often highlight otherwise overlooked, but very real and relevant, problems with the proposed policy.

Isabel Campos, a Denver teacher who also participates in the New Millennium Initiative, offers another compelling argument regarding the connection between the classroom and policy:

Why do we force good teachers to leave the profession if they want to become active leaders in educational reform? When teachers are asked to institute policy without any voice in its design, it leads us to the current state of disconnect and frustration we are in.

As Ariel Sacks has pointed out previously (see her blog/article "Earthlings Voyage to Planet Policy"):

> The disconnect between policymakers and teachers is remarkably similar to the disconnect between students and teachers in many classrooms. Policies are out of sync with teachers just like teaching in too many classrooms is out of sync with the needs of students. No wonder teachers leave teaching and students drop out of school. By not allowing teachers of proven expertise to have a voice in policy, we are pushing ambitious teacher-leaders out of teaching—and in doing so, keeping up a wall between policy and the classroom of "right now." Active classroom teachers would be amazing incubators of education reform, policy, and best practice.

Teacherpreneurs for Community

Julianna Dauble, also a young educator in the New Millennium Initiative, provides a segue into our discussion of another teacherpreneurial role—that of the teacher who devotes a portion of her time to making the connections between what students are learning inside school walls and what's happening in the community outside those walls, where young people spend the majority of their time:

> A teacher could act as a wellness educator or family liaison/advocate to provide much needed parent education as identified by the school, teacher, student, or parent. . . . Parents could enroll [voluntarily] in seminars or hands-on learning experiences with students that would support all levels of student learning and school function and send important messages out into the community.

TLN member Sarah Henchey, another generation Y teacher, confirms the widening scope of support that Julianna envisions:

> In addition to academic-based roles, I believe schools will need to develop more social support services—motherhood consultants for our teenage mothers, emotional coaches for our students who never seem to be loved enough, financial experts to help students understand the economics of their world, college counselors to assist high school students in navigating the admissions process.

Veteran inner-city Los Angeles teacher Kathie Marshall agrees:

> The differentiation I'd like to see is an educational system that recognizes noninstructional issues and brings support through social and other services, many of which could land in the hands of those differentiated/hybrid teachers.

Teacherpreneurs might have a key role not just providing resources, education, and services, but mobilizing members of the community to capitalize on the resources of the school and bring their own community expertise—a precious resource—to the table. TLN member Larry Ferlazzo is a teacher of English for speakers of other languages at a diverse high school in Sacramento, California. The author of a book on school-parent engagement, Larry worked as a community organizer for 20 years before becoming a teacher. His firsthand experience gives him insight into how teachers could act as community organizers:

> Teachers would spend time, not just talking with parents about their children, but also trying to learn from those parents. Not only would they learn about the challenges parents and families face and what they worry about at night, but about their hopes and dreams for themselves. Through the conversations they have with parents, and the trust that they start with and can build upon, teachers can help parents connect with other parents who have those same hopes, dreams, worries, and challenges. In turn, they can help parents connect to other community institutions so they can launch effective public and collective action to accomplish those dreams and confront those challenges. Through this kind of proactive role, teachers can help confront the many school-related issues that have their basis outside the schoolhouse walls (unemployment, safety, health care, etc.) but that have a huge effect on what goes on in the classroom.
>
> Teachers would need to develop the capacity to recognize that they don't have all the answers—that, in terms of organizing communities for better education, their most important tools are their ears and not their mouths. They need to recognize that as they build the trusting and reciprocal relationships needed to move this kind of effort forward, they, not only have to listen to people's stories, they have to open up and share their own.

Larry is a community-oriented teacherpreneur who has practiced what he preaches—organizing a teacher home-visit program in Sacramento and helping launch a nationally recognized family literacy project. He understands, not just the potential that teachers have for acting in the community, but the special skills and dispositions required for the job—including humility. His observation that teachers need to recognize they don't have all the answers reminds us that teachers must constantly support and question one another about the important work they're doing. Each teacher with a specialized role is one connector in a tightly cross-linked web of activity and awareness.

For example, the teacher with a natural affinity (or substantial human services training) for advising might be a teacher who takes on a central role on a team of teachers guiding a student's learning in concert with his or her emotional, social, and health needs. We do not envision these teachers replacing social-services professionals, although we see a very clear place for community-centered schools richly resourced in health and social services. The advisor teacher would be an anchor for a student, a trustworthy point of contact who could coordinate the student's (and parents') interactions with content specialists and outside professionals. This would ensure that students are met with the right resources at the right times and also prevent the incoherence of students being shuffled from one specialist to another.

As teachers with a strong commitment to the concept of "whole child" education, we confess to having deep concerns about compartmentalizing too far—the way disconnected medical specialists study organs in isolation. As we suggested in Chapter 5, this could be disastrous if taken too far. The key to preventing any virtual isolation or specialist compartmentalization is collaboration among teachers themselves.

Collaboration is the glue. In 2030, we will put just as much emphasis on the concept of team teaching as we will on the idea of teachers taking on specialized jobs and teacherpreneurial roles. The team of teachers works together and is collectively responsible for the whole child, sharing insights and progress. The team model allows teachers to offer their key strengths to students while being fully aware of their particular place in the student's entire learning experience. Team teaching is the basis on which hybrid teachers and teacherpreneurs will succeed as leaders and collaborators. We have to build a system that interlocks teachers' strengths while freeing part of their time and minds for creative problem solving and innovation.

Creating a System of Teacherpreneurship

Anne Jolly, a veteran science teacher and former Alabama teacher of the year, is the author of the popular *Facilitator's Guide to Professional Learn-*

ing Teams, published by the National Staff Development Council. A TLN charter member, Anne entered teaching after a first career as a scientist in the private sector and went on to become co-moderator of the USDOE's online national teacher-leader community in the 1990s and, later, a PLC coach for schools across the Southeast. She dispels the myth that current teachers (and administrators) are the problem responsible for educational stasis. Rather, it is the structure of the system itself that stifles the creativity many practicing educators want to exert:

> Teachers work in a powerful status quo system that has successfully resisted widespread change for a century, despite local innovations and despite a rapidly changing world. I often work with local and district administrators now, and they, too, are restrained by outside forces and encouraged by policymakers and those who supervise them to do things the same way they've always done. I work with so many teachers who could become teacherpreneurs—but we have to find a way so they can tackle the possibilities head on while keeping them in the classroom. We have to continue to work on building a critical mass of teacherpreneurs and being intentional about providing a place for them to learn, grow, and draw encouragement from one another.

We also have to find a way to build demand for them, because we know that effective educational practices have not gone to scale—not because the ideas were not good, but because there was not enough demand for them by policymakers and administrators who control the purse strings and determine how scarce resources are spent.

Anne continues,

> We have to find a way to cultivate and grab these teacherpreneurs—and sustain them. This will require a whole new process of teacher preparation and ongoing professional learning—and a whole new way of thinking about how teachers are expected to use their time. I passionately believe that the greatest knowledge and potential for change rests with teachers—those who still have their feet resolutely planted in the classroom.

Our co-author Ariel Sacks draws on a current corporate example to suggest another way to restructure schools and roles around the critical issue of time, so the most accomplished teachers can spread their teaching expertise. Ariel points to Internet search giant Google's practice of setting aside a portion of its engineers' time to work on projects of their own invention and interest—a policy that produced, among other innovations, AdSense and Google Mail. Ariel writes,

> In order to break away from the hierarchical structures that keep us losing great teachers and moving at a snail's pace, we'll need to carve out significant time, like Google's 20%, or even up to 50% for some, to expand teachers' roles as leaders and innovators who are able to respond better and faster to the needs of students. Blogging on the company's Web site, Google employee Alex K writes: "You can use the time to develop something new, or if you see something that's broken, you can use the time to fix it." He fixed an annoying keyboard function on the Google Readers feature to allow him to skip sections of stories. He writes that "every time I use the new shortcut (*shift* and *N*), I get a . . . thrill at how easily I was able to get my idea implemented."
>
> Teachers do this kind of real-time problem solving constantly on a microscale—like finding a new way to reach a struggling student—but we rarely have the time to do it on large scale and share out what we learn. On a macrolevel, teachers have some of the best ideas around because we know our students. If given the time to develop ideas and create solutions to problems, teachers could be of much greater value to our schools. According to research by University of Michigan professor Theresa Welbourne, "company performance increases when more time is spent on 'noncore job roles'—for example, when leaders focus on roles such as innovator or team member." School organizations would benefit similarly, when teachers are allowed to spend time in roles outside of classroom teaching, developing ideas that could exponentially increase learning.

Teacherpreneurism, and the freedom it represents, will demand that attention be paid to the necessary diversity of teacher roles and that a high premium be placed on collective responsibility. Kilian Betlach uses an economics metaphor to describe the potential teacherpreneurism has for strengthening students' learning experiences and achievement:

> In the same way that a national economy based on a single industrial sector is inherently weaker than one that is sufficiently diversified, when the only job requirement for teachers is

classroom teaching, schools are inherently weaker than if some taught, some led, and some undertook a combination of the two.

The creation of hybrid roles allows for diversification of responsibilities based on teacher strengths. Teachers with exemplary abilities in curricular design could be given the freedom to plan units and courses of study for grade levels and departments. Teachers with the ability to coach and guide their peers could do so in afternoons, while teaching all morning. And those teachers who excel in the classroom, whose ability to grow student achievement trumps the other skills they undoubtedly bring to the table, would continue to teach at high levels.

The structures of team teaching and blended-learning environments create the flexibility that teacherpreneurs need both to develop their craft and to bring their expertise to their students and peers. Part of teachers' self-directed learning time, as described by Ariel, could be used to connect to a host of teacherpreneurs to develop special capacities to solve knotty problems or meet identified wide-scale learning needs.

Our co-author Emily Vickery points us to the thinking of media consultant and "digital ethnologist" Marc Pesce, who posits that we must "transform the classroom, from the inside out, melting it down, and forging it into something that looks quite a bit different from the classroom we've grown familiar with over the last 50 years."[16] Pesce imagines,

> In [the] near future world, students are the administrators. All of the administrative functions have been "pushed down" into a substrate of software. Education has evolved into something like a marketplace, where instructors "bid" to work with students.[17]

The key puzzle piece needed to complete Mr. Pesce's picture is the teacher, serving as the agent to empower students to negotiate a personalized, open-ended education—guiding them at every step along the way with deep content and pedagogical knowledge. Students, parents, and families, as well as a range of school districts and nonprofits, would be able to bid for the best teachers, who offer their knowledge and skill as individuals and collectives.

What we must not lose sight of, as TeacherSolutions 2030 team member Renee Moore has reminded us at crucial points, is the currency with which students from vastly different backgrounds are "bidding" for those services. This is also a role that teachers themselves can take on— helping governments and school districts make the best choices about where to allocate resources, and connecting students and parents to the vast opportunities available. The model of teacherpreneurism must not drive a wedge further between the haves and have-nots. With the right support and resources, teacherpreneurs can act as engines of reform, developing innovative ways to spread their expertise where it is needed most. Ultimately, teacherpreneurship is not so much about establishing a new income stream for individuals as it is about propagating a new culture of innovation and creativity in a sector—education—that has been woefully lacking in one. We are not just advocating for teachers—like some in South Korea—who launch their own lucrative tutoring businesses. Teacherpreneurship is not promoting a free-market vision for the profit of a few but how our society can invest substantially in teachers who can expertly serve millions of children and families who are not in the position to choose a better school somewhere else or find the most erudite online teacher anytime, anywhere. Teacherpreneurship is all about the public good, not private gain. Our colleague Renee Moore said it best:

> In creating teacherpreneurs, we as a society (yes, meaning with our government tax dollars) have the responsibility to make sure [that] what these expert teachers can do is done for all children, particularly those who have so few educational resources upon which to rely.

In closing, our vision of teacherpreneurism, unlike what many early 21st-century reformers have proposed, is of enterprising education professionals who are always grounded in classrooms, working daily on the front lines with students, their families, and their communities. Doing so will require a reinvented policy framework and teachers and administrators to break ranks with teaching's long arm of history.

CHAPTER 7

Policy Levers of Change: Accelerating Change and Transforming Teaching

> We have not often valued in federal or state policy the creativity in teachers or how we can best spread their expertise. Instead we have swung to *uniformity* as a way to control teachers, and in misusing standardized tests, we have reinstituted the lockstep curricula of bygone eras. It was as though we expected Wally and Beaver Cleaver to return to every classroom.
>
> —Shannon C'de Baca

We believe the ideas advanced here about the future of teaching can be realized. We are optimistic as we see positive shifts in the polling data on teachers' prestige. And we're energized by the sheer power of viral networking to not only spread the expertise of the nation's most effective teachers but to connect their ideas in a very direct way to the minds and hearts of the public.

There is no doubt that teaching has had a stormy and convoluted past—often framed by the struggle to determine who should teach, and what and how, and colored by the conditions under which they do so. The history of teaching has included long-standing control by laypersons, a lack of clarity and rigor in the process of becoming a teacher, and limited prestige and income.[1] These historical imperatives have constrained teaching and its professional possibilities. And the profession still is undermined by many of these same factors, although we are now in the second decade of the 21st century.

We are convinced that the future direction of teaching will depend, in part, on how well teacher-leaders can communicate to the larger public the choices we face in our education system and the potential of a fully-realized teaching profession to spark a learning renaissance in our public schools. Public opinion polls have revealed that most Americans want highly prepared teachers for all our children.[2] In 2002, the majority of Americans reported that they were firmly *against* the lowering of hiring standards for teachers.

In a 2004 poll Americans ranked "improving teacher quality" as the number one priority for school improvement (27%), far outstripping their desire to raise standardized test scores (2%) or let for-profit companies manage school districts (2%).

There are more good signs. For example, in 2009, 70% of American adults reported that they would like to see a child of theirs "take up teaching in the public schools as a career"—up from 48% in 1980.[3]

However, opinion polls also suggest that most Americans are largely uninformed about the policies being promoted that, intentionally or unintentionally, undermine the development of a profession. For example, over the last decade the public increased its support of higher standards and accountability while continuing to report little knowledge of No Child Left Behind laws.[4] Many Americans, reminiscing on their own public education, may wish for schools to improve, but they do not always want them to look any different or for teachers to take on more variegated roles. There seems to be little awareness of the growing complexities of teaching today and oftentimes the public expresses conflicting views on what path is most likely to lead us to better schools and an improved teaching profession.

Public perception is often framed by what the media reports—and that makes teacher professionalism a hard sell. High-profile journalists like Nicholas Kristof and David Brooks and popular magazines like *Newsweek* propose that the key to fixing what ails the teaching profession is to do away with schools of education and fire all the bad teachers.[5] What the public hears is that there is no knowledge base for teaching—any reasonably smart person can walk in and do it—so why invest in teacher

FIGURE 7.1. The American Public Wants Prepared Teachers

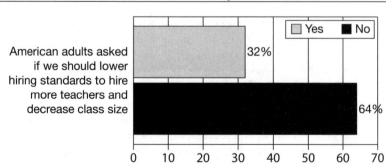

Source: Educational Testing Service. (2002). *A national priority: Americans speak on teacher quality*. Princeton, NJ: Author. Reprinted by permission of Educational Testing Service.

FIGURE 7.2. Public Priorities for School Improvement

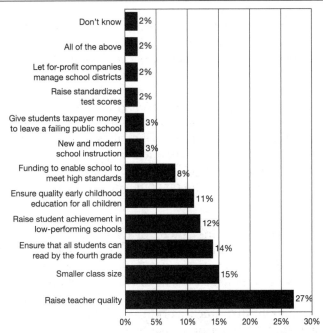

Top priorities for improvement from the American public, 2004

Source: Public Education Network. (2004). *Demanding quality public education in tough economic times: What voters want from elected leaders.* Washington, DC: Author. Reprinted by permission of Public Education Network.

education? Or they hear the schools are overflowing with incompetent teachers—like those characterized by Steven Brill in New York City's "rubber room" where grossly inept individuals were said to be "housed" with full pay because the union's iron grip on teacher evaluation and tenure kept them in the profession. It turned out that only about one-twentieth of 1% of the NYC's teaching workforce was actually on paid leave in the rubber room and not always because of incompetence. But this did not keep Jonah Goldberg of the *National Review* from claiming, "This is just a small illustration of a larger mess. America's school systems are a disaster . . . but of all the myriad problems with public schools, the most identifiable and solvable is the ludicrous policy of tenure for teachers."[6] This kind of reckless hyperbole, which is widespread on the Internet and in the "responsible" media, raises the hackles of unions considerably. They fight back, protecting teachers—good and bad—even more. The upshot, of course, is that the public sees and hears round after round of the same old policy gridlock. It's a lose-lose strategy.

We believe the vision developed and advanced here offers a "different way" for seeing the future of teaching and transforming the profession. Our vision imagines big policy changes over the next 2 decades—changes that we all recognize do not come about easily. Speaking in another context about another divisive social issue—health care—conservative commentator and former George W. Bush aide Peter Wehner noted:

> America in general is fairly non-ideological and pragmatic, and we tend to play within the 40-yard lines. Big policy changes don't come along very often, and when they do come along, especially when dealing with entitlement programs, you need a kind of civic propulsion to drive them through. If you don't have that intense public sentiment on your side, you're not going to get it through.[7]

Helping the public to think differently is a precursor to getting them to push policymakers to act differently. And changing the public's thinking means rallying practitioners to communicate the true complexity of their work. Our most accomplished teachers, who are held in high regard by the public, are the logical leaders in making this happen. The 2009 MetLife poll leaves no doubt that much work needs to be done to move teacher voices center stage: Only 2% of the nation's teachers strongly agreed that they have a voice in the current debates on public education and their profession.[8]

FIGURE 7.3. Teacher Voice: Are Teachers Heard When It Comes to Current Debates on Education

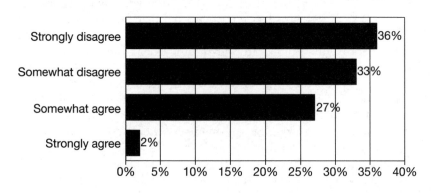

Source: MetLife survey of the American teacher: Collaborating for student success. (2009). New York: Author. Reprinted by permission of MetLife.

All too often "teacher voice" on matters of teaching policy and school reform surfaces through their unions, which typically focus on a narrow and often very local set of issues. As a result, good ideas from the classroom and insights about low-functioning schools from the "forward observers" rarely make it into the debate over teachers and teaching, and even less into the crafting of public policy.

If teaching is to emerge as the 21st-century profession we have envisioned here, then several challenges must be met and at least six interlocking levers of change need to be developed and used. They are

1. Engaging the public with a new vision for teaching and learning;
2. Rethinking school finance so it drives new investments and partnerships;
3. Redefining preparation and licensing to ensure truly highly qualified and effective teachers;
4. Cultivating working conditions that make high-needs schools "easier to staff";
5. Reframing accountability for transformative results; and
6. Transforming teacher unions into professional guilds.

All are critical. However, new forms of unionism—whereby old-guard labor/management divisions morph into results-oriented partnerships among equals—will be paramount if the public is to get behind teachers and make the investments essential to prepare a professional workforce for the decades to come.

Change Lever #1:
Engage the Public with a New Vision for Teaching and Learning

Engaging the public around a 21st-century teaching profession is a must—and a great deal of re-learning must take place, not just among policymakers, community members, parents, and business leaders, but also practitioners themselves.

Over time America's collective view of teaching has been confounded by the occupation's large size—which makes it very difficult to change—and the fact that teachers are expected to fulfill a number of custodial responsibilities in the service of children and their families.[9] Additionally, as workers in America's most widespread and visible public enterprise, K–12 educators are easy targets for those who are angry and frustrated about the nation's perceived shortcomings and looking for someone to blame.

Most Americans have attended schools for 13 years—and have watched teachers teach for more than 15,000 hours. The way they were taught in the past is assumed to be the way others will be taught in the future. The teacher in front of the classroom blackboard is a familiar and static norm in the American story—even if the blackboard becomes a "smartboard." On the other hand, most Americans have seldom seen doctors practice medicine all day, lawyers prepare a brief, or accountants negotiate an income tax dispute with the IRS. Doctors, lawyers, and accountants possess specialized knowledge. Highly effective teachers do, as well—but it is not obvious, especially when so many teachers enter teaching without it and those with it are rarely recognized or elevated as experts.

In point of fact, America's familiarity with teaching may breed some contempt. When expert teachers teach effectively, teaching looks easy. When teachers teach poorly, their performance suggests that anyone with average intelligence and a strong work ethic can get by.

Dan Lortie, the well-known education sociologist, called it the "apprenticeship of observation"—where the public has seen so much teaching that it seems common and simple. Lortie documented how so many teachers themselves, as a result of their own childhood "internship," believe that effective teachers are born, not made, and that they have little to learn from formal, professional pedagogical coursework.[10]

The mass media, including Hollywood, have for the most part worked against a professional image of teaching—one in which teachers are viewed as well-prepared experts and in which intellect and preparation are critical to effectiveness and growth in student learning. Instead, decades of popular movies have most often painted portraits of teachers either as inspired lunatics, such as Richard Mulligan as the multicostumed Mr. Gower in the 1984 film *Teachers*, or as stupefying bores, like the economics teacher played by Ben Stein in the 1986 comedy classic *Ferris Bueller's Day Off*.

The media and the public do have an affinity for teachers who are presented as anti-establishment heroes defying all odds—like Sidney Poitier as Mark Thackery in *To Sir with Love* (1967) or Robin Williams as John Keating in *The Dead Poets Society* (1989). Even depictions of real-life teachers like Jaime Escalante, played by Edward James Olmos in *Stand and Deliver* (1988), and Erin Gruwell, played by Hilary Swank in *Freedom Writers* (2007), portray noble individuals who work alone, always against the system, and use their intellect and commitment to help students learn, improving lives despite the less-committed teachers who surround them. The implication, of course, is that such teachers are a rare commodity and come into our schools by chance.

The problem is that by 2030 our nation's schools (both virtual and physical) will demand more than 4 million teachers—many of whom will need to teach more than the few years that Ms. Gruwell did in the mid-1990s. Can we find 4 million self-sacrificing superheroes to staff every classroom in 100,000 schools and/or community centers of learning? Answering with a "not likely" would be an understatement. But we *can* create the conditions that will allow ordinary individuals to do the extraordinary work required to teach effectively in the 21st century.

We have a reservoir of public sentiment that could be intensified to create the "civic propulsion" for change alluded to by political strategist Peter Wehner. A 2008 Gallup poll suggests that the general public views teachers very favorably by comparison with other occupations—ranking them third in a list of most honest and ethical professions, just behind nurses and pharmacists. The public has more faith in teachers to do the right thing than even medical doctors, the clergy, or police officers. And the public thinks *much more highly* of teachers (65%) than lawyers (18%), labor union leaders (16%), members of Congress (12%), and business executives (12%).[11]

A 2008 Harris Poll measured public perceptions of the prestige associated with certain jobs. The pollsters found that firefighters, scientists, doctors, teachers, and nurses are seen as the most prestigious on a list of 23 professions and occupations.[12] Interestingly, when the Harris Poll asked the public this question in 1977, only 29% rated teaching as a prestigious profession. With a 23-percentage-point jump over 3 decades, the public's respect for teaching has increased more than any other profession. This trend is matched by changes in teachers' own attitudes. MetLife has surveyed teachers annually for 25 years. Among the many intriguing findings in MetLife's 2008 poll is that teachers—despite mass media portrayals—believe they are earning more social esteem. In 1984, only 47% of American teachers felt respected (with only 10% agreeing strongly). In 2008, two-thirds (66%) believed that the American people had respect for their work, including 17% who agreed strongly.

All this data suggest that there has never been a better time to elevate teacher voices in new venues where both policymakers and the public listen, hear, and embrace teachers on matters of school reform and transforming their profession. Seasoned expert teachers as well as today's new millennials (or tomorrow's iGeneration) could "tip" the conversation—engaging the public in powerful and provocative ways. Much like the way Malcolm Gladwell has described the beginning of other social epidemics, highly successful teachers—specially prepared as connectors, mavens, and publicists—could market the 21st-century profession that students deserve.[13]

FIGURE 7.4. Teachers' Opinions of Their Profession

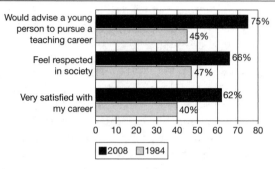

Source: *MetLife survey of the American teacher: Past, present and future.* (2008). New York: Author. Reprinted by permission of MetLife.

Selling a bold new vision of teaching and learning is far from impossible. The American people have the capacity to let go of old patterns of thinking when the evidence is well presented and compelling. Consider how our nation's adult population changed its collective mind about cigarette smoking. In the early 1960s, cigarettes were "very cool" and the Marlboro Man, portrayed as a rugged cowboy, gave cigarettes a free-spirited, back-to-basics, all-American image. Cigarette smoking was common and often viewed as an important accessory to one's lifestyle. Then studies began to identify empirical links between smoking and cancer. The Federal Communications Commission's Fairness Doctrine (equal time for controversial issues) allowed antismoking advertisements to blanket network television. Early antismoking commercials, starring "Johnny Smoke," showed cowboys keeling over with poisonous fumes in their lungs—parodying the Marlboro Man. Public awareness grew and behavior began to change as TV ads for cigarettes were banned and the Surgeon General's warnings on cigarette packages became more visible and stark. Over the ensuing 40 years, the percentage of American adults smoking cigarettes decreased from 45% to 20%.

So what might be the components of a long-term campaign to remake the image of teaching—a campaign of sufficient intensity to convince Americans that teachers are not primarily an education problem but important contributors to the policy solution? Part of this messaging needs to emphasize that effective teachers are not accidents of birth but the products of smart actions by decision makers in support of comprehensive teacher development. We begin by following a basic tenet of good marketing: Show, don't tell. The media and the public have yet to see consistent images of good teaching or observe expert teachers as they illustrate what works and why in our nation's most challenging schools.

Viral networks and Web 2.0 (and soon Web 3.0) tools are creating the environment for expert teachers to make high-quality teaching and learning transparent. New statistical applications can link a range of student learning measures to different teaching in different contexts. Teachers, parents, and students can use handheld devices to share information and forge new forms of public accountability. Multimedia presentations of student learning products can encapsulate a richer variety of achievement data and inform a deeper understanding among policymakers and practitioners as well as the public and the media.

If we push forward with this vision of teaching's future, parents will, not only be able to access a classroom calendar and group wiki on their child's school website, but also privately view and comment on their child's work and teachers' observations about his or her progress. Teachers, beginning with sites like YouTube and Facebook, can create and upload their own minidocumentaries—telling stories of reform that link research to real-life practices and possibilities. Videos of effective teaching can be shared among teachers, but just as importantly among parents and other education stakeholders who serve as an informal but large-scale accountability mechanism, driving continuous improvement in teaching quality. The George Lucas Foundation and its *Edutopia* website, using a growing set of multimedia tools, is already documenting and disseminating exciting tales of teaching practice they have captured in classrooms across the nation—modeling ways that teachers can tell their stories using images that can inform and inspire new policies.

As expert teachers witness the power of their own voices, more and more will step up to share their insights and advocate for their students and their profession through blogs, forums, policy development opportunities, and ever more-potent viral networks. Poorly prepared and less competent teachers will be more easily identified. The most effective practitioners will support these colleagues' improvement, and when necessary, serve in peer-review roles to remove them from the profession. As a result the public will have even more trust in teachers—and be more willing to support deeper investments in teacher compensation, beginning with a professional pay system consistent with 21st-century teaching and learning.

Change Lever #2: Rethink School Finance

In American public education the wealth of a particular geographic community still determines the extent to which students have access to a quality education and a stable source of effective teachers. Given that local governments provide almost half of the cost of K–12 education, differences in taxable wealth among communities translate into large differences in what is spent per student—and often times affluent suburban school districts spend two or three times more on the education of their children than either urban or rural communities can afford.

Some critics of public education (and governmental spending) lament that by the end of the first decade of the 21st century, American taxpayers were spending about $500 billion a year on public education or, on average, about $11,000 per student.[14] For some, especially those Americans who seek to undermine public schools (and government's investment in other people's children), this seems like a lot of money. It is not—especially in light of the $300 billion of public monies lost annually due to the cost of dropouts, incarceration linked to illiteracy and school failure, and low productivity in the workforce.[15] In fact, the American people consistently point to the lack of funding—not the lack of rigorous academic standards or insufficient numbers of good teachers—as the number one problem facing public education.[16]

FIGURE 7.5. Public Perception of the Number One Problem Facing Public Education

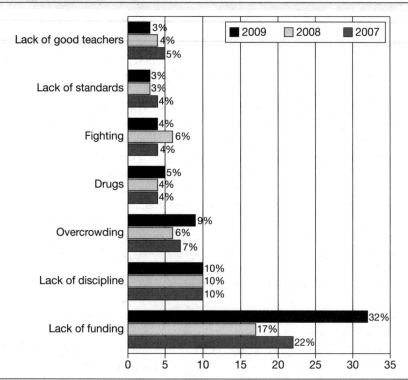

Source: Bushaw, W. J., & Gallup, A. M. (2009). *Americans speak out: Are educators and policy makers listening?* Bloomington, IN: Phi Delta Kappan. Reprinted by permission of Phi Delta Kappan.

In addition, what critics of public-education spending often overlook are the wildly different amounts states, districts, and schools spend on students. For example, the state of Utah spends about $5,500 per student while the per-pupil expenditure in New Jersey reaches more than $14,000.[17] In a recent study, per-pupil spending from district to district *within* states varied considerably as well—from a difference of up to $2,000 in North Carolina to nearly $4,500 in Ohio.[18] The disparities in base spending per student result in part from local tax revenue, but much more so from the large differences in the property tax base upon which local governments draw. Historically, state government aid has only slightly compensated poor school districts for the often dramatic differences in funding between those districts and wealthier districts with a richer property tax base.[19]

These financial inequities mean that our most vulnerable communities cannot compete in the teacher labor market because they lack the money to entice talent or develop and retain top-notch instructors. In America, recruiting and retaining effective teachers has a lot to do with one's zip code. And while policymakers and reformers continue to push for all students to reach higher academic standards regardless of where they live, most states have not equalized the funding needed to ensure the equitable distribution of effective teachers and equal access to quality curriculum. For example, median salaries in suburban Scarsdale, New York, are almost twice the amount offered to teachers in New York City. This disparity positions the district serving more-affluent students to pay top dollar for qualified and experienced teachers, and it forces expert teachers who feel a social responsibility to work in high-needs schools to accept considerably less salary for doing so.[20] This must change.

Throughout the history of public education, school financing has been a source of hot debate and a string of adequacy lawsuits. Arthur Wise, who in 1968 penned *Rich Schools, Poor Schools: The Promise of Equal Educational Opportunity,* made the pathbreaking case for the courts to begin intervening in order for less affluent school districts to close the resource gap as well as the achievement gap. Some researchers have claimed that for most of the 20th century there was "no evidence" that additional investments in public education improve student performance.[21] However, most of these studies ignore key research findings and do not account for the context in which school funding dollars are spent.[22] No doubt every school system should "demand innovation and continuous improvement, keeping what works and discarding what does not."[23] But the reality is that while per-pupil expenditures have increased over time, there has been little change in the amounts spent on instruction and teacher development.[24] It's not about "throwing money at the problem," it's about investing money to address the *right* problems.

Teachers, despite their well-documented importance, cannot do it alone. Other nations, whose students outperform ours on international assessments, not only invest more in teachers, but also in students. These nations are willing to embrace the fact that much of the student achievement gap is explained by what takes place not only in schools but in families, communities, and society.[25] High-performing nations like Finland invest not just in schools and teachers but also in housing, medical care, social services, and community development.[26] Rethinking school finance will include spending *more* on students who need the most help to succeed—as well as reallocating resources for teaching, making new and different investments in teachers, and fusing education and community efforts and funding.

Spending More on the Students Who Need the Most. Just spending more money on anything in education does not mean better outcomes for students. Often critics point to districts like Washington, D.C., where per-pupil spending far exceeds the national average while yielding dismal student achievement results.[27] As Linda Darling-Hammond has noted, "It is certainly true that money can be spent unwisely, and dollars spent on patronage, bloated bureaucracies, football fields, and swimming pools are less likely to translate into learning than dollars spent on sound instruction." However, she also notes that education costs must account for the higher costs of living in many urban areas, as well as the deep and diverse needs of students living in poverty. To close the achievement gap, many students will require investments, not just in their teachers, but also on nutrition, health care, and before- and after-school care, as well as year-round learning opportunities. Current school-funding models do not account sufficiently for the diversity of students entering our nation's schools. Diversity increases costs. Districts with a small tax base and considerable diversity require extra support to serve a larger than average proportion of students who need specialized services.

To address the existing inequities in services and teacher distribution, our nation's school finance system must operate on a more precise per-pupil weighting formula that provides extra funds for disadvantaged students at the school level. Expert teachers have reported their willingness to move to high-needs schools if they were to have smaller class sizes, lighter teaching loads, and more opportunities to work with their colleagues in serving both students and their families. All teachers who work in highly challenged school communities need more time and more in-depth training to teach effectively. Both create new costs, but they can be offset somewhat by different resource reallocations.[28]

Reallocating Resources for Teaching. Nations whose students academically outperform students in the United States spend far more on teachers and teaching. In America, barely 50% of the $500 billion spent annually on public education is focused on instruction and only about 43% of all of the nation's education staff are classroom teachers. In high-performing nations, about 75% of the education resources spent go directly to instruction, and classroom teachers represent somewhere between 60 and 80% of all staff.[29] Why? We employ lots of nonteachers, in part, because American policymakers see every scare headline as a new problem facing our public schools. For every problem, they create a special program that requires a slew of administrators—befitting of the top-down, hierarchical school organization our nation has put into place. For example, the Los Angeles Unified School District serves over 688,000 students, who are taught by over 36,000 teachers. The district also employs over 36,000 administrators, supervisors, and support staff. Could not the district's executive leadership think more creatively about how to use the resources committed to over 72,000 adults in the school system? We emphatically think so.

In other nations (and in selected American schools) most administrators are expected to teach at least part of the time. Many of the teacherpreneur roles needed for 21st-century teaching and learning could be created if more of the nation's education dollars went directly into classrooms and fewer were spent on administrators who do not teach students.

In addition, in the future, American teachers could accomplish more if they were expected to restructure face time spent with students and devote more time to improving their practice and sustaining high teaching standards. For example, U.S. teachers currently work fewer days per year but spend many more hours teaching students (180 days and 1,080 hours) than teachers in nations like South Korea (200 days and 800 hours) where more time is allotted to improving teaching and spreading pedagogical expertise. And Korean teachers, based on international assessments, get better student achievement results. A relatively simple reallocation of teacher time can begin to leverage the transformation of the teaching profession. The Generation Schools Network (www.generationschools.org) has already shown how new school designs can reduce class size and increase teachers' time to learn from one another.

Let's remember that a large portion of the cost of public education, from 60 to 80%, is wrapped up in paying teachers, administrators, and other school personnel (from teaching assistants to bus drivers to cafeteria workers). Some elements of these labor costs are not easily linked to achievement outcomes for students and probably shouldn't be. But others deserve close scrutiny.[30] A recent analysis has shown that the "near-universal practice of compensating teachers for earning [any] master's degree" has little relationship to improved student achievement.[31] It has been estimated that almost $8 billion annually is spent on paying teachers for an advanced degree that may not have much bearing on their teaching. While some may earn a graduate degree in reading and literacy, many teachers end up earning school administration credentials, which mean virtually nothing for student achievement.[32] While these dollars represent only 1% to 2% of the monies spent on teacher salaries each year, they could be put to better use and leverage changes needed to spread teaching expertise.

Making New and Different Investments in Teachers. Spending around $300 billion a year on teachers' salaries seems like a big number. But the reality is that even with an average salary of slightly more than $51,000 (in 2008 dollars), public school teachers "face a large and growing pay gap."[33] Midlevel accountants, computer analysts, and engineers, on average, earn approximately $10,000 to $20,000 more than teachers.[34] And during the first decade of the 21st century, the salary differences between these professionals and teachers were getting larger.[35]

In 2005, Lou Gerstner, then chair of the Teaching Commission, called for raising an additional $30 billion annually for teacher salaries in order to provide across-the-board increases, as well as performance pay.[36] This was not a reform plan developed by teacher unions but by the former chief executive officer of IBM. In launching his blue ribbon panel, Gerstner was quite blunt in posing the question, "How do you rustle up—and better yet, hold onto—legions of superb teachers when they could probably make a lot more money doing something a lot less challenging?"[37] (Gerstner's profound question has been largely ignored in the teaching quality debate ever since.)

Paying for the most accomplished teachers to lead and spread their expertise might add more than Gerstner's proposed $30 billion to the cost of public education. But the cost is well within the reach of the American taxpayer. Doubling Gerstner's proposal, $60 billion would ensure that at least 10% of the nation's most well-prepared and effective classroom teachers could earn more than $125,000 a year (in 2010 dollars) and that all teachers would be paid a professional salary. These are modest numbers given that the cost of the Iraq War is now more than $800 billion, with the cost to deploy *one* soldier approaching $400,000 annually.[38]

More money needs to be invested in teachers' salaries. However, it is critical that those who are paid well be those who are well prepared and effective. And this will require considerable rethinking of investments in teacher education.

Currently, there are more than 1,200 colleges and universities that prepare teachers, and they produce about 170,000 teachers annually.[39] In addition, there is a booming number of new teachers—prepared in a variety of alternative ways—coming from community colleges, for-profits like

Kaplan University and the University of Phoenix, nonprofits like Teach for America and the New Teacher Project, and school districts themselves. There are more than enough teachers being "produced" (in absolute numbers) for the vacancies at hand. However, with both traditional *and* alternative teacher education programs there is a serious lack of resource management and quality control in the supply chain.

First of all, at the universities that prepare teachers, only one-half of entering candidates actually graduate, and about 70% of those who do graduate actually enter teaching.[40] One reason is that most universities offer just about every kind of teacher education major, irrespective of the local labor market and the needs of area districts looking for new recruits. In some "teacher surplus" states, universities graduate far too many teachers prepared for subjects and areas in low demand (e.g., elementary, physical education, social studies), while math, science, and special education vacancies continue to haunt practitioners as well as parents.[41] One large teacher education provider in Michigan still graduates more than 1,000 newly minted teachers a year, but only places a handful in the nearby Detroit public schools.

Second, while many of the new alternative certification providers are more likely to match up their recruits to the specific needs of school districts, they often do not prepare them sufficiently well for the job at hand, especially in terms of how to teach subject matter in ways that diverse students can deeply understand and apply. As a result, districts subsequently see a much higher than average turnover among the teachers placed by these programs. As one research report recently concluded, in a rush to get the right teacher in the classroom as quickly and as cheaply as possible, most alternative-certification programs that offer only a few weeks of preservice training ignore both "quality ceilings and floors."[42]

Regardless of the route they enter into teaching, ill-prepared teachers are more likely to leave. This costs districts and states big money that could be invested in the reforms needed to make teaching a 21st-century profession. Districts lose about $15,000 to $20,000 in hiring costs each time a novice teacher leaves. When education productivity losses are included, the price tag can reach somewhere between $33,000 and $48,000 for each early departure.[43] A 2000 study in Texas, a state which routinely recruits large numbers of underprepared teachers via alternative programs, found that the cost of turnover ranges from $329 million to $2.1 billion per year, depending on the cost model used.[44]

Imagine the cost savings that could be created if universities prepared teachers needed by school districts (both locally and nationally), and did so only in partnership with them. Universities could then afford to more deeply prepare teachers for high-needs schools, because they would not be expected to prepare as many as they do now. School districts would be expected to develop new teachers, both individually and in teams, drawing on the expert knowledge and skills already present within their systems. With a more focused approach to teacher development, districts could afford to give teachers more time to learn on the job. And with less turnover among teachers, districts could invest the dollars recovered from lower hiring costs and greater productivity into teacher education and professional growth.

Fusing Education and Community Efforts and Funding. Much of the current K–12 finance system in this nation is decoupled from the higher-education system that recruits and prepares teachers. And both K–12 and higher-education services are disconnected from the social and health care services essential to serving both students and their families well. As Lisbeth Schorr has noted, the conventional approach to solving social inequities in America has been to focus on singular remedies to what are unfortunately viewed as discreet problems. But as she noted in the early 2000s,

> As social problems have become deeper and more complex over the last 20 years, interventions that could respond to the growing burden of risk have also become increasingly complex—and therefore harder to assess by traditional means. Interventions that change only one thing at a time often fail *because* they change only one thing at a time.[45]

Schorr argues that initiatives, and their funding sources, need to aim collectively at "strengthening families, rebuilding neighborhoods, reforming schools, enhancing youth development, and ensuring that disadvantaged 4- and 5-year-olds are ready for school."[46] Her work reminds us that much of the current school-reform effort—including President Obama's Race to the Top initiative—rests on the assumption that students learn mostly in school, but that is not the case.

Efforts to integrate the social, health, and educational services provided by communities to underserved and poor children are critical to improving student achievement. In Chapter 3, we highlighted several examples of such integration—like the Harlem Children's Zone—which offer compelling evidence that unified approaches make a difference. Other efforts, like Communities in Schools (CIS), coordinate resources for students and families through programs that take place before and after school. With almost 200 affiliates in 26 states and the District of Columbia, CIS has produced impressive outcomes. If their integrated approach to service delivery is implemented with "fidelity," then the students they serve are more likely to reach proficiency in 4th- and 8th-grade reading and math and graduate from high school on time.[47]

Both the HCZ and CIS models could do more if they could systematically draw upon bundled funding from each of the service sectors (health, social, and education) in their respective communities. Few current policies are in place to ensure the alignment and connection of out-of-school supports to the PreK–12 curriculum. But powerful results and efficiencies could be created if our nation's school finance system fully integrated the work and staff of health care and social work inside of the schools and the universities that serve specific communities.

New federal legislation, including significant changes to the Elementary and Secondary Education Act (formerly labeled the No Child Left Behind Act) are needed so partnerships of school districts, universities, and nonprofits, as well as other agencies, can use Title I, Supplemental Educational Services (SES), and other funding streams, such as the 21st Century Community Learning Centers Fund and the Child Care and Development Fund, to link services for students. The current R2T focus on developing data systems to link teacher and student records for accountability purposes should be expanded to include other measures and related outcomes that drive different agencies to work in concert, not at cross-purposes as they so often do now. Granted, federal efforts such as those operating as a part of the Full Service Community Schools Act are important breakthroughs, but as some researchers have suggested they "are not sufficient to push (out of school) learning from the shallows into the mainstream of education reform."[48]

In making our case for a seamless blend of virtual and brick-and-mortar learning systems, we've described our vision of community-centered "hub" schools staffed by many hybrid teachers who are fully prepared to grapple with complex educational and social issues. If policymakers can succeed in aligning federal, state, and local programs that serve school-age children, they will provide the leverage for hub schools to become thriving enterprises in our most vulnerable communities and neighborhoods.

Change Lever #3:
Redefine Teacher Education and Licensing
to Advance the Spread of Effective Teaching

Most other professions, like medicine, law, architecture, and now nursing have created preparation and licensing systems to ensure that all new entrants are ready to begin professional practice. In these fields, preparation and licensure standards vary little from state to state and national exams ensure quality control to a large extent—at least in terms of making sure all newly certified recruits are safe to practice.[49]

However, the United States currently does not have a teacher-education licensing *system*, only a patchwork of uneven programs run by universities, school districts, and nonprofits and further hampered by a jurisdiction-specific mishmash of rules and regulations that determine who enters teaching, how, and when. While a growing number of teacher-education programs—such as those at George Washington University, Stanford University, the University of Pennsylvania, and the University of Chicago—have actually created new urban schools in partnerships with school districts and community organizations "to demonstrate state-of-the-art practices and to serve as training grounds for teachers," they are still the exceptions.[50] In addition, a number of education schools, led by the cutting-edge research of University of Michigan dean Deborah Ball and her colleagues, are developing new programs to focus teacher pre-service preparation on high-leverage instructional practices in specific content areas and to offer clinical training so novices can be deliberately taught and explicitly coached with the skills to reach a wide range of learners.[51]

However, the trailblazing efforts of teacher-education programs, while growing steadily, are not well known by policymakers and the public, making it all the more difficult for their innovations to be better known, funded, and replicated.

Granted, too many of the nation's education schools continue to have too-low admission standards and offer an incoherent curriculum run by "disconnected" faculty.[52] Historically, university presidents have expected their education schools to train as many teachers as cheaply as possible, rather than invest in more rigorous and, frankly, more expensive training. Many still do, and much needed investments in the clinical preparation of future teachers in partnerships and community-based organizations go wanting.

At the same time, the growing number of alternative certification programs (estimated at 600 nationwide in 2009) typically offer even more-jumbled and truncated pedagogical training for tens of thousands of newly minted teachers, who receive a few weeks of preservice training to be followed up later by piecemeal college coursework and mentoring.[53]

To make matters more complicated, currently while 43 states require teachers to pass written tests in their content area, only 5 require them to demonstrate their knowledge of subject-specific pedagogy.[54] According to some analysts, most content-area teacher tests are generally viewed as too easy or irrelevant, and passing scores vary widely.[55] But given that these state licensure tests are quite inexpensive (ranging from $80 to $110 in 2010), policymakers and the public should not expect them to do more than assess competence in a narrow set of skills and make a crude split between prospective teachers who are unqualified and those who are minimally qualified."[56]

It gets worse: Only 39 states require student teaching—ranging from 8 weeks in Wyoming to 18 weeks in Wisconsin and 20 weeks in Maryland—and only 15 states actually require other clinical training that would prepare a candidate for a formal student-teaching experience.[57] There are no state standards for who gets to supervise student teachers and no requirements that the supervisors themselves are effective teachers who know how to mentor new recruits. What's more, there are no substantive standards for what student teachers have to demonstrate before they earn the right to teach—and as a result too few end up knowing how to use the most effective instructional strategies to increase student learning in diverse areas like teaching fractions or understanding the causes of the Civil War. In addition, only 17 states require teacher preparation programs to be accountable for classroom performance of their graduates—but, then again, only 20 states have the capacity to match teacher and student records so programs could possibly determine where their graduates actually end up teaching.[58]

Current teacher-education and licensing systems, at best, prepare teachers for (and measure whether they are minimally qualified to teach in) late 20th-century schools—not ones filled with second language learners and students who are growing up in a Web 2.0 world. A reconceptualized system, built on a new generation of partnerships and performance assessments, can offer opportunities for individuals from many backgrounds to enter teaching through different routes, while also promoting the spread of effective teaching and the identification of our most expert teachers—all in support of the redesigned profession we identify in Chapter 5.

The emergence of urban teacher residencies (UTRs) has begun to drive changes in pedagogical preparation and the public perception of how much training teachers need to be effective early in their careers (see Chapter 4). UTRs are beginning to bridge the best of both university-based and alternative preparation and are modeling how to get serious about specialized preparation for high-needs schools. But while UTRs are a cost-effective policy tool for the long run, there's not much of a tradition among policymakers for making serious investments in teacher education on the front end and waiting patiently for the big payoff.

Progressive politicians and school, university, and foundation leaders can help change that mindset with serious investments of about $50,000 per recruit (which includes a $30,000 stipend to learn to teach and commit to teaching locally).[59] As more UTR programs demonstrate the power of the concept, they will leverage the idea that teachers need to be deeply prepared and offer a clear path for how to do so.[60]

The return on each dollar invested will be multiplied many times over if UTR interns and graduates are connected via the Web in professional networks the members of which share a profound understanding of successful teaching in high-needs environments. The use of Internet tools, videos, and podcasting can, not only help a growing number of talented recruits to learn from each other by analyzing lessons, assignments, and student work, but also spread teaching expertise faster and farther from one locale to another. A new generation of networked UTR recruits would not only serve as lead teachers but also have future roles as teacher educators, policy advocates, and community organizers who are skilled and prepared to connect effective teaching to a range of other student and family services and the other professionals who deliver them. Many would become experts in student assessment—and without them there will not be sufficient numbers of accomplished teachers needed to drive the development and use of 21st-century tests and accountability. These teachers would play key roles in implementing a wide array of school- and community-based assessments, now commonly found in high-achieving countries.

A $50,000 price tag per UTR recruit seems like a great deal of money. However, offering 10,000 of these service scholarships per year nationally would cost only a half a billion dollars. And over the next 20 years the nation would have 200,000 of these expert teachers ready to lead their schools and communities. Coupled with more-traditional service scholarships, school districts would no longer have to rely on emergency credentialed and out-of-field teachers. Teaching residencies would not have to be limited to high-needs urban settings—several initiatives are now underway to develop a rural teaching residency model, including a California partnership led by Bard College and supported by very modest federal Teacher Quality Partnership grants. While considerable, a $10-billion investment over 20 years would pale in comparison to those high-achieving countries that essentially underwrite all the expense of teacher education.

To go to scale, such a preparation system will require assessments of teaching that go far beyond the crude instruments in use today. These sophisticated assessments would use multiple measures of teaching effectiveness to identify teachers' strengths and determine when they are ready to teach independently. As a result, some teachers would earn their initial license sooner than others based upon performance data—gathered over time in electronic portfolios—that include value-added achievement data, analyses of student work, and video-taped teaching performances, as well as student engagement data. Teacher-leaders will be directly engaged in identifying effective teachers through this multi-layered process, which will also include evidence of the new teacher's leadership potential.

This work is already beginning to emerge. With the Performance Assessment for California Teaching (PACT), new teachers are expected to demonstrate their knowledge of content and how to teach it in real life circumstances and context. PACT, drawing on some of the assessment protocols of the National Board for Professional Teaching Standards, is now spreading to other states. Proven as a valid measure of individual teacher competence, the PACT design is useful for teacher licensure and can be a powerful tool for teacher learning and program improvement.[61] The assessments require teachers to demonstrate that they know how to effectively teach diverse students, for example, by showing how they teach specific content to second language learners and analyze achievement data on the progress students made.

The key to effective teaching is not just helping students achieve more on a given assessment, but knowing what to do based on evidence of learning, which may come from standardized and other achievement measures. PACT-like performance assessments have the potential to focus teacher evaluation on student learning without the distortions caused by the singular use of standardized test scores. For example, a much-needed revision of the National Board's advanced certification system will place a greater premium on teachers who advance student learning and spread their expertise to others. As new tools emerge from this revision process, they will likely influence improvements in teacher-assessment practices generally.

Sophisticated assessment tools will also help policymakers and educators know which teachers are ready to lead. And new technologies will make it much simpler to assemble the multiple measures needed for school and teacher-leaders to determine which teachers should be paid more—and to ensure that all of their colleagues are teaching effectively.

Change Lever #4: Cultivate Working Conditions That Make High-Needs Schools "Easier to Staff"

Under the American Recovery and Reinvestment Act, the Obama administration spearheaded the multibillion-dollar Race to the Top initiative to fund new approaches for improving schools, with a sharp focus on intensive support for the lowest performing schools.[62] States, school districts, and nonprofit organizations are receiving funding to radically change the teacher labor market in an effort to ensure a truly equitable distribution of effective teachers. Conventional wisdom suggests that if policymakers could somehow attract "smarter" individuals to teaching, or if principals had more hiring-and-firing authority, or if school districts used merit-pay systems, then hard-to-staff schools would become simple to staff and student achievement would improve. The reality is more complex. Overwhelming evidence suggests that improving the working conditions that support learning is the real key to recruiting and retaining effective teachers for high-needs schools.

In a recent poll of teachers, 86% agreed that "teaching is exactly what I want to be doing." Yet more than 90% of them also agreed that "teaching is so demanding, it's a wonder that more people don't burn out." For them, by far the "biggest drawback to teaching" is "too much testing."[63] When asked which conditions would most improve their teaching effectiveness, the nationwide sample of teachers pointed primarily to schools instituting more-proactive approaches for students with serious behavior problems, reduced class sizes (by at least 5 pupils), and opportunities to develop their own skills to adapt instruction for diverse learners. Last on their list were eliminating tenure and tying teacher rewards to student performance.

FIGURE 7.6. Teachers Rank Reform Proposals in Terms of Improving Teacher Effectiveness

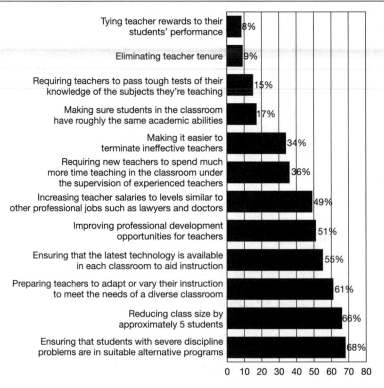

Percent of teachers ranking measure as very effective

Source: Learning Point Associates and Public Agenda. (2009). *Retaining Teacher Talent website— Report 2: Teaching for a living*. Washington, DC: Authors. Retrieved March 14, 2010, from http://www.learningpt.org/expertise/educatorquality/genY/TeachingforaLiving/results.php. Reprinted by permission of Learning Point Associates.

At the Center for Teaching Quality, our own most recent research has shown that several working conditions are essential for teachers to be successful in high-needs schools. Teachers need high-quality preparation for working with special-needs students and those who are learning English as a second language. They also need to develop knowledge about how to manage reform mandates as part of their daily teaching practice. They need to learn specific instructional strategies to work with growing numbers of transient students—many of whom enter, exit, and reenter schools routinely in a given year. In addition, our research suggests that teachers need more preparation to work with a variety of community organizations and *outside-of-the-traditional* school providers—such as Communities in Schools. Finally policymakers and administrators need to make sure these teachers are not placed in an out-of-field teaching assignment.[64]

In this book, we have discussed at length the inevitable impacts of a constantly connected world on future learning systems. We have demonstrated that, very soon, teachers will no longer focus solely on imparting siloed information to students in discrete classrooms. Teachers' educational experiences will include coordinating diverse sources of learning beyond the standard text and lecture—both in virtual settings and in brick-and-mortar school buildings. Creating school environments that support this kind of effective teaching go well beyond the traditional "working conditions" issues of time, class size, and the length of the workday. Increasingly, research points to the fact that it is not just *what* teachers can access but *how* they use those accessed resources to advance instructional excellence that will determine their effectiveness and their longevity in the profession. Unfortunately, the term *working conditions* is viewed negatively by many policymakers and members of the media, who believe the phrase reveals evidence of a self-interested focus on the adults in a school, at the expense of students. This must change. The Center for Teaching Quality has always concentrated on the teacher working conditions that promote *student learning*. And CTQ's conclusion, after much research, is that teachers cannot help students learn at high levels if the conditions under which they teach keep them from acting on what they know.

Most policymakers do not realize that teaching in a high-needs school is often a frenetic experience. Many teachers need to put in well over 60 hours a week to manage multiple interventions, meet the social and emotional needs of their students, mediate conflicts when out-of-school turmoil spills over into the classroom, cope with the complexity of teaching highly mobile students, and deal with the constant pressure to prepare for high-stakes tests. Many young recruits in high-needs schools must work 12-hour days, every day (plus additional weekends and late nights), to get all the work done and serve the needs of the children and their families. And they cannot work like this forever.

The human price, all too often, is the kind of professional and personal burnout described by a former Teach For America recruit, Sarah Fine, who resigned from teaching because administrators "steadily expand(ed) the workload and workday" while "more and more major decisions were made behind closed doors, and more and more teachers felt micromanaged rather than supported."[65] Ms. Fine is not alone.

Researchers have shown the tight relationship between teachers' preparation to make informed decisions and retention in the profession.

The same researchers also have found a tight relationship between retention in the profession and teachers' influence over their work.

There are many examples of how schools are organized for both student and teacher success. Like the Harlem Children's Zone, New York City's Julia Richman Education Complex integrates a hands-on approach to learning with wraparound services for the students they serve. The Ohio-based KnowledgeWorks Foundation, working closely with both administrators and union leaders, has designed full-service schools or hubs that can create new opportunities for teachers to know their students (and families) and integrate K–12 and after-school learning. These structures position teachers to support the full spectrum of students' learning needs.

Raising the quality of teaching and boosting student achievement in high-needs schools requires an intensive focus on other working conditions as well. They include appropriate teaching assignments; adequate

FIGURE 7.7. Attrition Rate of Beginning Teachers, by Extensiveness of Teacher Education (number of preparation components)

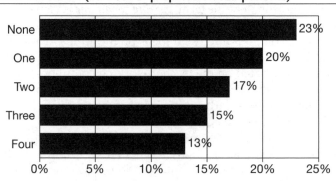

Source: Ingersoll, R., & Smith, T. (2004, April). *What are the effects of teacher education, preparation and training on beginning teacher attrition?* Paper presented at the annual meeting of the American Educational Research Association, San Diego. Reprinted by permission of CPRE.

Note: Preparation components considered in this study were coursework in selection of instructional materials, coursework in learning theory/child psychology, observation of others' classes, and feedback on teachers' own teaching.

FIGURE 7.8. Effects of Faculty Decision-Making Influence on Teacher Turnover

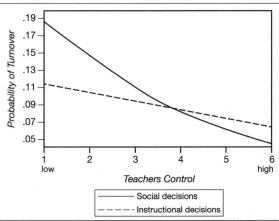

Reprinted by permission of the publisher from *Who Controls Teachers' Work? Power and Accountability in America's Schools* by Richard M. Ingersoll, p. 205, Cambridge, Mass.: Harvard University Press, Copyright © 2003 by the President and Fellows of Harvard College.

time to work with colleagues and students; professional development that focuses on systemic, sustained, and collective study of student work; access to information, materials and technology; and regular helpful feedback on teaching.[66] In 2005, a six-state survey of National Board–certified teachers found that factors such as strong principal leadership, a collegial staff with a shared teaching philosophy, access to adequate resources, and strategies to work with parents were the most powerful incentives for them to consider moving to high-needs schools.[67]

As states create new accountability frameworks, "opportunities to teach effectively" standards should be put into place. Just as teachers are expected to help students learn more, administrators and policymakers would be expected to maintain the conditions necessary to do so. Based upon a wide range of evidence, these "opportunities to teach effectively" standards would include: (1) principals who cultivate and embrace teacher leadership; (2) time and tools for teachers to learn from each other; (3) specialized preparation and resources for the highest needs schools, subjects, and students; (4) an absolute zero tolerance policy on out-of-field teaching assignments; (5) teaching loads that are in sync with the diversity and mobility of students taught; and (6) opportunities to test out new ideas and take risks.

The "Benwood" schools in Chattanooga, Tennessee, offer compelling evidence of the right kind of preparation and support needed to teach effectively in high-needs schools.

Initially, reformers in Chattanooga assumed that teachers already working in the then-struggling schools were the problem, and the solution would be to recruit "better" teachers from elsewhere. However, over time, as an analysis by Education Sector found, some of the most impressive student achievement gains were associated with the growing effectiveness of teachers *who were at the Benwood schools before reform efforts began*. With more-effective leadership, better training, quality peer assistance, and a specialized master's degree in urban education, these teachers improved their teaching, and their students performed at much higher levels. The powerful lesson: *Effective teachers can be cultivated within high-needs schools, not just recruited to them.*

While some of these critical working conditions will cost more, most will not. The Benwood experience suggests that the keys to making high-needs schools "easier to staff" are reallocated time, open collaboration, and school administrators who value and utilize teacher leaders.

Change Lever #5:
Reframe Accountability for Transformative Results

In public education, American policymakers seem to respect what we assess, as opposed to assessing what we respect. As for the public itself, polling data reveal that Americans are not sold on the idea that standardized tests can accurately assess student performance. In fact, in a 2009 national poll, both parents and the general public reported that student work samples and teacher observations were better measures than the current once-a-year, multiple choice tests that have been driving high-stakes accountability.[68] And their skepticism has been increasing.

Since the release of *A Nation at Risk* in 1983, the United States has pursued increasingly intensive efforts to raise academic standards and measure more precisely, in highly quantitative ways, whether or not students are learning more and if the achievement gaps are closing. This is a good thing. And no doubt the No Child Left Behind Act reinforced the use of high-stakes testing and accountability to objectively measure academic performance and determine which schools were serving students well and which were not. However, NCLB did a lot more, promoting among both major political parties "as secular gospel the idea that testing and accountability would necessarily lead to better schools."[69] Initially, NCLB mandated annual tests in math and reading in grades 3 through 8 and a single test each of reading and math in high school. And beginning in 2007, states were required to give tests in science at least once in elementary, middle, and high school.

NCLB not only required all states to create strict timelines for all of their students to reach proficiency by 2014 but also imposed a "series of

FIGURE 7.9. Public and Parent Perceptions of the Most Accurate Measures of Students' Academic Progress

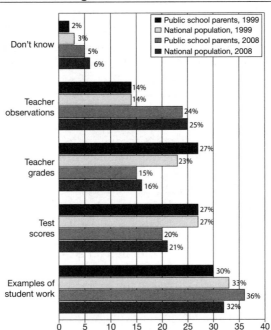

Source: Bushaw, W. J., & Gallup, A. M. (2008). *Americans speak out: Are educators and policy makers listening?* Bloomington, IN: Phi Delta Kappan. Reprinted by permission of Phi Delta Kappan.

increasingly onerous sanctions" for schools (e.g., the firing of principals and teachers, state or private management takeover, or conversion to charter status) if they did not pass muster.[70]

Teacher associations and educational researchers consistently raised questions about the quality of tests and the metrics used. Certain multiple choice questions, designed with early 20th-century-psychometric principles in mind, are definitively biased against certain students—mostly minorities and new immigrants to America. Other tests are badly worded and incorrectly scored—and they do not always correspond to the state standards.[71] Year-to-year gains for students often vary in unpredictable ways. In addition, tests can be invalidated if teachers teach to the test. And sometimes, when students who pass one basic skills test and then take another one focused on the same content but with a higher-order thinking bent, they fail.[72] For example, assessment expert Lorrie Shepard showed, in a hard-hitting analysis, how 80% of a national sample of 8th-graders could accurately determine the product of 9 × 9 on a bubble-in, multiple choice test, but only 40% of them could then correctly answer a simple word problem requiring them to compute the square footage of a 9 × 9 foot room.[73] As Diane Ravitch, once a strong proponent of high-stakes accountability and NCLB, noted, "The problem with using [these current standardized] tests to make important decisions about people's lives is that [the tests] are not precise instruments."[74] Testing experts have always warned policymakers to use standardized tests in consequential ways only with other measures of performance.

But hardly any policymaker seemed to listen—and school administrators continued to focus on making sure teachers would teach to the once-a-year standardized tests that would determine whether or not they would keep their jobs. The nation's testing industry grew, with the General Accounting Office reporting that states spent at least $2 billion on just NCLB-mandated, multiple choice tests between 2002 and 2008—and the costs could be 8 to 15 times higher if the estimates included the time and money spent on practice tests. Both states and districts added benchmark (and other) tests to ensure that schools were on track to do well on the annual high-stakes, bubble-in tests. Another estimate pegged states, in 1 year (2005–2006), having to spend $517 million on NCLB and related testing.[75] And under the pressure of NCLB accountability demands and limited resources, states and districts turned to the testing industry to produce "fast and cheap assessments that focus on basic skills."[76] A 2009 report from the Forum on Education and Democracy concluded that "as tests have been used for accountability purposes, they have increasingly shaped teaching, reducing the amount of time students spend reading real books, writing essays, and conducting research."[77] Hard evidence has proved the point. In 2007, the nonpartisan, D.C.-based think tank, the Center for Education Policy, found that more that 44% of the nation's school districts had reduced instructional time in science, social studies, and the arts.[78]

And as NCLB reforms took hold, test score gains on the National Assessment of Educational Progress (NAEP), a more rigorous test of academic skills, were—for the most part—nonexistent. Although recent NAEP trend data suggested that minority students are scoring higher than they had in the past, most of their gains were accrued well before the advent of the higher-stakes accountability system imposed by NCLB.[79] The law allowed states to develop their own tests and set their own benchmarks for proficiency—and it showed. In Mississippi, the state's NCLB test results reported that 89% of the state's 4th-graders were proficient in reading; but on the NAEP only 18% of Mississippi's 4th-graders scored at the proficient level. Only a few states had comparable percentages of students scoring proficient on their tests as well as on the NAEP. Even the Fordham Foundation, known for its avid support of NCLB and high-stakes accountability, came to question the system. The often-partisan think tank called NCLB an "accountability illusion" given the evidence that a school that made "adequate yearly progress" in its own state might not make it in another one.[80]

Twenty-first-century teaching and learning—that capitalizes on the potential of the teachers of 2030—will require a dramatically different school accountability system. Much like in other high-scoring nations today, America's system of testing must focus on students' abilities to *apply* what they know to new problems and situations, and its accountability schemes must identify more than who is doing well or not. It must send clear signals as to why students are performing at proficiency (or better) or not—and what educators should do next in order to help them improve. This kind of system is already in the reach of American policymakers and the practitioners who implement it. As we note in Chapter 3, the know-how is already in place to create assessments that include research projects and science investigations as well as the development of student products.

These assessments will cost more, but sound accountability systems do not require that every student take every test—and by providing a larger number of teacherpreneurs and others in hybrid roles to develop and score these assessments, students will be pushed to learn 21st-century skills, and policymakers as well as parents and employers will know more precisely what they know and can do. New technologies that we have described herein can document what and why students learn, assembling data on how they address multistep problems and generating descriptive data about strategies used to arrive at solutions.[81]

Much like with River City (a MUVE), an assessment tool we highlighted in Chapter 3, the Calipers project is using technology-based simulations to develop and study a new generation of assessment systems. For example, assessment requires students to find out the proper angle and speed to rescue an injured skier on an icy mountain. The assessments are designed to provide data to teachers to inform instruction and to students to increase their own awareness of how they are learning (metacognition). Bill Tucker, an analyst with Education Sector, a D.C.-based think tank that initially promoted NCLB-style accountability, has called for an overhaul of current multiple choice tests. Tucker pointed to how "the U.S. Army has 'instrumentalized' many of its war games and other performance exercises, using video and sensors to gather multiple sources of data about what is happening and when." These tools drive serious school improvement and 21st-century skill development among students.[82] The Cisco Networking Academy, which uses advanced technologies in training more than 600,000 high school and college students each year worldwide, is developing tools to take these applications to scale.[83]

But as Larry Cuban, an education historian, notes, the "persistent dream of technology driving school and classroom changes has continually foundered in transforming teaching practices."[84] Much more needs to be done, including transforming the context of how teachers work and the incentives that promote more ambitious teaching. Two things need to happen: First of all, more teachers need to be involved in creating and scoring these assessments and, second, the accountability system needs to surface information on why students perform as they do and what steps practitioners and policymakers need to take in order to close achievement gaps.

The New York Performance Standards Consortium, since 1998, has been doing both. The assessments include literary essays that demonstrate analytical thinking, as well as problem solving in mathematics that demonstrates high-level conceptual knowledge. The assessments are scored by teachers with detailed rubrics and with outside reviewers serving as an additional layer of external accountability.[85]

If states work together on these assessments, as opposed to in 50 different policy and practice silos, the costs of them would drop remarkably.[86] As we note in Chapter 3, the Obama administration is spending $350 million to support consortia of states in developing a new generation of assessments. And while the need is recognized for states to use new assessments that measure a broader range of students' knowledge and skills, there is no plan yet to draw on teacher-leaders to implement them. As Darling-Hammond noted, high-achieving nations "measure performance in authentic ways and with intensive teacher engagement throughout the assessment process, as teachers work with others to develop, review, score, and use the results of assessments."[87] Their accountability systems report on a comprehensive set of indicators on both student learning results and opportunities for teachers to teach effectively.

And if the nation's accountability system begins to include a range of indicators, such as if teachers and administrators have the time and the skills for using data to improve student learning and engagement, then policymakers and the public will be able to understand why schools are doing better or not. Sam Chaltain, in his former role as national director of the Forum for Education and Democracy, called for the federal government to create a reciprocal accountability system that hones in on five universal measurement categories—achievement, balance, climate, democratic practices, and equity.[88] The system does not have to be cumbersome. As Chaltain noted, "If each school identified between three and ten different data points (including, but not limited to, test scores) to assess their overall learning environment, we might start to see 'achievement' as a broader set of measures, and evaluate the full extent to which we are supporting the young people we serve."[89] Such an accountability system would not only capitalize on the potential of the teachers of 2030 but also help cultivate them.

Change Lever #6:
Transform Teacher Unions Into Professional Guilds

Any discussion of teacher unions is sure to elicit some controversy. For more than 50 years teacher unions have been powerful forces in American public education, especially in collective-bargaining states where they can and usually do define a web of far-reaching classroom work rules. But they are not the national, monolithic organizations some envision, uniformly dictating the specifics of local bargaining contracts. Each local union—and its leadership—can be very different. Issues that are common to teachers across America—the problems of teacher evaluation and tenure as well as professional pay and seniority transfer rights—tend to manifest themselves in similar ways from one district to the next no matter whether teachers work under a collective-bargaining agreement.

Some brief history is in order. Prior to the 1960s, public employees did not have authorization to engage in collective bargaining. Since then teacher unions have used that authority and their political clout to resist managerial indiscretions. Diane Ravitch, one of our nation's most re- spected education historians, has documented how, yesterday and today, unions have been necessary to protect teachers against the "arbitrary ex- ercise of power by heavy-handed administrators."[90] In 2005, for example, the New York City union had to include in contract provisions language to explicitly keep administrators from dictating rules related to the format of bulletin boards, the arrangement of classroom furniture, and the "exact duration" of classroom lessons.[91] Yes this was in 2005, not 1905.

This history notwithstanding, at the beginning of the second decade of the 21st century, the teacher unions—more than any other group—have been portrayed as the sinkhole on the path to improving teaching and clos- ing the student achievement gap. Pundit after pundit paints unions—with their insistence on due process rights for members (and job placement pref- erences for the most senior ones)—as the primary reason effective teachers cannot be recruited and rewarded and ineffective ones fired expeditiously. Even well-respected journalists like Mr. Kristof have gone to war over the teacher unions—claiming that they block the expansion of charter schools, are primarily responsible for the system in which poor students and those of color are taught by the most ineffective teachers, and protect their incom- petent members religiously from termination.[92] Organizations such as the Center for Union Facts have been launched to denigrate organized labor—

charging, for example, that unionized teachers are willing to "hold children hostage" in order to gain inordinate salary raises and job protections.[93]

Emotions and vitriol often trump the real facts. For example, researchers have shown that while unionized teachers do earn more than their nonunionized counterparts, the differences are not large—5 to 12%.[94] While unions have not always been able to secure professional salaries for their members, it is true that they *have* been able to protect more senior teachers (who have literally paid more dues) with reduction-in-force provisions. In unionized districts, the student-teacher ratio is generally lower,

FIGURE 7.10. Teachers' Views on Their Unions and Teaching Quality

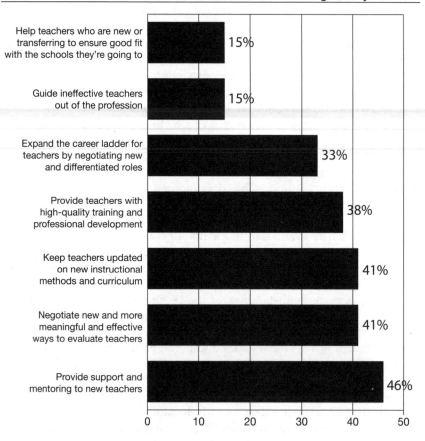

Percent of teachers agreeing that unions take such action

Source: Duffet, A., Farkas, F., & Rotherham, A. J., & Silva, E. (2008). *Waiting to be won over: Teachers speak on the profession, unions and reform.* Washington, DC: Education Sector. Reprinted by permission of Education Sector.

FIGURE 7.11. Teachers' Opinions of Their Unions, New and Veteran Teachers

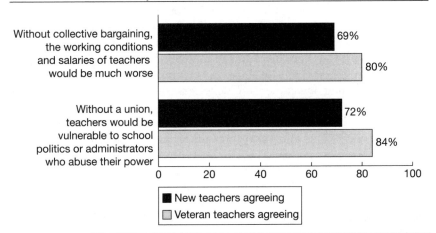

Source: Duffet, A., Farkas, F., & Rotherham, A. J., & Silva, E. (2008). *Waiting to be won over: Teachers speak on the profession, unions and reform.* Washington, DC: Education Sector. Reprinted by permission of Education Sector.

approximately 7% to 12%—but many reform advocates would argue that a lower ratio can be a positive for learning. Research has revealed that unionized schools drive up instructional costs (but only about 8% to 15% higher) and "restrict the discretion of administrators." But the evidence does *not* suggest that these restrictions on administrative power lead to less effective schools.[95]

In reality very little evidence exists connecting the actions of teacher unions and student achievement. For one, it is not easy to disentangle the host of factors involved in defining and measuring the relationship between collective-bargaining arrangements and student learning outcomes. But researchers *have* found that students in unionized locals, compared to their peers in nonunionized districts, generated a 5% higher student achievement gain on standardized tests.[96] While the measured effects of unions are not large, it's worth noting that one of our nation's highest performing states, Massachusetts, also has one of the most unionized teacher workforces. Also notable is the fact that teachers in Finland, the highest-scoring nation in the world, are 100% unionized.[97]

There is no question that teachers, especially younger ones, want more from their unions. They want to see unions involved in far more than just bread-and-butter issues like salary, health care, and traditional workplace concerns such as smaller class size, adequate planning periods, and limited doses of cafeteria and lunch duty. In a recent poll, teachers reported seeing little emphasis on quality teaching from their unions.[98]

At the same time, these poll results, assembled in 2008, also reveal that teachers were more likely than 5 years before to describe their unions as "essential." The jump in the numbers of new teachers (with less than 5 years of experience) who pointed to the essential role of unions is especially noteworthy, given the claims of many reformers that unions are not important to generation Y teachers. In fact, while there are generational differences among newcomers and veterans when it comes to unions, they are marginal and in no way, shape, or form suggest that teachers do not want and need a collective voice on matters of policy and practice.

Do all these facts and survey results mean that unions, as currently construed, are what is needed for a 21st-century profession? Not at all.

Less than half of the nation's teachers believe that their unions provide substantive opportunities for them to become a better teacher—and newcomers to the profession are most interested in them doing so. More than half (55%) of all teachers report that it's too difficult to let go of teachers who shouldn't be teaching and many believe unions could do more to protect children and the profession in this regard.[99]

Some union leaders have acknowledged that they have a "mixed record on fighting for an equitable and quality education for all children" and "too often have been accomplices in maintaining an unsatisfactory status quo."[100] Don Cameron, a former National Education Association official, has lamented that the nation's largest union has suffered from a governance structure that does not favor a strong, centralized leadership and often "hunkers down" to oppose education policies that members believe are ill-conceived rather than using the vast know-how of their membership to find solutions to endemic problems.[101] As a result, it has been relatively easy to characterize teacher unions as always saying "no"—rather than seeking ways to say "yes." Bob Chase, a former president of the NEA, wrote more than a decade ago:

> While some of NEA's critics aim only to dismantle public education, many others care about our schools, and we have been too quick to dismiss their criticisms and their ideas for change. The fact is that in some instances we have used our power to block uncomfortable change, to protect the narrow interests of our members, and to hold back on advancing the interests of students and schools.[102]

There is positive movement, however. For example, in January 2010, Randi Weingarten, president of the American Federation of Teachers, called for the unions to work with administrators on using student achievement data in evaluating teachers, while also ensuring that the process remained "fair and transparent" as well as "expedient" in identifying and "dealing with" those who are ineffective.[103] At the National Education Association's

2010 convention, president Denis Van Roekel launched a Commission on Effective Teachers and Teaching, which would break new ground by distinguishing excellence among its ranks. At the same time, Van Roekel warned the Obama administration that it cannot focus its efforts on just using test scores to identify winning and losing teachers and schools.[104]

These union initiatives are encouraging and come at a critical time. Nationwide, very few teachers (newcomers, 11%; veterans, 27%) claim to be involved with their local unions.[105] Only slightly more in each category (newcomers, 23%; veterans, 39%) believe their unions provide "feelings of pride and solidarity."[106] What if teachers were involved in their unions and felt more connected? And what would it mean for public support if collectives of teachers demonstrated how expert practitioners can drive student success, school improvement, and a results-oriented profession of teaching? The teacher unions have high visibility—and understandably so. In many ways they control the public perception of teaching. If the American people continue to perceive the teacher unions as recalcitrant or untrustworthy, then they may continue to resist investments that could transform the profession.

For the public to get behind teachers as a collective force for good, the unions must organize their members as "mind workers," not industrial workers subject to micromanagement.[107] In the post-industrial age, teachers need professional organizations that defend not only their rights but their profession's commitment to high standards, the interests of children, and a public education system that protects American democracy.

Decades ago the nation's most honored teacher-union-leader, the late Al Shanker, believed that teachers should firmly establish and enforce standards among their ranks.[108] While Shanker was known for leading industrial-style teacher strikes, he also called for peer review, and late in his life he put forth the argument that unions should no longer resist the fair use of student test scores in teacher evaluation systems. In the 1990s he called for a demanding examination, administered nationwide, that teachers would have to pass in order to gain union membership.[109] In recent comments both AFT's Weingarten and NEA's Van Roekel have expressed much of this same reform sentiment—suggesting that teachers can take the lead in focusing, not just on bread-and-butter issues, but also on what matters most for students and their learning.

Imagine that by 2030, fueled by viral networking and the emergence of new generations of leaders, teacher unions have evolved into professional guilds in which membership is based on proven levels of performance. Imagine that a wide variety of contractual arrangements frame the work and compensation of teachers. As artist and craft guilds have defined a career path from apprentice to novice to journeyman to master, teaching guilds would do the same for teachers—and even more.

In the late 1990s, C. T. Kerchner and colleagues called for school-based compacts that loosen up the traditional union-district contract and replace it with "slender agreements" where "most of the decisions that lie at the heart of teaching and learning would shift to the schools."[110] Setting school schedules, making teacher assignments (such as hybrid roles), and determining supplemental pay would be done in partnership with teachers at the school, not at the district level. These are important first steps—but insufficient to fully establish teaching as a 21st-century profession.

Building off of the ideas posed by Shanker, imagine that teachers would earn differentiated membership into their unions, based on the quality of their teaching as demonstrated by the same sophisticated multiple measures discussed in Lever 3. Union leaders would be selected for their classroom expertise as well as their leadership skills and organizational prowess. No longer would spending enough time in the union ranks ensure higher responsibility. At the local, state, and national levels, only the most effective and principled teachers would rise to the rank of union leader.

In addition, much like in medicine and law, the new union would focus on identifying and elevating the very best teachers. Unions currently highlight the achievements of a small percentage of excellent teachers, including those who are teachers of the year or become National Board certified. But these union designations are most often ceremonial—the recognized teachers are not marketed as experts and they are surely not expected to spread their expertise in ways found in other professions. Imagine how the image of teachers—and the substance of the unions—would change if *expert teachers* were accurately identified and well utilized. The legal profession has drawn on "Super Lawyers"—so designated through a national process of both independent research evidence and peer review—to spread expertise, assist clients in getting expert assistance, and elevate the profession. Versions of *Super Lawyers* magazine are published in all 50 states and reach more than 13 million readers nationwide.[111] Perhaps in the not-distant future, guild-published editions of *Expert Teacher* will be disseminated through social media, highlighting the accomplishments (based on a wide range of metrics) of the most effective teachers in every community, teaching in virtual and physical learning spaces. Professional teacher guilds would wield even more influence among their members than traditional unions—and drive the kinds of public-engagement campaigns needed to trigger major policy changes in school finance as well as teacher education, licensing, and compensation. Professional guilds could also guide the profession through a seamless transition to blended virtual and brick-and-mortar teaching. They would take a major role in virtual peer mentoring—connecting expert teachers with novices and other colleagues who need a variety of supports in content and teaching (as well as working with students and families in and out of cyberspace). In doing so, excellent teaching would become far more visible to teachers as well as to the public and to policymakers.

Guilds would continue to represent the individual and collective interests of members as well. Successful teacher leaders would call upon the resources of trusted professional guilds to broker complex roles for them to play in schools and across the nation and beyond—including assisting them in becoming the teacherpreneurs a 21st-century teaching profession demands. Professional guilds would help forge new kinds of school-based and virtual teaching jobs for their members, breaking through the current tight organizational and geographic boundaries of today's schools and helping them earn the salaries and prestige they deserve based upon the quality of their individual and collaborative work.

Imagine that well before 2030, federal and state policy backed off its relentless obsessions with narrow test score gains and actually placed a premium on teacher creativity and the spread of teaching expertise, making teacherpreneurs the reality they must become. Imagine that in the 2030 MetLife Survey of the American Teacher, more than 90% of the responding teachers believed that their teaching guild helped them become better teachers, and the guild's collective efforts were rated as "almost always" in the best interests of its members and the students those members serve. There would no longer be a reason to ask if teachers felt pride and solidarity as guild members. The answer would be obvious in the day-to-day interactions among teachers and in the role they play with the public in breaking new historical ground in their evolution from low-paid caretakers and industrial age automatons to results-oriented professionals needed for the public schools of 2030.

CHAPTER 8

Taking Action
for a Hopeful Future

We began this book admitting that we had no special skills in predicting the future. Clearly we are not technology prophets like Ray Kurzweil, with special insight into how intelligent machines and nanotechnology might create a boon for teaching and learning.[1] But we already see the potential of students designing their own web-based learning programs, which will develop their knowledge and skills as well as their understanding, creativity, and career opportunities. And we imagine that Teachbots,[2] or virtual assistants that currently help online customers find what they are seeking in the world of web-based retailing, can help *real teachers* provide even more personalized guidance when and where students need it, freeing them up to spread their expertise to others and providing leadership for both reforms in pedagogy and policy.

Soon, not just students, but also their teachers will prefer just-in-time virtual learning opportunities that will break up their longstanding isolation from each other and escalate the possibilities for excellent teaching to spread from one classroom to another. We can only be hopeful that our teaching profession can catapult beyond its troubled past and the deep divides that define our present policy environment. By exploiting the possibilities of a growing viral circle of like-valued colleagues, and the infusion of new millennium teachers into the profession, we believe that teaching can overcome its convoluted history and the monotony of recent two-sided debates over teaching quality. A recent poll has revealed that America's youngest adults, who will be the teachers of tomorrow, are "confident, connected, and open to change" and remain the most likely of any generation alive today to support a progressive domestic social agenda.[3] But there is more to creating the 21st-century teaching profession than just calling new recruits to serve the nation's public schools for a few years of teaching prior to entering more lucrative careers.

The profession's hopeful future is emerging with the visibility of new researchers who are beginning to surface the fact that peer learning among small groups of teachers (not individuals) seems to be the most powerful predictor of student achievement over time.[4] Another study has found that teachers who are effective in one school will not necessarily be effective in another—pointing to the fact that varying school conditions may account for 25% of teacher effects on student learning.[5] This research affirms that there is more to creating a results-oriented teaching profession than over-hauling teacher evaluation and judging individual teachers on the basis of how well their students perform on 20th-century standardized tests.

Other sentiments are beginning to shift as well. A 2010 report from a diverse group of education leaders, including those who have previously argued against professionalizing teaching, concluded that 21st-century school reforms depend less on alternative certification and merit pay and much more on "teachers working in teams to analyze student data, tailoring instruction to diverse student needs, delivering content in multiple ways, and quickly measuring their students' progress (as well as their own)."[6] And we believe that many teachers, like the co-authors of this book, will help turn this idea into action and reframe the conversation about the future of the profession.

In addition, in 2010, the Bill and Melinda Gates Foundation launched a $335-million investment in teacher effectiveness, with major grants to three large school districts and two public charter school networks to transform their systems of professional development, tenure, evaluation, and compensation. Working collaboratively with both administrators and unions—not just one or the other—the Gates-fueled approach to teacher effectiveness will rest not only on standardized test score data but other metrics derived from new tools that gauge student engagement and analyze teaching practices in depth. The Gates research and development agenda, along with a new initiative by the Ford Foundation, also will focus on more precise measures of teacher working conditions that will allow policymakers and practitioners to have a better understanding of the school context that allow teachers to teach—and students to learn—most effectively.

We are also enthusiastic about the growing interest of policymakers and business leaders, many of whom were once fervent supporters of standardized testing, to promote performance assessments that emphasize the 21st-century skills students need to learn and use. These purposeful assessments will serve as better indicators of the value-added impact of teachers and teacher teams on student achievement. Polling data suggest that most teachers embrace accountability, if their work is assessed using authentic, fair, and reliable student learning measures.

Finally, both top-flight schools of education and a growing number of urban residency programs are beginning to document more carefully how they are preparing future teachers and how effective their graduates are in boosting student learning in high-needs schools. These latter efforts, we believe, can help policymakers transcend the current dysfunctional disputes over the merits of university-based teacher education versus abbreviated-training regimes led by nonprofits.

While we are optimistic, caution is in order as well. We know that empirical evidence and high-profile think tank reports alone will not transform education policy—especially in the teaching arena, where the perspectives of many policymakers are deeply rooted in social custom and their experiences as students in America's schools. And it is too early to tell whether the current reforms of the federal government and major philanthropies will actually expand beyond narrow definitions of effective teaching, past and present, and embrace and truly cultivate teacher-leaders as drivers of the transformation of their own profession. There are many think tanks with a policy agenda built on viewing teachers as inexpensive labor—not as empowered, well paid, and respected professionals. We anticipate that these think tank analysts will seek to continue the current dysfunctional debates on the proper role of teachers in the nation's schools—primarily to fuel the media's recent obsession with teacher unions as the sole "enemy of reform" and innovation in public education.[7]

It is also too soon to determine whether teachers will have the time or flexibility to help fully develop much-needed performance assessments in ways that assist practitioners in improving their teaching and inform policymakers and the public about which students are learning and why. Finally, while we hope that with new technologies and investments policymakers will have a better idea of who is ready to teach and what role they should play if they do, we are not sure if policymakers will have the political courage to close down the preparation programs (both traditional and alternative) that consistently fall short of the mark.

As the 21st century's second decade begins, a shift in outlook inside unions is also becoming more visible. The American Federation of Teachers, through its Innovation Fund, is supporting community-centered schooling, union-partnership charter schools, and school-based teacher contracts as well as performance-pay systems that avoid the merit pay mistakes of the past. A number of National Education Association local affiliates are on the move as well. In 2010, the leadership of the Illinois Education Association helped enact statewide legislation that created a student results-oriented teacher evaluation system. And in Colorado, the Jefferson County Education Association has been instrumental in forging, with administrators, an ambitious approach to performance pay that can connect student achievement with teacher learning *and* leadership.

Although the mainstream media's attack on teacher organizations has not abated, we sense a coming change. Despite last-ditch efforts to paint teachers and unions as the source of all problems plaguing America's public schools, we predict a surge of positive public opinion on behalf of making teachers part of the solution. Growing numbers of teacher-leaders, with union backing, are already opening their own schools designed to close the achievement gap. As teacher-run schools continue to make "strides in autonomy, creativity, and collective decision making,"[8] they will also be working diligently on innovative ways to measure their efficacy. If they are successful in showing results that matter for students, in very convincing ways, then the movement toward teacher professionalism will be reenergized—and perhaps led by our very best teachers for the first time in America's stormy educational history.

A lot more must get done. So we begin our campaign to turn the ideas in this book into productive action by specifically asking administrators, union leaders, policymakers, university presidents, community leaders, parents, students, and fellow teachers to get involved in transforming the teaching profession to meet the demands of the 21st century.

What You Can Do to Build a 21st-Century Teaching Profession

First, we ask *school administrators* to leave their offices and spend more time in classrooms teaching students and *embracing teacher leadership*. We call on principals, in particular, to begin blurring the lines of distinction between those who lead schools and those who teach in them. We realize that some administrators still believe teachers belong at the bottom of the school organizational pyramid. Given today's classroom challenges, others are beginning to see the value of sharing some decision making with teachers. But we urge school leaders to go well beyond current conceptions of distributed leadership and begin to obscure the deep demarcation between management and labor. Teacher-leaders who are welcomed as peers and colleagues will make it possible for administrators to lead in more powerful ways, opening a portal for increasing numbers of practitioners to work in and out cyberspace on behalf of students and their families.

Second, we ask *union leaders* to get beyond their limiting, 20th-century conceptions of teacher work rules (lockstep pay and seniority-based hiring and placement) and embrace efforts to establish and enforce standards of quality among the teaching ranks. If unions are to transform into professional guilds, a new generation of leaders must emerge, ready to champion excellence in teaching and learning, to uphold the principles of social justice, and to reframe collective bargaining as a tool to support effective teaching, identify expertise, and spread that expertise through teacher leadership and entrepreneurial spirit.

Third, we ask *policymakers* to invest in hybrid teaching roles—a strategy that can quickly escalate the number of expert teachers available to lead reforms from the classroom to the Capitol. Our co-author Kilian Betlach is performing in an hybrid position today, teaching 7th-grade math as well as serving in a more traditional assistant principalship role that includes managing student behavior and completing countless compliance forms. Kilian notes that his hybrid role builds trust and credibility among administrators, teachers, and students—but his school is not funded and organized at a level that allows him to maximize these benefits. Policymakers have it in their power to provide the new and reallocated funding necessary to recruit and develop 600,000 teacherpreneurs by 2030 and promote the *right kind* of performance-pay systems that will help spread their expertise. To ensure that these teacher change agents are equitably distributed in the years ahead, high-needs schools and districts must have the financial resources to compete in a dynamic teacher labor market. Policymakers must "just say no" to hiring under-prepared teachers while also promoting policies that allow hybrid teachers to lead and supervise a wide array of adults who are part of a differentiated teaching profession with multiple pathways and careers.

Fourth, we ask *university presidents* to invest in teacher-education very differently in the future by rewarding their faculty in education schools, arts and sciences, and allied professions who work more closely with PreK–12 schools and community-based organizations. Universities, which serve as hot houses of innovation in so many fields, must finally fulfill their promise of developing teacher-leaders who can challenge the pedagogy of curriculum compliance that dominates many of today's school districts. With new fused financial models that intertwine PreK–12 and higher education funding, the best of these classroom teachers, using a variety of advanced digital tools, can also serve as the next generation of teaching educators, ready to transform university-based preparation programs and to work more closely with researchers to investigate teaching policies that will improve student learning.

Fifth, we ask *community leaders* to step up and embrace teacher-leaders, offering them encouragement and support as they work to transcend the current labor/management divides that impede the development of teaching as a full profession. Bridging the current chasm between unions and administrators (and think tanks) will take time, and new millennium teachers need partners who will help them cultivate their leadership potential. In particular, we have high hopes for local education funds, which have solid reputations for moving beyond the "teachers are the problem" mindset, to serve in this role. They can create unique connections between teacher-leaders and the public—bypassing the frequent discord that takes place among unions, administrators, and reformed-minded teachers and establishing powerful "three-way" alliances to advance effective teaching policies for the 21st century.

Sixth, we ask *parents and students* to speak up about the many effective teachers who currently teach in our nation's schools. Many parents, as co-author Shannon C'de Baca says, "give us the safe harbor to do the right thing for their children, despite ill-conceived administrative dictates from above." We need to work even more closely with you now. Help us dispel the myth that the key to improving America's schools is just to fire bad teachers. No one will be better at shifting the conversation about the future of teaching than those who are the ultimate beneficiaries of the profession. Parents and students, working with teacher-leaders and a wide array of community-based organizations, can lead the public-engagement campaign necessary for our vision for the teachers of 2030 to become a reality.

Finally, *teachers* need to band together to *document their professional practice* and assemble both empirical evidence and compelling stories about what works in their classrooms and communities—and, therefore, what most matters for public policy. If teaching is to become the results-oriented profession that students truly deserve, then classroom practitioners, not just researchers and think tank analysts, must weigh in on what it means to be an effective teacher. Armed with inexpensive digital cameras and media training, effective teachers can begin to capture powerful images from their teaching and make strong connections between policy and pedagogy. We call on the growing numbers of new millennium teachers, who grew up on YouTube and digital media, to organize themselves via the Internet and spread a new message about excellent teaching—making the nuances of effective practice much more visible and understandable. The public, which has always had respect for teachers, will begin to pay attention as never before and invest in the profession in ways that make a difference for student learning.

Margaret Mead posed a simple claim with regard to social change: "Never doubt that a small group of thoughtful, committed citizens can change the world. Indeed, it is the only thing that ever has." While her postulate may seem a cliché after so many repetitions over the years, there's a reason for its staying power. *It rings true.* If teaching, by 2030, is to develop into the profession that the students of the new millennium deserve, small groups of committed people all over America must begin to lead the way.

And consider this: The dynamic potential of small-group leadership is a thousand times greater than in Mead's day. The connectivity made possible by the Internet and Web 2.0 tools is unprecedented and powerful. Of course it's true that many of the most promising leaders and activists are very busy people. Even so, consider the novel thinking about "cognitive surplus" offered by social networking experts Clay Shirky and Dan Pink. During the last half of the 20th century, they say, restless minds turned to television to "while away the hours." Today, minds hungry for engagement are turning to the Internet—and many of us are seeking out like-minded people to pursue causes we care about. By 2009, Pink and Shirky estimated, individuals and small groups had invested more than 100 million volunteer hours in the development of Wikipedia. Imagine the champions of teaching doing something similar. What might be accomplished?

Our writing team has begun to build an action agenda based on the ideas in this book—both at our *Teaching 2030* social website (www.teaching2030.org) and by connecting up with other policy-minded teacher groups like the Center for Teaching Quality's New Millennium Initiative (www.teachingquality.org). We are eager for teachers, parents, community activists, and everyone else who wants a great future for all kids in our public schools to join the conversation. Come to our website, share your ideas, and help us sharpen both the dialogue and the agenda. Pass this book along to colleagues. Use it as a discussion starter in book study groups. Blog and twitter about it. Let it spark your own thinking and best solutions about how we can move the teaching profession forward together.

Finally . . .

As the founder of an organization dedicated to elevating the voices of excellent teachers, **Barnett Berry** would like to give you the opportunity to eavesdrop on our team conversation as we transition from book writing to community-building and activism. Think of the comments below as the beginning of our interactive discourse with you and many others at the Teaching 2030 networking site. We hope to see you there and find ways to take action together.

Jose Vilson: As we continue this conversation about the future of teaching and learning, we need to keep in front of us the many social and economic, as well as education, policies of inequity that perpetuate the gaps between the haves and have-nots in our nation. We have high hopes that technology will help close the gap. But we must remember that *quantity* of access does not equal *quality* of access.

Remaking public education is about more than setting up social networking sites and employing ever-increasing cool tools of technology. It is about strengthening the pedagogical skills of all of us who teach students. If we do not focus on this core proposition we will have learned nothing from our exploration into Teaching 2030 and beyond.

Cindi Rigsbee: We are entering an era in education in which we finally have the tools in place that will enable students to learn in ways that are best for them, individually. We also have the capacity to utilize teacher talents, whatever they may be, so that educators can grow and flourish in a supportive environment. What we must strive for is recognition, both financially and in ways that promote leadership opportunities. We must "expect" respect for the job that leads to all other jobs. That goal that can only be reached once the world begins to look at teaching as a different profession than it was when our great-grandmothers taught school.

Jennifer Barnett: When I look out on the everyday world, it looks much the same as it did 20 years ago. But the way I and most everybody else thinks about the world has changed completely. Therefore, our world really must be different. In so many ways, this paradox defines our nation. We must look past the ordinary and see how profound the change is. Have we even stopped to wonder what "the new American mind" will do for our world? For our students and schools? What it's already doing?

Emily Vickery: Across the country's urban, suburban, and rural spectrums, the importance of a local community's role in educating and caring for its children will increase dramatically over the coming years. There may be celebration in that. Yet, there is also a caution. Let's remember that today's public schools are more segregated than when *Brown v. Board of Education* was decided more than 50 years ago. An intensified resurgence of neighborhood schools coupled with a rise in "greening practices" will diminish busing, bringing about an increase in segregated schools. This change in living and learning patterns may also lead to further racial, ethnic, and socioeconomic isolation, perhaps bringing a rise of intolerance with it. Grappling with growing cultural stratification will challenge those in the teaching profession even more. So, I ask, how can you engage your community and state leaders in the imperative of being vigilant and stemming the growth of segregated learning? How will you engage community leaders in ensuring equitable opportunities for all youth to learn from and contribute to a diverse population both locally and globally?

Carrie J. Kamm: I look out an inner-city school window and gaze at the chain link fence that surrounds an empty lot. Upon that empty lot once stood a tall housing project that has now been demolished. It has shaken our students and families, but I believe it has not shattered their hopes for full, purposeful lives. When our students and families are shaken and vulnerable, as teachers we need to help them remember their strength and support them as they learn to fight for themselves. We need to push back against those forces that crowd in on our most vulnerable students, by protecting them, but more importantly, by arming them with an education that will support them when they move beyond us.

Ariel Sacks: As Carrie's comments illustrate, the future is so uncertain for our students today. We cannot possibly equip them with all the factual knowledge they will need to meet the challenges we've yet to imagine. But we must teach them to look carefully, to problem solve critically, to work together, and to create new and better realities. The most essential step in accomplishing this mission is to set up structures that support teachers as critical thinkers and skillful problem solvers. Only then can our profession truly fulfill the charge of leading the nation's youth to meet the future with bravery, compassion, and innovation.

Shannon C'de Baca: The simple truth is that we are all part of the problem and all part of the solution. We know the world is changing and yet we hold on to an ineffective system of education because it is comfortable—and because any change in the system impacts so many other parts inside and outside of that system. Every school has some exceptionally talented and effective teachers who, rather than wait for more cohesive and focused leadership, are marching ahead against a tide of confusing directives and making a difference for their students. Their success and the amazing wisdom and sanity in their efforts are minimized by the structure of our school systems. Schools as we know them must change. The key is to find out what we want to do and to align our efforts so that we are moving in the same direction and not against each other. We must empower those on the front lines to innovate. The kids I see every day deserve something better.

John M. Holland: Maybe it is because I have always taught 4-year-olds that I see the future in the faces of small children. I have always felt the weight of the unintended consequences of decisions I make in my classroom. That's why we need to think about and create what we want education to be like in 2030—not next year, or in 5 years, or even 10 years from now. When we really think long-term about education, it will likely change our strategy and our approach. We need to start being proactive instead of reactive. It is the reactionary approach to adjusting policy based on what is happening now, instead of what we want to happen in the future, that has kept our schools in constant crisis. I once heard a former state superintendent say that if she could have gazed into the future and seen how state-level tests were going to make school such an unenjoyable place to be, she might not have made the decision to support them as much as she did.

Laurie Wasserman: I remember when I first wanted to become a teacher, I had a vision for myself of inspiring students, of helping young men and women reach their full potential as learners, of teaching them to honor their learning differences, and of finding ways to help them using their strengths. After 30 years of holding onto that dream, I've come to realize that it's not just what we as educators want to inspire in our students that counts, it's also our ability to respond to their own hopes for the future. It's respecting them fully as young people by giving them the tools they require for the best possible education. The same goes for the larger community. All adults need to invest in the best future for our students, with no more cuts in vital educational resources and full support for the professional growth of their teachers

Susie Highley: The accuracy of our vision for 2030 may ultimately depend upon who is in charge. While we may anticipate student self-directed learning, power struggles among local entities and state and federal governments will affect curricula, school structure, and more. This is why it is imperative for teacher leadership to take hold now. As educators, we need to find ways to demonstrate that we are indeed experts who deserve decision-making powers. We need to advocate for our students and our profession, so that our voices will be heard and acted upon. It is no longer enough to simply shut the classroom door and teach to the best of our abilities.

Renee Moore: We stand on the cusp of a great opportunity to end generations of educational discrimination and inequity, finally to fulfill the promises of our democratic republic. I believe the noblest teachers, students, and leaders of 2030 will be remembered by future generations as those who surged over the barriers to true public education and a fully realized teaching profession—while myopic former gatekeepers staggered to the sidelines of history.

The End

Notes

Prologue

1. KnowledgeWorks Foundation. (2006). *Map of future forces affecting education.* Retrieved September 9, 2009, from http://www.kwfdn.org/map/
2. Hargreaves, A. (2009). The fourth way of change: Towards an age of inspiration and sustainability. In A. Hargreaves & M. Fullan (Eds.), *Change wars* (p. 40). Bloomington, IN: Solution Tree.
3. Alvarez, R. (2009). *The Wire: Truth be told.* New York: Grove Press, p. 5.

Chapter 1

1. Prensky, M. (2001). *Digital natives, digital immigrants, part II: Do they really think differently?* Retrieved September 9, 2009, from http://www.rutherfordschools.org/rhs/social/hermitagefiles/Prensky2.pdf
2. Stone, B. (2010, January 9). The children of cyberspace: Old fogies by their 20s. *New York Times.* Retrieved March 4, 2010, from http://www.nytimes.com/2010/01/10/weekinreview/10stone.html?scp=1&sq=old%20fogies&st=cse
3. Pew Internet and American Life Project. (2010, February). *The future of the internet IV.* Washington, DC: Author. Retrieved March 2, 2010, from http://www.pewinternet.org/Reports/2010/Future-of-the-Internet-IV.aspx
4. Bowker. (2009, May 19). *Bowker reports US book production declines 3% in 2008, but "on demand" publishing more than doubles.* Retrieved March 2, 2009, from http://www.bowker.com/index.php/press-releases/563-bowker-reports-us-book-production-declines-3-in-2008-but-qon-demandq-publishing-more-than-doubles
5. Quitney, J., & Rainie, L. (2010, February 19). *The future of the internet.* Washington, DC: Pew Research Center's Internet and American Life Project. Retrieved March 4, 2010, from http://www.pewinternet.org/~/media//Files/Reports/2010/Future%20of%20internet%202010%20-%20AAAS%20paper.pdf, p. 10.
6. See http://www.q2l.org/node/13
7. Forum on Education and Democracy. (2008). *Democracy at risk: The need for a new federal policy in education.* Washington, DC: Author. Retrieved March 4, 2008, from http://www.google.com/url?sa=t&source=web&ct=res&cd=1&ved=0CAYQFjAA&url=http%3A%2F%2Fforumforeducation.org%2Ffiles%2Fu1%2FFED_ReportRevised415.pdf&rct=j&q=%22the+need+for+major+transformation%22%22forum+for+education+and+democracy%22&ei=kraPS5GkLo-YtgeH2_CgCw&usg=AFQjCNH_rIzfNwgamDO2a2CnihCFxmpsPw&sig2=FAhsvbm7ueENNLL-m5Cn9g
8. Dede, C. (2007, February). *Transforming education for the 21st century: New pedagogies that help all students attain sophisticated learning outcomes.* Raleigh, NC: Friday Institute.

215

9. Kurzweil proposes that nanotechnology will make it possible for "experience beamers" to transmit the entire flow of their sensory experiences to others via the web.

10. Martin, M. (2007, April 11). *My personal learning environment. The Bamboo Project.* Blog retrieved September 9, 2009, from http://michelemartin.typepad.com/thebambooprojectblog/2007/04/my_personal_lea.html

11. Hoffman, N. (2003). *Women's true profession: Voices from the history of teaching.* Cambridge: Harvard Education Press.

12. Bradley, A. (2000). The not-quite profession. In *Education Week* (Ed.), *Lessons of a century: A nation's schools come of age* (p. 2). Bethesda, MD: Editor.

13. Rheingold, H. (2002). *Smart mobs: The next social revolution.* Cambridge, MA: Basic Books.

14. Shirky, C. (2008). *Here comes everybody: The power of organizing without organizations.* New York: Penguin.

15. Hales, D. (2007, October). *Emergent networks as a distributed reputation system.* Lecture at Department of Computer Science, University of Bologna. Retrieved March 2, 2010, from http://videolectures.net/eccs07_hales_end/

16. Center for Teaching Quality. (2009). *The math and science leadership academy.* Retrieved March 4, 2010, from http://www.teachingquality.org/newsroom/node/588

17. Hu, W. (2009, June 8). Connecticut district tosses algebra textbooks and goes online. *New York Times.* Retrieved March 4, 2010, from http://www.nytimes.com/2009/06/08/education/08math.html

18. Lankford, H., Loeb, S., & Wyckoff, J. (2002). Teacher sorting and the plight of urban districts: A descriptive analysis. *Education Evaluation and Policy Analysis, 24*(1), 37–62.

19. Center for Social Organization of Schools. (2010). *The graduation gap.* Retrieved March 4, 2010, from http://web.jhu.edu/CSOS/graduation-gap/gradgap.html; Eduwonkette (2008, April 1). *AERA continued: Dropout factories.* Message posted to http://blogs.edweek.org/edweek/eduwonkette/2008/04/aera_continued_dropout_factori.html

20. Schofield, J. W. (1995). *Computers and classroom culture.* Cambridge, UK: Cambridge University Press.

21. Holley-Walker, D. (2008). Educating at the crossroads. *Ohio State Law Journal.* Retrieved March 4, 2010, from https://litigation-essentials.lexisnexis.com/webcd/app?action=DocumentDisplay&crawlid=1&doctype=cite&docid=69+Ohio+St.+L.J.+911&srctype=smi&srcid=3B15&key=b5ee864ed017e2125756eb105976d12a

22. Ladson-Billings, G., & Tate, W. F. (Eds.). (2006). *Education research in the public interest: Social justice, action, and policy.* New York: Teachers College Press.

23. Weiss, H. B., Little, P., Bouffard, S. M., Deschenes, S. N., & Malone, H. J. (2009). *The federal role in out-of-school learning: After-school, summer learning, and family involvement as critical learning supports.* Cambridge, MA: Harvard Family Research Project.

24. National Center for Education Statistics (2003), p. 11.

25. National Center for Education Statistics (2003), p. 11.

26. DeNavas-Walt, C., Proctor, B. D., & Lee, C. H. (2005). *Income, poverty and health insurance coverage in the United States, 2005.* Washington DC: U.S. Census Bureau.

27. Campaign to End Child Homelessness. (2010). Homepage. Retrieved March 4, 2010, from http://www.homelesschildrenamerica.org/

28. DeNavas-Walt, Proctor, & Lee (2005); at the completion of this manuscript major health care legislation was passed and the number of uninsured Americans may finally decrease, somewhat.

29. Herbert, B. (2010, February 8). The worst of pain. *New York Times.* Retrieved March 4, 2010, from http://www.nytimes.com/2010/02/09/opinion/09herbert. html?th&emc=th

30. Goodman, P. (2010, May 23). Cuts to child care subsidy thwart more job seekers. *New York Times.* Retrieved May 24, 2010, at http://www.nytimes.com/2010/05/24/business/economy/24childcare.html?th&emc=th

31. Zigler, E., Gilliam, W., & Jones, S. (2006). *A vision for universal preschool education.* Cambridge, UK: Cambridge University Press.

32. Institute of Educational Sciences. (2008). *Turning around chronically low-performing schools.* Washington, DC: U.S. Department of Education. Retrieved March 4, 2010, from http://74.125.47.132/search?q=cache:hncXU8vuaxEJ:ies.ed.gov/ncee/wwc/pdf/practiceguides/Turnaround_pg_04181.pdf+low+performing+schools+USDOE&cd=1&hl=en&ct=clnk&gl=us&client=safari

33. Darling-Hammond, L. (2010). *The flat world and education: How America's commitment to equity will determine our future.* New York: Teachers College Press.

34. Gladwell, M. (2000). *The tipping point: How little things can make a big difference.* New York: Little Brown.

35. Asia Society and Council of Chief State School Officers. (2010). *International perspectives on U.S. education policy and practice: What we can learn from high-performing nations?* Washington, DC: Author.

36. VUCA is an acronym initially coined by the Army War College to frame how the military made strategic decisions about training, leading, and stationing forces. The "Map of Future Forces Affecting Education" developed by KnowledgeWorks Foundation and the Institute for the Future has used the same concept to consider how policymakers, practitioners, and the public must respond to public schooling in the years ahead. The visionary thinkers at KWF and IFTF have been important influences on our work.

Chapter 2

1. Lortie, D. (1975). *Schoolteacher.* Chicago: University of Chicago Press.

2. Lortie (1975).

3. Bradley, A. (2000). The not-quite profession. *Education Week, 19*(2), 31–36.

4. Rousmaniere, K. (2005). In search of a profession: A history of American teachers. In D. Moss, W. Glenn, & R. Schwab (Eds.), *Portraits of a profession: Teaching and teachers in the 21st century* (pp. 1–26). Westport, CT: Praeger, p. 3.

5. Hoffman, N. (2003). *Women's true profession: Voices from the history of teaching.* Cambridge: Harvard Education Press.

6. Sedlak, M. W., & Schlossman, S. (1986). *Who will teach? Historical perspectives on the changing appeal of teaching as a profession.* Santa Monica, CA: Rand.

7. Sedlak & Schlossman (1986).

8. J. Fraser (personal communication, February 7, 2010).

9. Angus, D., & Mirel, J. (2001). *Professionalism and the public good: A brief history of teacher certification.* Washington, DC: Fordham Institute. Retrieved April 13, 2010, from http://www.edexcellence.net/doc/angus.pdf

10. Apple, M. W. (1985). Teaching and "women's work": A comparative historical and ideological analysis. *Teachers College Record, 86*(3), 445–473.

11. Clifford, G. J. (1989). Man/women/teacher: Gender, family, and career in American educational history. In D. Warren (Ed.), *American teachers: Histories of a profession at work* (pp. 293–343). New York: Macmillan; Rury, M. W. (1989). Who became

teachers? The social characteristics of teachers in American history. In D. Warren (Ed.), *American teachers: Histories of a profession at work* (pp. 9–48). New York: Macmillan.

12. Finkelstein, B. (1989). *Governing the young: Teacher behavior in popular primary schools in 19th century United States.* Philadelphia: Falmer Press.

13. Rousmaniere, K. (2005). *Citizen teacher: The life and leadership of Margaret Haley.* Albany: State University of New York Press.

14. J. Fraser (personal communication, February 7, 2010).

15. Angus & Mirel (2001).

16. Angus & Mirel (2001).

17. Elmore, R. (1996). Getting to scale with good educational practice. *Harvard Educational Review, 66*(1), 1–26.

18. Callahan, R. E. (1962). *Education and the cult of efficiency.* Chicago: University of Chicago Press, p. 81.

19. Callahan (1962).

20. Terman, L. (1916). *The measurement of intelligence: An explanation of and a complete guide for the use of the Stanford revision and extension of the Binet-Simon intelligence scale.* Boston: Houghton Mifflin.

21. Kridel, C., & Bullough, R. V. (2007). *Stories of the eight-year study: Reexamining secondary education in America.* Albany: State University of New York Press.

22. The "eight-year" reference reflects the study's focus on the relationship between what students experience in high school and college over the 8 years students typically spent in the respective educational institutions.

23. Butts, R. F., & Cremin, L. A. (1953). *A history of education in American culture.* New York: Holt, Rinehart and Winston.

24. Labaree, D. F. (2004). *The trouble with ed schools.* New Haven, CT: Yale University Press.

25. National Commission on Teacher Education and Professional Standards (TEPS). (1961). *Journey to now, 1946–1961: The first fifteen years of the professional standards movement in teaching as reflected in keynote addresses.* Washington, DC: National Education Association.

26. Toppo, G. (2007). Sputnik heralded space race, focus on learning. *USA Today.* Retrieved June 1, 2008, from http://www.manitowoc.org/vcb/New_Images/Sputnik%20-%20USA%20TODAY.htm

27. Fraser, J. W. (2007). *Preparing America's teachers: A history.* New York: Teachers College Press.

28. Sykes, G., & Dibner, K. (2009). *Fifty years of federal teacher policy: Looking back, looking ahead.* Washington DC: Center for Education Policy.

29. Coleman, J. S., Campbell, E., Hobson, C., McPartland, J., Mood, A., Weinfeld, F., & York, R. (1966). *Equality of educational opportunity.* Washington, DC: U.S. Government Printing Office.

30. MacPhail-Wilcox, B., & King, R. A. (1986). Resource allocation studies: Implications for school improvement and school finance research. *Journal of Human Resources, 11,* 416–432.

31. Wisconsin Center for Education Research. (2007). *Coleman report, forty years on.* Retrieved June 12, 2009, from http://www.wcer.wisc.edu/news/coverStories/coleman_report_40_years.php

32. Levine, D. U., & Lezotte, L. W. (1990). *Unusually effective schools: A review and analysis of research and practice.* Madison, WI: The National Center for Effective Schools Research & Development.

33. Angus & Mirel (2001).

34. Kahlenberg, R. D. (2008). Albert Shanker and the future of teacher unions. *Phi Delta Kappan, 89*(10), 712–720. Retrieved July 31, 2009, from http://www.pdkintl.org/kappan/k_v89/k0806kah.htm

35. Kahlenberg (2008).

36. Kerchner, C. T., & Koppich, J. (2007). Negotiating what matters most: Collective bargaining and student achievement. *American Journal of Education, 113*, 349–365.

37. Angus & Mirel (2001).

38. Waller, W. (1932). *The sociology of teaching.* New York: Russell & Russell.

39. Eberts, R. (2007). Teachers unions and student performance: Help or hindrance? *The future of children, 17*(1), 175–200.

40. Hess, F. M., & West, M. (2010). *A better bargain: Overhauling teacher collective bargaining for the 21st century.* Retrieved April 13, 2010, from http://www.hks.harvard.edu/pepg/PDF/Papers/BetterBargain.pdf

41. Eberts (2007).

42. Eberts (2007).

43. Angus & Mirel (2001).

44. Baratz-Snowden, J. (2009). *Fixing tenure: A proposal for assuring teacher effectiveness and due process.* Washington, DC: Center for American Progress.

45. *Phi Delta Kappan.* (1970). PDK/Gallup poll. *Phi Delta Kappan, 52*, 1–10.

46. Bradley (2000).

47. Johnson, S. M., Donaldson, M., Munger, M. S., Papay, J., & Qazilbash, E. K. (2009). *Leading the local: Teachers union presidents speak on change, challenges.* Washington DC: Education Sector.

48. Finn, C. E. (2003). High hurdles. *Education Next, 3*(2). Retrieved March 1, 2004, from http://educationnext.org/highhurdles/

49. Johnson, Donaldson, Munger, Papay, & Qazilbash (2009).

50. Gallup. (2009). *Honesty/ethics in the professions.* Retrieved March 16, 2010, from http://www.gallup.com/poll/1654/honesty-ethics-professions.aspx

51. *Education Week.* (2007, December 6). *Vouchers.* Retrieved March 16, 2010, from http://www.edweek.org/rc/issues/vouchers/; Gallup. (2009). *Public says better teachers are key to improved education.* Retrieved March 16, 2010, from http://www.gallup.com/poll/122504/Public-Says-Better-Teachers-Key-Improved-Education.aspx

52. Bushaw, W. J., & NcNee, J. A. (2009). *The 41st annual Phi Delta Kappa/Gallup poll of the public's attitudes toward public schools.* Bloomington, IN: Phi Delta Kappan International and Gallup.

53. National Commission on Excellence in Education. (1983). *A Nation at Risk.* Washington, DC: Author. Retrieved February 2, 2010, from http://www2.ed.gov/pubs/NatatRisk/index.html

54. Astin, A. W., Green, C. C., & Korn, W. S. (1987). *The American freshman: Twenty year trends.* New York: American Council of Education.

55. Carnegie Forum on Education and the Economy. (1986). *A nation prepared: Teachers for the 21st century.* Washington, DC: The Task Force on Teaching as a Profession, pp. 66–67.

56. Berry, B. (2007). *The National Board for Professional Teaching Standards and the future of a profession.* Arlington, VA: NBPTS.

57. National Commission on Teaching and America's Future. (1996). *What matters most: Teaching for America's future.* New York: Author.

58. Dillon, S. (2010, February 7). With federal stimulus money gone, many schools face budget gaps. *New York Times.* Retrieved February 8, 2010, from http://www.cbpp.org/cms/index.cfm?fa=view&id=2220; Johnson, N., Koulish, J., & Oliff, P. (2009). *Most*

states are cutting education. Center on Budget and Policy Priorities. Retrieved February 8, 2010, from http://www.nytimes.com/2010/02/08/education/08educ.html

59. McMurrer, J. (2007). *Implementing the No Child Left Behind teacher requirements*. Washington, DC: Center for Education Policy.

60. Ingersoll, R. (2008). *Core problems: Out-of-field teaching persists in key academic courses and high-poverty schools*. Washington, DC: Education Trust. Retrieved March 8, 2009, from http://www.edtrust.org/sites/edtrust.org/files/publications/files/SASSreportCoreProblems.pdf

61. Darling-Hammond, L. (2006). Constructing 21st-century teacher education. *Journal of Teacher Education, 57*(3), 300–314.

62. Finn, C., & Wilcox, D. (1999, August 9). *Board games: Failure of National Board for Professional Teaching Standards to accomplish objective of improving quality of teaching in the US*. Retrieved June 30, 2008, from http://www.edexcellence.net/foundation/publication/publication.cfm?id=161

63. Heilig, J. V., & Jez, S. J. (2010). *Teach for America: A review of the evidence*. Boulder, CO: Education and the Public Interest Center & Tempe, AZ: Education Policy Research Unit. Retrieved June 1, 2010, from http://epicpolicy.org/publication/teach-for-america

64. Feistritzer, E. (2010, February). *Alternative routes to teacher certification*. Paper presented at the annual meeting of the American Association of Colleges of Teacher Education, Atlanta, GA.

65. Chait, R., & McLaughlin, M. (2009). *Realizing the promise: How state policy can support alternative certification programs*. Washington, DC: Center for American Progress.

66. Humphrey, D. C., & Wechsler, M. E. (2007). *Characteristics of effective alternative teacher certification*. Menlo Park, CA: SRI International; Humphrey, D. C., & Wechsler, M. E. (2005, September 2). Insights into alternative certification: Initial findings from a national study. *Teachers College Record*. Retrieved September 14, 2005, from http://www.tcrecord.org [ID Number: 12145].

67. Gitomer, D. (2007). *Teacher quality in a changing policy landscape: Improvements in the teacher pool*. Princeton, NJ: Education Testing Service.

68. National Research Council. (2010). *Preparing teachers: Building evidence for sound policy*. Washington, DC: Author. Retrieved June 1, 2010, from http://www.nap.edu/catalog.php?record_id=12882#description

69. Finn, C. (2003). High hurdles. *Education Next*. Retrieved September 1, 2009, from http://www.educationnext.org/20032/62.html

70. Democrats for Education Reform. (2007). *Statement of principles*. Retrieved May 1, 2010, from http://www.dfer.org/2007/11/statement_of_pr.php#more

71. Dede, C. (2010). *Transforming schooling via the 2010 National Educational Technology Plan*. New York: Teachers College Press. Retrieved July 21, 2010, from http://www.tcrecord.org/Content.asp?ContentID=15998

72. Winerip, M. (2010). A popular principal, wounded by government's good intentions. *New York Times*. Retrieved July 19, 2010, from http://www.nytimes.com/2010/07/19/education/19winerip.html?_r=1&th&emc=th

73. Braun, H. (2005). *Using student progress to evaluate teachers: A primer on value-added models*. Princeton, NJ: Education Testing Service; McCaffrey, D. M., Lockwood, J. R., Mariano, L., & Setodji, C. (2005). Challenges for value-added assessment of teacher effects. In R. Lissitz (Ed.), *Value added models in education: Theory and applications* (pp. 111–144). Maple Grove, MN: JAM Press; Sass, T. R. (2008, November). *The stability of value-added measures of teacher quality and implications for teacher compensation policy*.

Retrieved January 21, 2010, from http://www.caldercenter.org/partners/florida.cfm.

74. Springer, M. G., Ballou, D., Hamilton, L., Le, V., Lockwood, J. R., McCaffrey, D., Pepper, M., & Stecher, B. (2010). *Teacher pay for performance: Experimental evidence from the Project on Incentives in Teaching.* Nashville, TN: National Center on Performance Incentives at Vanderbilt University.

75. Sawchuk, S. (2010). NEA's Delegates Votes "No Confidence" in Race to the Top. *Education Week.* Retrieved July 21, 2010, from http://blogs.edweek.org/edweek/teacherbeat/2010/07/neas_delegates_vote_no_confide_2.html

Chapter 3

1. Rosenbaum, S. (2009, January 4). *5 trends that will change media in '09.* Retrieved March 15, 2010, from http://www.huffingtonpost.com/steve-rosenbaum/5-trends-that-will-change_b_155119.html

2. Bridgeland, J., Dilulio, J., & Morison, K. (2006). *The silent epidemic: Perspectives of high school dropouts.* Washington, DC: Civic Enterprises.

3. Pew Internet and American Life Project. (2010, February). *The future of the internet IV.* Washington, DC: Author. Retrieved March 2, 2010, from http://www.pewinternet.org/Reports/2010/Future-of-the-Internet-IV.as

4. Oracle Education Foundation Thinkquest. (2010). Homepage. Retrieved March 15, 2010, from http://www.thinkquest.org/en/

5. Edutopia. (2010). *Digital media empower youth.* Retrieved March 16, 2010, from http://www.edutopia.org/digital-generation-youth-network-video

6. Rheingold, H. (2010). *Invite to the community of practice.* Retrieved March 16, 2010, from http://socialmediaclassroom.com/index.php/invitation-to-the-community-of-practice

7. Owston, R. (2009). Digital immersion, teacher learning and games. *Educational Researcher, 38*(4), 270–273.

8. The River City Project. (2009). Homepage. Retrieved on December 31, 2009, from http://muve.gse.harvard.edu/rivercityproject/curriculum.htm

9. Tapscott, D. (2010, March 4). *Teaching kids democratic values.* Retrieved March 16, 2010, from http://dontapscott.com/2010/03/04/teaching-kids-democratic-values/

10. The Education Arcade. (2008). *About the Education Arcade.* Retrieved March 15, 2010, from http://www.educationarcade.org/about

11. Facebook. (2010). *Statistics.* Retrieved March 16, 2010, from http://www.facebook.com/press/info.php?statistics

12. Alpert, J., & Hajaj, N. (2008, July 25). *We knew the web was big . . .* Retrieved March 16, 2010, from http://googleblog.blogspot.com/2008/07/we-knew-web-was-big.html

13. comScore. (2010, February 11). *comScore releases January 2010 U.S. search engine rankings.* Retrieved March 16, 2010, from http://www.comscore.com/Press_Events/Press_Releases/2010/2/comScore_Releases_January_2010_U.S._Search_Engine_Rankings

14. Wikipedia. (2010). *Google Books.* Retrieved March 16, 2010, from http://en.wikipedia.org/wiki/Google_Books

15. Siegler, M. G. (2009, May 20). *Every minute, just about a day's worth of video is uploaded to Youtube.* Retrieved March 16, 2010, from http://techcrunch.com/2009/05/20/every-minute-just-about-a-days-worth-of-video-is-uploaded-to-youtube/

16. Radwanick, S. (2010, February 8). *The 2009 digital year in review.* Retrieved March 16, 2010, from http://www.comscore.com/Press_Events/Presentations_Whitepapers/2010/The_2009_U.S._Digital_Year_in_Review

17. Executive Office of the President Council of Economic Advisers. (2009, July). *Preparing the workers of today for the jobs of tomorrow.* Washington DC: Author. Retrieved March 16, 2010, from http://www.whitehouse.gov/assets/documents/Jobs_of_the_Future.pdf

18. Ferriter, B. (2009, March 13). *Do something funny for money day.* Retrieved March 16, 2010, from http://docs.google.com/Doc?id=dgq5xrkg_175ft5tgbfk

19. *Powering your classroom with the iPad, part 2.* (2010, April 4). Retrieved April 7, 2010, at http://misterteacher.blogspot.com/

20. Gladwell, M. (2007). *Blink: The power of thinking without thinking.* New York: Little, Brown and Company.

21. Siemens, G. (2004, December 12). *Connectivism: A learning theory for the digital age.* Retrieved March 16, 2010, from http://www.elearnspace.org/Articles/connectivism.htm

22. Siemens, G. (2010, February 16). *Teaching in social and technological networks.* Retrieved March 16, 2010, from http://www.connectivism.ca/?p=220

23. United States Department of Education. (2010). *Transforming American education: Learning powered by technology.* Office of Education Technology. Retrieved June 30, 2010, from http://www.ed.gov/sites/default/files/NETP-2010-final-report.pdf

24. Darling-Hammond, L., & Rustique-Forrester, E. (2005). The consequences of student testing for teaching and teacher quality. In J. Herman & E. Haertel (Eds.), *The uses and misuses of data in accountability testing* (pp. 289–319). Malden, MA: Blackwell; Diamond, J., & Spillane, J. (2002). *High stakes accountability in urban elementary schools: Challenging or reproducing inequality?* Evanston, IL: Northwestern University Institute for Policy Research.

25. Darling-Hammond, L. (2010). *The flat world and education: How America's commitment to equity will determine our future.* New York: Teachers College Press.

26. Darling-Hammond, L. (2010). *The flat world and education.*

27. California Department of Education. (2009). 2003 through 2008 CST released test questions. Retrieved March 16, 2010, from http://www.cde.ca.gov/ta/tg/sr/css05rtq.asp

28. Silva, R. (2008, November 10). *Measuring skills for the 21st century.* Washington, DC: Education Sector. Retrieved March 16, 2010, from http://www.educationsector.org/research/research_show.htm?doc_id=716323

29. *USA Today.* (2010). Education Dept. to give $350M to states that revamp testing. Retrieved April 7, 2010, from http://www.usatoday.com/news/education/2010-04-06-school-tests_N.htm

30. Darling-Hammond, L., & Wentworth, L. (2010). *Benchmarking learning systems: Student performance assessment in international context.* Stanford, CA: Stanford University, Stanford Center for Opportunity Policy in Education.

31. Center on Education Policy. (2007, July). *Choices, changes, and challenges: Curriculum and instruction in the NCLB era.* Washington, DC: Author.

32. Hoffman, J. V., Assaf, L. C., & Paris, S. G. (2001). High stakes testing in reading: Today in Texas, tomorrow? *The Reading Teacher, 54*(5), 482–492.

33. Silva (2008, November 10).

34. Public Broadcasting System. (2008, February 18). *The new business of education—Standardized testing.* Retrieved March 18, 2010, from http://www.pbs.org/nbr/site/onair/transcripts/080218a/

35. Ferriter, B. (2009, June 21). *Assessing learning the Danish way . . .* Retrieved March 16, 2010, from http://teacherleaders.typepad.com/the_tempered_radical/2009/06/assessing-learning-the-danish-way.html#more

36. Darling-Hammond (2010), *The flat world and education*, p. 70.

37. Forum for Education and Democracy. (2009). *Investing in a culture of learning.* Washington, DC: Author. Retrieved March 16, 2010, from http://forumforeducation. org/files/u48/Learning_Brief_010410.pdf

38. Organisation for Economic Co-operation and Development, Programme for International Student Assessment. (2006). *PISA 2006: Science competencies for tomorrow's world.* Paris: Author; Schmidt, W. (2008, Spring). What's missing from math standards: Focus, rigor and coherence. *American Educator.* Retrieved April 1, 2008, from http:// www.aft.org/pubs-reports/american_educator/issues/spring2008/Schmidt.htm

39. Hamilton, N. K. (1966). What can be done about the Carnegie Unit? *Educational Leadership.* Retrieved March 16, 2010, from http://www.ascd.org/ASCD/pdf/ journals/ed_lead/el_196601_hamilton.pdf

40. Robelen, E. W. (2010, February 9). Work begins on "next generation" of science standards. *Education Week.* Retrieved March 16, 2010, from http://www.edweek.org/ ew/articles/2010/02/10/21science.h29.html

41. Darling-Hammond, L. (2010). *Performance counts: Assessment systems that support high quality learning.* Washington, DC: CCSSO.

42. Vrasidas, C., & Zembylas, M. (2004). Online professional development lessons from the field. *Education and Training, 46,* 326–334.

43. Charalambos, V., Michalinos, Z., & Chamberlain, R. (2004). The design of online learning communities: Critical issues. *Educational Media International, 41,* 135–143.

44. Owston, R. (2009). Digital immersion, teacher learning and games. *Educational Researcher, 38*(4), 270–273.

45. Gloor, P. A. (2006). *Swarm creativity.* Oxford, UK: Oxford University Press; Williams, W. M., & Yang, L. T. (1999). Organizational creativity. In R. J. Sternberg (Ed.), *Handbook of creativity* (pp. 373–391). Cambridge, UK: Cambridge University Press.

46. Virtual Pioneers. (2010). Homepage. Retrieved March 16, 2010, from http:// virtualpioneers.ning.com/

47. Guzdial, M., Rick, J., & Kehoe, C. (2001). Beyond adoption to invention: Teacher-created collaborative activities in higher education. *Journal of the Learning Sciences, 10,* 265–279.

48. TeachScape. (2010). Homepage. Retrieved March 16, 2010, from http://www. teachscape.com/html/ts/nps/index.html

49. TeachScape. (2010).

50. Teachers.TV. (2010). *Teachers TV and me.* Retrieved March 16, 2010, from http:// www.teachers.tv/testimonials

51. Dede, C., Nelson, B., Ketelhut, D., Clarke, J., & Bowman, C. (2004). Design-based research strategies for studying situated learning in a multi-user virtual environment. In Y. Kafai, N. Enyedy, & B. Sandoval (Eds.), *Proceedings of the Sixth International Conference on the Learning Sciences* (pp. 158–165). Mahwah, NJ: Lawrence Erlbaum.

52. Bransford, J. D., Brown, A. L., & Cocking, R. R. (Eds.). (2000). Learning: From speculation to science. In *How people learn: Brain, mind, experience, and school* (pp. 3–27). Washington, DC: National Academy Press.

53. Institute for the Future. (2010). Homepage. Retrieved March 16, 2010, from http://iftf.org/

54. Jackson, C. K., & Bruegmann, E. (2009, July). *Teaching students and teaching each other: The importance of peer learning for teachers* [NBER Working Paper 15202]. Cambridge, MA: National Bureau of Economic Research.

55. Viadero, D. (2009). Top-notch teachers found to affect peers. *Education Week.*

Retrieved September 1, 2009, at http://www.edweek.org/ew/articles/2009/09/01/03peer.html?tkn=VQ[F91pv4%2Fm1H05QrumV3xEwIqnZkr5Dl8iG

56. The Quantified Self. (2010). Homepage. Retrieved March 16, 2010, from http://www.kk.org/quantifiedself/

Chapter 4

1. Cowan, K. (2009, January/February). Learning across distance. *Harvard Education Letter.* Retrieved March 22, 2010, from http://www.hepg.org/hel/printarticle/170

2. Christensen, C., Horne, M., & Johnson, C. (2008). *Disrupting class: How disruptive innovation will change the way the world learns.* New York: McGraw-Hill.

3. Christensen, C., & Horne, M. (2009). Revolution in the classroom. *Atlantic Monthly.* Retrieved January 5, 2010, from http://www.theatlantic.com/doc/200908u/race-to-the-top-education

4. Lohr, S. (2009, August 19). Study finds that online education beats the classroom. Retrieved March 22, 2010, from http://bits.blogs.nytimes.com/2009/08/19/study-finds-that-online-education-beats-the-classroom/?ref=education

5. Quitney, J., & Rainie, L. (2010, February 19). *The future of the internet.* Washington, DC: Pew Research Center's Internet and American Life Project. Retrieved March 4, 2010, from http://www.pewinternet.org/~/media//Files/Reports/2010/Future%20of%20internet%202010%20-%20AAAS%20paper.pdf, p. 13.

6. Graft, K. (2010, February 18). Zynga's Reynolds on "social" first and foremost. Retrieved March 22, 2010, from http://www.gamasutra.com/view/news/27310/DICE_2010_Zyngas_Reynolds_On_Social_First_And_Foremost.php

7. Dieterle, E., & Clarke, J. (in press). Multi-user virtual environments for teaching and learning. In M. Pagani (Ed.), *Encyclopedia of multimedia technology and networking* (2nd ed.). Hershey, PA: Idea Group.

8. Wikipedia. (2010). *Farmville.* Retrieved March 22, 2010, from http://en.wikipedia.org/wiki/FarmVille

9. Harvard Graduate School of Education. (2004, August 1). *Engaging viewers, virtually.* Retrieved March 22, 2010, from http://www.gse.harvard.edu/news/features/dede08012004.html

10. Digital Inspiration. (2009, May 30). *Web 3.0 concepts explained in plain English.* Retrieved March 22, 2010, from http://www.labnol.org/internet/web-3-concepts-explained/8908/

11. Kamenetz, A. (2010, April 1). *A is for app: How smartphones, handheld computer sparked an educational revolution.* Retrieved April 4, 2010, from http://www.fasteconomy.com/magazine/144/a-is-for-app.html

12. Educause. (2009, February 13). *7 things you should know about QR codes.* Retrieved April 4, 2010, from http://www.educause.edu/ELI/7thingsyoushouldknowaboutQRcod/163728

13. KnowledgeWorks Foundation. (2010). *Map of future forces affecting education.* Retrieved March 22, 2010, from http://www.kwfdn.org/map/

14. KnowledgeWorks Foundation. (2010). *How can you take action?* Retrieved March 22, 2010, from http://www.futureofed.org/taking-action/

15. Lefkowits, L., & Diamond, B. (2009). *Transforming urban education: Implications for state policymakers.* Cincinnati: KnowledgeWorks Foundation. Retrieved March 22, 2010, from http://www.futureofed.org/pdf/taking-action/PolicyBrief1.pdf

16. KnowledgeWorks Foundation. (2006). *Appendix A: 2006–2016 KWF/IFTF map of future forces affecting education.* Retrieved March 22, 2010, from http://www.ucucc.org/

Interim/Appendixes/A.%20%20KWF-IFIF%20Map%20of%20Future%20Forces%20
Affecting%20Education.pdf

17. Peck, D. (2010, March). How a new jobless era will transform America. *Atlantic Monthly.* Retrieved March 22, 2010, from http://www.theatlantic.com/doc/201003/jobless-america-future

18. Hindery, R. (2010, March 15). Pink slips sent to thousands of California teachers. *Business Week.* Retrieved March 16, 2010, from http://www.businessweek.com/ap/financialnews/D9EFBE3G0.htm

19. Peck (2010).

20. Lefkowits & Diamond (2009).

21. Moe, T., & Chubb, J. (2009). *Liberating learning: Technology, politics and the future of American education.* San Francisco: Jossey-Bass.

22. Moe, T., & Chubb, J. (2009). An interview with Terry Moe and John Chubb, authors of *Liberating Learning: Technology, Politics and the Future of American Education.* Retrieved March 22, 2010, from http://www.liberatinglearning.org/?page_id=20

23. Coalition for Community Schools. (2010). Homepage. Retrieved January 31, 2010, from http://www.communityschools.org/

24. Lefkowits & Diamond (2009).

25. Harlem Children's Zone. (2010). *100 blocks, one bright future.* Retrieved March 22, 2010, from http://www.hcz.org/about-us/the-hcz-project

26. Schorn, D. (2006, May 14). *How one man's vision to revitalize Harlem starts with children.* Retrieved March 22, 2010, from http://www.cbsnews.com/stories/2006/05/11/60minutes/main1611936.shtml

27. Wald, D. (2009, December 18). *Bonus video: Sopori, the little rich school.* Retrieved March 22, 2010, from http://learningmatters.tv/blog/featured/schools-in-the-recession-bonus-video-sopori-the-poor-little-rich-school/3644/

28. The National Commission on Excellence in Education. (1983, April). *A nation at risk.* Washington, DC: Author. Retrieved February 7, 2010, from http://www2.ed.gov/pubs/NatAtRisk/index.html

29. Steele, S., Quitney, J., & Rainie, L. (2010, February 19). *The future of the internet IV.* Retrieved March 1, 2010, from http://pewinternet.org/Reports/2010/Future-of-the-Internet-IV/Part-2Reading.aspx?r=1, p. 21.

30. Steele, Quitney, & Rainie (2010), p. 21.

31. National School Boards Association. (2007, July). *Creating and connecting: Research and guidelines on online social—and educational—networking.* Retrieved March 1, 2009, from http://www.nsba.org/site/docs/41400/41340.pdf

32. Rheingold, H. (2002). *Smart mobs: The next social revolution.* Cambridge, MA: Basic Books.

33. Used among friends, "Bonjou konpè-m" means *hello* in Haitian Creole.

Chapter 5

1. Marvel, J., Lyter, D. M., Peltola, P., Strizek, G. A., & Morton, B. A. (2007). *Teacher attrition and mobility: Results from the 2004–05 Teacher Follow-up Survey.* Washington, DC: NCES. Retrieved September 9, 2009, from http://nces.ed.gov/pubs2007/2007307.pdf

2. Boyd, D. B., et al. (2009). *Who leaves? Teacher attrition and student achievement* [CALDER Working Paper 23]. Washington, DC: National Center for Analysis of Longitudinal Data in Education Research; Goldhaber, D., Gross, B., & Player, D. (2008). *Are public schools really losing their best? Assessing the career transitions of teachers and their implications for the quality of the teacher workforce* [CALDER Working Paper 12].

Washington, DC: National Center for Analysis of Longitudinal Data in Education Research; Hanushek, E. A., et al. (2005). *The market for teacher quality* [NBER Working Paper 11154]. Cambridge: National Bureau of Economic Research.

3. Marvel, Lyter, Peltola, Strizek, & Morton (2007).

4. Berry, B. (2009). *Children of poverty deserve great teachers: One union's commitment to challenge the status quo.* Washington, DC: The National Education Association. Retrieved September 9, 2009, from http://www.teacherleaders.org/sites/default/files/CTQ-NEA%20Report%20Final.pdf

5. Betlach, K. (2008). *Teaching in the 408.* Retrieved September 9, 2009, from http://roomd2.blogspot.com/

6. Rockoff, J. (2003). *The impact of individual teachers on student achievement: evidence from panel data.* Retrieved on December 1, 2009, from http://ideas.repec.org/p/wpa/wuwppe/0304002.html

7. Hess, R. (2008). *The human capital challenge: Towards a 21st century teaching profession.* Paper prepared for the Gates Foundation.

8. Odden, A., & Kelly, J. (2008). *Strategic management of human capital in public education.* Madison, WI: CPRE.

9. See Drew Gitomer's recent analyses of the improved academic ability of teacher education candidates and graduates at http://www.ets.org/Media/Education_Topics/pdf/TQ_full_report.pdf

10. Thomas, E., & Wingert, P. (2010, March 6). Why we must fire bad teachers. *Newsweek.* Retrieved March 18, 2010, from http://www.newsweek.com/id/234590

11. Futernick, K. (2010). *Incompetent teachers or dysfunctional systems? Re-framing the debate on teacher quality and accountability.* San Francisco: WestEd.

12. Consortium for Policy Research in Education. (2008). *Strategic management of human capital case studies.* Madison, WI: Author.

13. Educational Testing Service. (2007). *Teacher quality in a changing policy landscape: Improvements in the teacher pool.* Princeton, NJ: Author.

14. Thomas & Wingert (2010, March 6).

15. Cohen, D. (2010). *Thanks for the test scores.* Retrieved March 30, 2010, from http://accomplishedcaliforniateachers.wordpress.com/2010/03/26/thanks-for-the-test-scores/

16. Wise, A. (2004, September 29). Teaching teams: A 21st-century paradigm for organizing America's schools. *Education Week, 24*(5), 32–44.

17. KnowledgeWorks Foundation. (2009). *2020 forecast: Creating the future of learning.* Retrieved March 11, 2010, from http://www.futureofed.org/forecast/

18. Public Agenda. (2007). *Lessons learned: New teachers talk about their jobs, challenges, and long range plans.* Washington, DC: Author. Retrieved April 13, 2010, from http://www.google.com/url?sa=t&source=web&ct=res&cd=1&ved=0CAoQFjAA&url=http%3A%2F%2Fpublicagenda.org%2Ffiles%2Fpdf%2Flessons_learned_2.pdf&rct=j&q=%22public+agenda%22%222007%22%22alternative+certification%22&ei=c3jES7SPNMT68AaKps2yDw&usg=AFQjCNGbdckOADL_-9MDnZ0s9AI-xfIzRA&sig2=qIhpnkhqZSLlycEtUDaEWw

19. Betlach (2008).

20. National school standards, at last. (2010, March 13). *New York Times.* Retrieved April 6, 2010, from http://www.nytimes.com/2010/03/14/opinion/14sun1.html

21. Levine, A. (2006). *Educating school teachers.* Washington, DC: Education Schools Project.

22. Newton, X. (2010). *Teacher effectiveness and pathways into teaching in California.* Berkeley: University of California-Berkeley.

23. J. Synder (personal communication, April 4, 2010)

24. Murnane, R., & Cohen, D. (1986, February). Merit pay and the evaluation problem: Why most merit pay plans fail and a few survive. *Harvard Educational Review, 56,* 1–17; Cuban, L., & Tyack, D. (2000, Summer). Merit pay: Lessons from history. *Rethinking schools, 14*(3), http://www.rethinkingschools.org/restrict.asp?path=archive/14_03/hist143.shtml

25. Springer, M. G., et al. (2010). *Teacher pay for performance.* Nashville, TN: National Center on Performance Incentives at Vanderbilt University.

26. Darling-Hammond, L. (2010). *The flat world and education: How America's commitment to equity will determine our future.* New York: Teachers College Press.

27. TED. (2009, August). *Dan Pink on the surprising science of motivation* [Video]. Retrieved September 10, 2009, from http://www.ted.com/talks/dan_pink_on_motivation.html

28. TED. (2009, August).

29. Lawler, E. (2008). *Strategic talent management: Lessons from the corporate world.* Madison: University of Wisconsin–Madison, SMHC.

30. Center for Teaching Quality. (2007). *Performance-pay for teachers. Designing a system that students deserve.* Retrieved September 9, 2009, from http://www.teachingquality.org/legacy/TSP4P2008.pdf

31. Think about Chiron, the centaur, who taught Jason, Heracles, Ajax, and Percy Jackson. This mythical teacher represented all things wise, kind, and equitable. He was noble, and his ability to teach allowed him to become immortal, earning him a place in the constellations.

Chapter 6

1. Hess, R. (2008). The supply side of school reform. In R. Hess (Ed.), *The future of educational entrepreneurship: Possibilities for school reform* (pp. 1–21). Cambridge, MA: Harvard Education Press.

2. Hess (2008).

3. Smith, K., & Petersen, J. L. (2006). What is educational entrepreneurship? Retrieved March 15, 2010, from http://www.newschools.org/files/EducationalEntrepreneurship.pdf

4. Seligman, M. (1991). *Learned optimism: How to change your mind and your life.* New York: Knopf.

5. Hassel, B. (2008). Attracting entrepreneurs to K–12. In R. Hess (Ed.), *The future of educational entrepreneurship: Possibilities for school reform* (pp. 45–64). Cambridge, MA: Harvard Education Press.

6. Dede, C. (2010). *Transforming schooling via the 2010 National Educational Technology Plan.* New York: Teachers College Press. Retrieved July 21, 2010, from http://www.tcrecord.org/Content.asp?ContentID=15998

7. Hess (2008).

8. Hu, W. (2009, November 14). Selling lessons online raises cash and questions. *New York Times.* Retrieved March 15, 2010, from http://www.nytimes.com/2009/11/15/education/15plans.html?_r=1&ref=us

9. Hu (2009, November 14).

10. Teachers Pay Teachers. (2010). Homepage. Retrieved March 15, 2010, from http://www.teacherspayteachers.com

11. We Are Teachers. (2010). *Management team and board of directors.* Retrieved March 15, 2010, from http://www.weareteachers.com/web/corporate/about

12. The other four pillars are an inspiring and inclusive vision, public engagement, no achievement without investment, and corporate educational responsibility.

13. Hargreaves, A. (2009). The fourth way of change: Towards an age of inspiration and sustainability. In A. Hargreaves & M. Fullan (Eds.), *Change wars*. Bloomington, IN: Solution Tree.

14. Available at http://lessonplans.blogs.nytimes.com/2008/09/09/teaching-the-government-down-the-road/?scp=1&sq=%22ken%20bernstein%22&st=cse

15. Cody, A. (2010, April 3). *From Facebook to YouTube, a teacher movement is born*. Retrieved April 13, 2010, from http://blogs.edweek.org/teachers/living-in-dialogue/2010/04/from_facebook_to_youtube_a_tea.html

16. Pesce, M. (2008, December 11). *Inflection points*. Retrieved September 9, 2009, from http://blog.futurestreetconsulting.com/?m=200812

17. Pesce, M. (2008). *Fluid learning*. Retrieved March 15, 2010, from http://blog.futurestreetconsulting.com/?p=94

Chapter 7

1. Lortie, D. (1975). *Schoolteacher*. Chicago: University of Chicago Press.

2. Education Testing Services. (2002). *A national priority: Americans speak on teacher quality*. Princeton, NJ: Author; Public Education Network. (2004). *Demanding quality public education in tough economic times: What voters want from elected leaders*. Washington, DC: Author; The Teaching Commission. (2005). *America's commitment to quality teaching in the public schools: A national survey conducted by Hart-Harris*. New York: Author.

3. Bushaw, W. J., & NcNee, J. A. (2009). *The 41st annual Phi Delta Kappa/Gallup poll of the public's attitudes toward public schools*. Bloomington, IN: Phi Delta Kappan International and Gallup.

4. Hess, F. M. (2007, February). *No Child Left Behind: What the public thinks*. Retrieved March 14, 2010, from http://www.aei.org/outlook/25667

5. Kristof, N. D. (2009, March 21). Education's ground zero. *New York Times*. Retrieved March 14, 2010, from http://www.nytimes.com/2009/03/22/opinion/22kristof.html?_r=2; Brooks, D. (2008, December 5). Who will he choose? *New York Times*. Retrieved March 14, 2010, from http://www.nytimes.com/2008/12/05/opinion/05brooks.html; Thomas, E., & Wingert, P. (2010, March 6). Why we must fire bad teachers: In no other profession are workers so insulated from accountability. *Newsweek*. Retrieved on March 6, 2010, from http://www.newsweek.com/id/234590

6. Goldberg, J. (2009, September 12). *Teacher tenure must go*. Retrieved January 4, 2010, from www.unionleader.com

7. Stevenson, R. (2009, September 6). Shake the government's helping hand. Or bite it. *New York Times*. Retrieved on September 6, 2009, from http://www.nytimes.com/2009/09/06/weekinreview/06stevenson.html?_r=1&scp=1&sq=&st=nyt

8. MetLife. (2009). *MetLife survey of the American teacher: Collaborating for student success*. New York: Author.

9. Grant, G., & Murray, C. (1999). *Teaching in America: The slow revolution*. Cambridge, MA: Harvard University Press.

10. Lortie, D. (1975). *Schoolteacher: A sociological study*. Chicago: University of Chicago Press.

11. Gallup. (2008). *Honesty/ethics in professions*. Retrieved September 9, 2009, from http://www.gallup.com/poll/1654/honesty-ethics-professions.aspx

12. Harris Poll. (2008). *Prestige paradox: High pay doesn't necessarily equal high pres-*

tige. Retrieved June 1, 2009, from http://www.harrisinteractive.com/harris_poll/index.asp?PID=939

13. Gladwell, M. (2000). *The tipping point: How little things can make a big difference.* New York: Little Brown.

14. National Center for Education Statistics. (2008). *The condition of education 2008* (Indicator 35). Washington, DC: U.S. Department of Education.

15. Darling-Hammond, L. (2010). *The flat world and education: How America's commitment to equity will determine our future.* New York: Teachers College Press.

16. Phi Delta Kappan. (2009). *Americans speak out: Are educators and policymakers listening?* Bloomington, IN: Author.

17. Prante, G. (2007, June 30). *K–12 spending more reliant on federal government since No Child Left Behind act.* Retrieved March 14, 2010, from http://www.taxfoundation.org/research/show/22519.html

18. Viadero, D. (2008, December 2). Study calls for tightly tying funding to strategic goals. *Education Week.* Retrieved March 14, 2010, from http://www.edweek.org/ew/articles/2008/12/02/15finance.h28.html?tmp=1471072516

19. Darling-Hammond (2010); Consortium for Policy Research in Education. (2007*). School finance inequities.* Retrieved March 14, 2010, from http://cpre.wceruw.org/finance/inequities.php

20. Darling-Hammond (2010). *The flat world and education.*

21. Hanushek, E., & Raymond, M. (2003). Improving educational quality: How best to evaluate our schools? In Y. Kodrzycki (Ed.), *Education in the 21st century: Meeting the challenges of a changing world* (pp. 193–224). Boston, MA: Federal Reserve Bank of Boston.

22. Darling-Hammond (2010). *The flat world and education.*

23. National Working Group on Funding Student Learning. (2008, October). *Funding student learning: How to align education resources with student learning goals.* Bothell, WA: School Finance Redesign Project. Retrieved March 14, 2010, from http://www.crpe.org/cs/crpe/download/csr_files/pub_sfrp_wrkgrp_oct08.pdf

24. Wisconsin Center for Education Research. (2008, August). *CPRE's school finance research: 15 years of findings.* Retrieved March 14, 2010, from http://www.wcer.wisc.edu/news/coverStories/cpre_school_finance_research.php

25. Nichols, S. L., & Berliner, D. C. (2007). *Collateral damage: How high-stakes testing corrupts America's schools.* Cambridge, MA: Harvard Education Press.

26. Hargreaves, A. (2009). The fourth way of change: Towards an age of inspiration and sustainability. In A. Hargreaves & M. Fullan (Eds.), *Change wars* (pp. 11–45). Bloomington, IN: Solution Tree.

27. Reuters. (2007, May 24). U.S. spends $8,701 per pupil on education. Retrieved March 14, 2010, from http://www.reuters.com/article/idUSN2438214220070524

28. Berry, B. (2009). *Children of poverty deserve great teachers: One union's commitment to changing the status quo.* Washington, DC: National Education Association and Center for Teaching Quality.

29. Organisation for Economic Cooperation and Development. (2005). *Education at a glance: OECD indicators, 2005.* Paris: Author.

30. Roza, M. (2007, January.). *Frozen assets: Rethinking teacher contracts could free billions for school reform.* Washington, DC: Education Sector. Retrieved March 14, 2010, from http://www.educationsector.org/usr_doc/FrozenAssets.pdf

31. Wasley, P., & Roza, M. (2009, December 1). The "Master's pay bump": Why ending it shouldn't frighten ed schools. *Education Week, 29*(13), 26–27.

32. Sawchuk, S. (2009, August 26). Halt urged to paying teachers for earning masters degrees. *Education Week*. Retrieved March 14, 2010, from http://www.edweek.org/ew/articles/2009/07/21/37masters.h28.html?r=1762965371

33. American Federation of Teachers. (2008, March 7). *EPI report: Teachers face large and growing professional pay gap.* Retrieved March 14, 2010, from http://archive.aft.org/news/2008/epi-report.htm

34. American Federation of Teachers. (2008, March 7).

35. Allegretto, S. A., Mishel, L., & Corcoran, S. P. (2008, March 5). *The teaching penalty: Teacher pay losing ground.* Washington, DC: Economic Policy Institute. Retrieved March 14, 2010, from http://www.epi.org/publications/entry/book_teaching_penalty/

36. The Teaching Commission. (2004). *Teaching at risk: A call to action.* New York: Author.

37. Winter, G. (2003, January 22). New panel to begin a quest to upgrade teaching. *New York Times.* Retrieved March 14, 2010, from http://www.nytimes.com/2003/01/22/us/new-panel-to-begin-a-quest-to-upgrade-teaching.html

38. White, D. (2010, February). *Iraq war facts, results and statistics as of February 16, 2010.* Retrieved March 14, 2010, from http://usliberals.about.com/od/homelandsecurit1/a/IraqNumbers.htm

39. Levine, A. (2006, September). *Educating school teachers.* The Education Schools Project. Retrieved March 14, 2010, from http://www.edschools.org/pdf/Educating_Teachers_Report.pdf

40. Henke, R. R., Chen, X., & Geis, S. (2000, January). *Progress Through the Teacher Pipeline: 1992–93 College Graduates and Elementary/Secondary School Teaching as of 1997.* Washington, DC: National Center for Education Statistics. Retrieved March 14, 2010, from http://nces.ed.gov/pubs2000/2000152.pdf

41. *Education Week*. (2003). *Quality Counts 2003: If I can't learn from you: Ensuring a highly qualified teacher for every classroom.* Bethesda, MD: Author.

42. Levine (2006, September).

43. Milanowski, A., & Odden, A. (2007). *A new approach to the cost of teacher turnover.* Seattle, WA: Center on Reinventing Public Education.

44. Benner, A. D. (2000). *The cost of teacher turnover.* Austin: Texas Center for Educational Research.

45. Schorr, L. B. (2003, February 26). *Determining "what works" in social programs and social policies: Toward a more inclusive knowledge base.* Washington, DC: Brookings Institute. Retrieved March 14, 2010, from http://www.brookings.edu/papers/2003/0226poverty_schorr.aspx

46. Schorr (2003, February 26).

47. Communities in Schools. (2010). *National evaluation.* Retrieved March 14, 2010, from http://communitiesinschools.org/subpage.php?rsid=17&p=About

48. Weiss, H. B., Little, P. M. D., Bouffard, S. M., Deschenes, S. N., & Janc Malone, H. (2009). The federal role in out-of-school learning: After-school, summer learning, and family involvement as critical learning supports. *Voices in Urban Education.* Retrieved March 14, 2010, from http://www.annenberginstitute.org/VUE/Summer09/Weiss.php

49. Berry, B. (forthcoming). NCATE Blue Ribbon Panel on Teacher Education.

50. Darling-Hammond (2010). *The flat world and education.*

51. Ball, D. (2010, May 4). *Supporting America's educators: The importance of quality teachers and leaders.* Testimony and responses to follow-up questions from the U.S. House Committee on Education and Labor Hearing on Teacher Quality, Washington, DC.

Retrieved July 17, 2010, from http://www-personal.umich.edu/~dball/presentations/DBall-testimony-House-EducationLabor-Comm_May2010.pdf

52. Levine (2006, September).

53. Feistritzer, E. (2010, February). *Alternative routes to teacher certification.* Presentation at the annual meeting of American Association of Colleges of Teacher Education, Atlanta.

54. *Education Week.* (2010). *Quality counts: Fresh course, swift current.* Bethesda, MD: Author.

55. Brennan, J. (2009). *Study finds teacher licensure tests are mostly high school level: If this is all we expect teachers to know, why do we make them go to college?* Washington, DC: Education Trust. Retrieved December 1, 2009, from http://www.edtrust.org/dc/press-room/press-release/study-finds-teacher-licensure-tests-are-mostly-high-school-level-if-this

56. Mitchell, K. J., Robinson, D. Z., Plake, B. S., & Knowles, K. T. (Eds.). (2001). *Testing teacher candidates: Licensure exams play limited role in boosting teacher quality.* Retrieved December 1, 2009, from http://www8.nationalacademies.org/onpinews/newsitem.aspx?RecordID=10090

57. Mitchell, Robinson, Plake, & Knowles (Eds.). (2001).

58. Mitchell, Robinson, Plake, & Knowles (Eds.). (2001).

59. Estimated in 2010 dollars, based on the cost of preparing residents at the Academy for Urban School Leadership, a UTR that has demonstrated considerable success in recruiting, preparing, and retaining effective teachers for the Chicago school community.

60. Berry, B., Montgomery, D., Curtis, R., Hernandez, M., Wurtzel, J., & Snyder, J. (2008). *Creating and sustaining urban teacher residencies: A new way to recruit, prepare, and retain effective teachers in high-needs districts.* Washington, DC: Aspen Institute.

61. Pechone, R., & Chung, R. (2006). Evidence in teacher education: The performance assessment for California teachers. *Journal of Teacher Education, 57*(1), 22–36.

62. U.S. Department of Education. (2009, April 3). *The American Reinvestment and Recovery Act.* Retrieved March 15, 2010, from www.ed.gov/policy/gen/leg/recovery/presentation/arra.ppt

63. Learning Point Associates and Public Agenda. (2009). *Report 2: Teaching for a living.* Washington, DC: Authors. Retrieved March 14, 2010, from http://www.learningpt.org/expertise/educatorquality/genY/TeachingforaLiving/index.php

64. Berry, B., Daughtrey, A., & Wieder, A. (2009). *Teaching effectiveness and the conditions that matter most in high-needs schools.* Hillsborough, NC: Center for Teaching Quality. Retrieved April 13, 2010, from http://www.teachingquality.org/sites/default/files/Tch_effective_twc_final.pdf

65. Fine, S. (2009, August 9). Schools need teachers like me. I just can't stay. *Washington Post.* Retrieved August 9, 2009, from http://www.washingtonpost.com/wp-dyn/content/article/2009/08/07/AR2009080702046.html

66. Little, J. W. (1996, April). *Organizing schools for teacher learning.* Paper presented at the annual meeting of the American Educational Research Association, New York.

67. Humphrey, D. C., Koppich, J. E., & Hough, H. J. (2005). Sharing the wealth: National Board Certified Teachers and the students who need them most. *Education Policy Analysis Archives, 13*(18), 1–50. Retrieved June 1, 2005, from http://epaa.asu.edu/epaa/v13n18/; Koppich, J. E., & Humphrey, D. C. (2006, April 3). Making use of what teachers know and can do: Policy, practice, and National Board Certification. *Education Policy Analysis Archives, 15*(7). Retrieved June 1, 2006, from http://epaa.asu.edu/epaa/v15n17/

68. Bushaw, W. J., & Gallup, A. M. (2009). *Americans speak out: Are educators and policy makers listening?* Bloomington, IN: Phi Delta Kappan.

69. Ravitch, D. (2010). *The death and life of the great American school system.* New York: Basic Books, p. 95.

70. Ravitch (2010), p. 97.

71. Toch, T. (2006, January 31). *Margins of error: The testing industry in the No Child Left Behind era.* Washington, DC: Education Sector. Retrieved March 30, 2010, from http://www.educationsector.org/research/research_show.htm?doc_id=346734

72. Koretz, D. (2008). *Measuring up: What educational testing really tells us.* Cambridge, MA: Harvard University Press.

73. Shepard, L. (1997). *Measuring achievement: What does it mean to test for robust understandings?* Princeton, NJ: Educational Testing Service.

74. Ravitch (2010), p. 152.

75. Jackson, J. M., & Bassett, E. (2005). *The state of the K–12 state assessment market.* Boston: Eduventures.

76. Toch (2006, January 31).

77. Forum for Education and Democracy. (2009). *Beyond standardized tests: Investing in a culture of learning.* Washington, DC: Author. Retrieved March 30, 2010, from http://forumforeducation.org/files/u48/Learning_Brief_1209_v1.pdf

78. Mcmurrer, J. (2007, December). *Choices, changes and challenges: Curriculum and instruction in the NCLB era.* Washington, DC: Center for Education Policy. Retrieved March 30, 2010, from http://www.cep-dc.org/index.cfm?fuseaction=document.show DocumentByID&nodeID=1&DocumentID=212

79. Dillon, S. (2009, April 28). "No Child" law is not closing a racial gap. *New York Times.* Retrieved March 30, 2010, from http://www.nytimes.com/2009/04/29/education/29scores.html?_r=1

80. Thomas B. Fordham Institute. (2009, February 19). *The accountability illusion.* Washington, DC: Author. Retrieved March 30, 2010, from http://edexcellence.net/index.cfm/news_the-accountability-illusion

81. Pellegrino, J. W., Chudowsky, N., & Glaser, R. (Eds.). (2001). *Knowing what students know: The science and design of educational assessment.* Washington, DC: National Academies Press.

82. Tucker, B. (2009, February 17). *Beyond the bubble: Technology and the future of student assessment.* Washington, DC: Education Sector. Retrieved March 30, 2010, from http://www.educationsector.org/research/research_show.htm?doc_id=826893

83. Tucker (2009, February 17).

84. Cuban, L. (1996, October 9). Techno-reformers and classroom teachers. *Education Week, 16*(6), Retrieved April 12, 2010, from http://www.edweek.org/ew.articles/1996/10/09/06cuban.h16.html

85. Foote, M. (2007, December 10). *Testimony before the Education Committee of the New York City Council hearings on the DOE's School Progress Reports.* Retrieved August 11, 2010, from http://timeoutfromtesting.org/TOFT_Foote_Dec1007.pdf

86. Gewertz, C. (2010, March 2). Experts lay out vision for future assessments. *Education Week.* Retrieved March 30, 2010, from http://www.edweek.org/ew/articles/2010/02/23/23assessment.h29.html?tkn=NYNFS3cNOFAbhSuNXLLv%2BIRe%2BuOyOE54H4KT&cmp=clp-edweek

87. Darling-Hammond, L. (2010). *Performance counts: Assessment systems that support high quality learning.* Washington, DC: CCSSO.

88. Chaltain, S. (2010, February 3). The big picture on school performance.

Huffington Post. Retrieved March 30, 2010, from http://www.huffingtonpost.com/sam-chaltain/the-big-picture-on-school_b_446865.html

89. Chaltain (2010, February 3).

90. Ravitch, D. (2007, Winter). They protect teachers' rights, support teacher professionalism, and check administrative power. *American Educator.* Retrieved September 9, 2009, from http://www.aft.org/pubs-reports/american_educator/issues/winter06-07/includes/ravitch.htm

91. Ravitch (2007, Winter).

92. Kristof, N. (2009, October 14). Democrats and schools. *New York Times.* Retrieved March 15, 2010, from http://www.nytimes.com/2009/10/15/opinion/15kristof.html?_r=1

93. Teachers Union Facts. (2010). *Teachers unions oppose education reform.* Retrieved March 15, 2010, from http://teachersunionexposed.com/blocking.cfm

94. Baugh, W. H., & Stone, J. A. (1982).Teachers, unions, and wages in the 1970s: Unionism now pays. *Industrial and Labor Relations Review, 35*(3), 368–376; Hoxby, C. (1996). How teachers unions affect education production. *Quarterly Journal of Economics, 111,* 671–718.

95. Eberts. R. (2007). Teachers unions and student performance: Help or hindrance? *The Future for Children, 17*(1), 175–200. Retrieved March 15, 2010, from http://muse.jhu.edu/login?uri=/journals/future_of_children/v017/17.1eberts.html

96. Eberts (2007).

97. Ravitch, D. (2009, May 19). *Diane Ravitch on "The Massachusetts miracle and the teachers union."* Retrieved March 15, 2010, from http://www.edexcellence.net/flypaper/index.php/2009/05/diane-ravitch-on-the-massachusetts-miracle-and-the-teachers-union/

98. Duffet, A., Farkas, F., & Rotherham, A. J. (2008). *Waiting to be won over: Teachers speak on the profession, unions and reform.* Washington, DC: Education Sector.

99. Duffet, Farkas, & Rotherham (2008).

100. Peterson, B., & Charney, M. (1999). *Transforming teacher unions: Fighting for better schools and social justice.* Milwaukee, WI: Rethinking Schools.

101. Cameron, D. (2005). *The inside story of the teacher revolution in America.* New York: Scarecrow Press.

102. Chase, B. (1999). The new NEA: Reinventing the teacher unions. In B. Peterson & M. Charney (Eds.), *Transforming teacher unions: Fighting for better schools and social justice* (p. 108). Milwaukee, WI: Rethinking Schools.

103. Anderson, N. (2010, January 12). *Union head to propose tying test scores, teacher evaluations.* Retrieved January 13, 2010, from http://www.washingtonpost.com/wpdyn/content/article/2010/01/11/AR2010011103691.html?wprss=rss_education

104. Hirsch, M. (2010). Teachers union chief blasts Obama administration's education policies. *The Times-Picayune.* Retrieved July 19, 2010, from http://www.nola.com/education/index.ssf/2010/07/teachers_union_chief_blasts_ob.html

105. Duffet, A., Farkas, F., & Rotherham, A. J. (2008). *Waiting to be won over: Teachers speak on the profession, unions and reform.* Washington, DC: Education Sector.

106. Duffet, Farkas, & Rotherham (2008).

107. Kerchner, C. T., Koppich, J. E., & Weeres, J. G. (1997). *United mind workers: Unions and teaching in the knowledge society.* San Francisco: Jossey-Bass.

108. Kahlenberg, R. D. (2008, June). Albert Shanker and the future of teacher unions. *Phi Delta Kappan, 89*(10), 712–720. Retrieved July 31, 2009, from http://www.pdkintl.org/kappan/k_v89/k0806kah.htm

109. Kerchner, Koppich, & Weeres (1997).

110. Kerchner, Koppich, & Weeres (1997).

111. Super Lawyers. (2010). Homepage. Retrieved March 15, 2010, from http://www.superlawyers.com/index.html

Chapter 8

1. Kurzweil, R. (2005). *The singularity is near: When humans transcend biology*. New York: Viking Press.

2. See http://www.elzware.com/us/index.us.html for more information on Teachbots.

3. Pew Research Center. (2010). *The millennials: Confident. Connected. Open to change.* Retrieved May 20, 2010, from http://pewresearch.org/pubs/1501/millennials-new-survey-generational-personality-upbeat-open-new-ideas-technology-bound

4. Jackson, C. K., & Bruegmann, E. (2009). *Teaching students and teaching each other: The importance of peer learning for teachers* [NBER Working Paper 15202]. Washington, DC: National Bureau of Economic Research.

5. Jackson, C. K. (2010). *Match quality, worker productivity, and worker mobility: Direct evidence from teachers* [NBER Working Paper 15990]. Washington, DC: National Bureau of Economic Research.

6. SMHC. (2010). *Taking human capital seriously: Talented teachers in every classroom, talented principals in every school*. Madison, WI: University of Wisconsin–Madison.

7. Brill, S. (2010, May 23). The teachers' unions last stand: How Obama's race to the top could revolutionize public education. *New York Times Magazine*, 32–39, 44–47.

8. Abowd, P. (2009, November 25). Tired of teacher-bashing, union educators grow their own schools. *Labor Notes*. Retrieved December 1, 2009, from http://www.labornotes.org/2009/12/tired-teacher-bashing-union-educators-grow-their-own-schools

About the Authors

 **Barnett Berry** is president and CEO of the Center for Teaching Quality, Inc., based in Hillsborough, North Carolina. Founded in 1999, CTQ seeks to improve student learning and advance the teaching profession by cultivating teacher leadership, conducting timely research, and crafting smart policy.

A former high school teacher, Barnett created, with John Norton, the Teacher Leaders Network—a dynamic virtual community designed to elevate the voices of expert teachers on matters of education policy that impact their profession and the students they serve.

Barnett also has worked as a social scientist at the RAND Corporation, served as a senior executive with the South Carolina State Department of Education, and directed an education policy center while he was a professor at the University of South Carolina. In the 1990s, he helped launch the work of the National Commission on Teaching and America's Future—and its state partnership efforts.

Barnett has authored numerous academic reports and publications and many articles for the popular education press. He frequently serves in an advisory capacity to organizations committed to teaching quality, equity, and social justice in America's schools. For example, in 2010 he was advising the National Council of Accreditation of Teacher Education's Blue Ribbon Panel on Clinical Preparation, Education Testing Service and its Teacher Leadership Initiative, Urban Teacher Residencies United, the NEA Foundation's Institute for Local Innovation in Teaching and Learning, and the Bush Foundation and its teacher-education reform initiative.

At the time of publication, Meredith, Barnett's wife of 34 years, serves as a special education teacher in the Chapel Hill–Carrboro City Schools. Meredith and Barnett are the proud parents of Joseph, a political organizer for the Working Families Party (New York City), and Evan, an organic farmer in the Pacific Northwest.

After teaching more than a dozen different language arts and social science courses in two Alabama school systems, **Jennifer Barnett** recently assumed the role of school-based technology integration specialist in rural Talladega County at Winterboro School. A veteran teacher of nearly 20 years, she was selected as Alabama's District III Teacher of the Year in 2001 and received the Marbury Technology Innovation Award, Alabama's most prestigious award recognizing technology innovation by a classroom teacher, in 2008. Leading a project-based learning initiative on global warming, Jennifer's team was selected to attend Microsoft's Innovative Teachers Forum in 2007. She designed and continues to lead a 21st-century learning initiative for her school system, implementing a protocol for integrating 21st-century skills with content standards. Her work with the highly effective Alabama Best Practices Center and presence on the Web has afforded Jennifer the opportunity to work with teachers on technology integration throughout the world. Jennifer is a member of the Teacher Leaders Network.

Kilian Betlach is the assistant principal of Elmhurst Community Prep (ECP), a small middle school in Oakland, California. An alumnus of Teach for America, Kilian taught 7th-grade language arts and English language development for 6 years in San Jose, California, experiences that were chronicled in the blog Teaching in the 408 – twice named one of the top education blogs in the country by the *Washington Post*. He has worked extensively in teacher training and development with the Oakland Teaching Fellows, Alliant International University, and Teach For America. Kilian is the author of *This Feels Like A Riot Looks*, a punk rock love story, and most recently *We Are Almost Always on the Verge*, a collection of short stories.

Shannon C'de Baca is a 31-year teaching veteran (K–12 science) who moved from face-to-face teaching to teaching online years ago. She developed a lab intensive chemistry course for Iowa students who did not have an available chemistry teacher. She has worked with seven states and two national organizations in the development of science standards and

teacher professional development. Shannon's teaching has been recognized with honors from the Milken Family Foundation, National Science Teachers Association (NSTA), the Iowa Department of Education, Sertoma, and PBS.

She hosted the Annenberg television series, *"The Missing Link in Mathematics."* She has also worked with the PBS series *NOVA* and served as a consultant for the National Education and the Economy, the Council of Chief State School Officers, the National Education Association, the NSTA, the U.S. Mint and the U.S. Department of State. Shannon currently serves as one of two citizen ambassadors to Bahrain. She has worked as a designer and a facilitator for the Iowa statewide "Every Learner Inquires" initiative and guided development of the science component of the Iowa Core Curriculum. Shannon continues to pursue her passion for equitable access to exceptional online courses for all students through work with the Iowa Technology Task Force and Iowa Learning Online. Her essay on teaching online appeared at *Teacher Magazine* online.

After 23 years as a science teacher, **Susie Highley** moved into the media center at Creston Middle School in Indianapolis to take advantage

of exciting advances in technology and to see what she could do to help students develop a love for reading. She has received the Golden Apple Award, Lilly Endowment Teacher Creativity Fellowship, GTE GIFT Grant, and Indiana Teacher Technology Fellowship and was her district Teacher of the Year (TOY) in 1999. She is a graduate of the Teacher Leadership Academy (TLA), a unique program sponsored by the Central Indiana Educational Service Center (CIESC) in which teachers from several counties embark upon a specialized 2-year program. TLA incorporates current research and best practices while developing and providing leadership opportunities. She serves on the board of directors for the Indiana Middle Level Educators Association (IMLEA), the Association of Indiana Media Educators (AIME), and her local library board. Susie has also participated as a Teacher Academy Fellow and consultant at Indiana State University and has been a member of the Teacher Leaders Network since its inception.

John M. Holland is an artist, a teacher, a writer, and an innovator. He has dedicated his career to serving the neediest and youngest school children of Richmond, Virginia. After 12 years as a preschool teacher of 3- and 4-year-olds from Richmond's toughest neighborhoods, John recently left the classroom to take a position as Early Head Start/Head Start Program child development specialist for Richmond Public Schools, supporting the teachers who serve those children. John is one of a handful of male National Board–certified pre-Kindergarten teachers in the country. He was the lead blogger for the Pew Charitable trust blog Inside Pre-K from 2008–2010 and currently writes about pre-K issues on his blog Emergent Learner. John is a member of the Teacher Leaders Network and the Center for Teacher Leadership at Virginia Commonwealth University (VCU) where he is the moderator for the Virginia Forum, an online community of accomplished teachers. John is pursuing a Ph.D. in educational leadership at VCU where he has served as a National Board coach, mentor, workshop presenter, and university student teaching supervisor. He is president of VCU's Educational Leadership Doctoral Association and was recognized in 2009 as one of Richmond's Top 40 Under 40 by *Style Weekly*. John's teacherpreneur company is rightSTART Solutions LLC. His passions include educational policy, teacher leadership, creativity, and 21st-century learning.

Carrie J. Kamm is a mentor-resident coach for the Academy for Urban School Leadership's (AUSL) Urban Teacher Residency (UTR) program at National Teachers Academy, a Chicago Public School. Carrie began her career in Chicago teaching 4th and 5th grades at R. N. Dett Elementary School for 4 years and then became a 4th-grade mentor-teacher at the Chicago Academy Elementary School, an AUSL resident teacher training academy, for 5 years. During that time, she earned her National Board–certification as a middle childhood generalist and mentored several cohorts of teachers going through the NBC process. She earned her Ed.D. in curriculum and instruction from Loyola University Chicago in May 2007. In her current role as mentor-resident coach she coordinates her site's resident teachers, provides coaching and support to mentor- and resident teachers, and provides professional development to the teachers in the AUSL schools network.

Renee Moore has taught English in the Mississippi delta for 20 years. The 2001 Mississippi Teacher of the Year, she is also a Milken Education Award winner and National Board Certified. Renee is a Writing Project Fellow and has received numerous awards and grants, including $30,000 from the Spencer Foundation (Chicago) for her work on teaching standard English to African American students. Actively involved in teacher-research, Renee is also a Writing Project Fellow and has received numerous awards and grants, including $30,000 from the Spencer Foundation (Chicago) for her work on teaching standard English to African American students. She was the first active K–12 educator to serve on the Board of the Carnegie Foundation for the Advancement of Teaching (California), and is on the Board of Directors for the National Board of Professional Teaching Standards. She also currently serves on the State Commission on Teacher Licensure. Active for many years in professional development, her writings have been published as chapters in four books and several professional journals.

Cindi Rigsbee has recently left her Literacy Coach position in Orange County, North Carolina to work as a Regional Education Facilitator, a "teacher-on-loan" to the North Carolina Department of Public Instruction. She works with a team of teachers in the Educator Recruitment and Development division. A former language arts teacher and reading specialist, Cindi was named North Carolina Teacher of the Year in 2008 and was a finalist for the 2009 National Teacher of the Year.

Cindi is a National Board certified teacher in the area of early adolescence/English language arts who enjoys writing about teaching. She has had several articles published by *Teacher Magazine* online, including "Grammar Interrupted," "Tips for New Teachers," and "What Makes a Principal Great." In addition, Cindi comments on education issues in her blog, the Dream Teacher, and is currently traveling the country sharing from her book *Finding Mrs. Warnecke: The Difference Teachers Make*.

Ariel Sacks has been teaching middle school English in New York City public schools for the past 6 years. She currently teaches 7th-grade English at a middle school in Sunset Park, Brooklyn. For the past 3 years she was team leader and English department chair at a public secondary school in Crown Heights, Brooklyn, and she previously taught English to transitional English language learners in a bilingual middle school in East Harlem. Ariel studied progressive pedagogy at Bank Street College of Education and is committed to implementing student-centered methods successfully in high-needs public schools. She has been developing and writing about the Whole Novels Program, a student-centered method of whole class literature studies, which she has presented at Bank Street College and the 2010 National Council of Teachers of English conference. Ariel has also been a panelist at conferences and workshops hosted by AACTE, Ford Foundation, Center for American Progress, and Great Teachers for Great City Schools, where she has discussed issues of teacher preparation and teacher leadership in urban public schools. Her articles have been published in *Teacher Magazine*, *NY Daily News*, and Bank Street College's Occasional Papers Series. She writes regularly about her teaching practice and educational issues at her TLN featured blog, On the Shoulders of Giants.

Emily Vickery in an innovator educator who has worked in a wide variety of settings, from teaching in an economically disadvantaged urban high school to serving as a consultant to a state governor. The constant in her work has been a love of teaching, learning, and technology. Emily has served on the Alabama Governor's Council on Education Technology and represented the state of Alabama on a task force for the U.S. Department of Education.

From 1997 to 2003, Emily served as a private educational consultant focusing on technology. Her clients included the governor of the State of Colorado, the Education Commission of the States, and Apple, Inc. In 2003, she accepted a fellowship with the award-winning Teaching Tolerance project of the Southern Poverty Law Center.

From 2004 to 2009, Emily served as a technology instructor and the director of 21st-century learning for a private academy in Alabama. In 2009, she accepted the position of 21st-century learning specialist at an innovative parochial school in Florida. There, she supports teachers in curriculum, instruction, assessment, learning management, and the use of digital tools.

Jose Vilson is a math teacher, coach, and data analyst for a middle school in the Inwood/Washington Heights neighborhood of New York, New York. He is beginning his 5th year as a teacher, having finished the New York City Teaching Fellows program in 2007. He graduated with a bachelor's degree in computer science from Syracuse University and a master's degree in mathematics education from the City College of New York. He has worked on creating professional development for his fellow teachers on such topics as working on goals for the classroom and using the ARIS system, a data management system under the NYC Department of Education. He's spoken at Lincoln Center as part of the NYC Teaching Fellows' induction ceremonies and writes regularly about education issues mainly at his blog. He is also a committed poet, Web developer, and mentor to new teachers. He can be found at http://thejosevilson.com.

Laurie Wasserman has been a special education teacher for the past 29 years working with students of all ages, many of whom have had a wide variety of learning and health disabilities. Teaching middle schoolers and sharing stories from the classroom are her passions. She currently teaches 6th-grade middle schoolers at The Andrews Middle School, in Medford, Massachusetts. Laurie mentors new teachers in her school district and has also mentored new teachers through a partnership with The Center for Teaching Quality and the University of Connecticut. She has written articles for *Teacher Magazine* and educationworld.com, and written book reviews for Teacher Leaders Network. This National Board–certified teacher is also part of the National Writing Project and the Teacher Leaders Network.

Teacher Contributors

A number of members of the Teacher Leaders Network participated in virtual conversations with our TeacherSolutions 2030 team that helped shape our ideas for this book. We are grateful for their time and contributions as well as their insightful writing. We are honored for their voices to be a part of the narrative for *Teaching 2030*.

Ellen Berg—Eighth-grade English and history teacher, San Diego, California

Ken Bernstein—National Board–certified social studies teacher, Greenbelt, Maryland

Dan Brown—High school English teacher, Washington, D.C.

Mark Clemente—Educator in residence, National Institute of Aerospace/Virginia; Beach City Public Schools, Virginia Beach, Virginia

Anthony Cody—Science coach, Oakland Unified School District, Oakland, California

David Cohen—NBCT, English teacher and academic advisor, Palo Alto, California

Julianna Dauble—Fifth-grade teacher and political action board director for Washington Education Association, Renton, Washington

Larry Ferlazzo—English and social studies for English language learners teacher, Sacramento, California

Bill Ferriter—Sixth-grade teacher, author and consultant, Apex, North Carolina

Jane Ching Fung—NBCT, mentor and kindergarten teacher, Los Angeles, California

Heather Wolpert Gawron—Middle School language arts and podcasting teacher, speech & debate coach, blogger, San Gabriel, California

Susan Graham—Consumer sciences teacher, Fredericksburg, Virginia

Jon Hanbury—Site-based math coach, W. T. Cooke Elementary, Virginia Beach, Virginia

Sarah Henchey—Middle school language arts teacher, Hillsborough, North Carolina

Bill Ivey—Middle school dean, Stoneleigh Burnham School, Massachusetts

Ben Jackson—High school English teacher and basketball coach, Denver, Colorado

Anne Jolly—Curriculum writer, learning team consultant, former middle grades science teacher, Warrior, Alabama

Laura Jones—Technology specialist, Herndon, Virginia

Patty Jordan—Instructional and resource teacher for academically gifted students, Poe Montessori, Raleigh, North Carolina

Kristoffer Kohl—Data strategist, Las Vegas, Nevada

Patrick Ledesma—School-based technology specialist and Special Education Department chair, Fairfax County, Virginia

Kathie Marshall—Grade 6 teacher, Pacoima Middle School, California

Anna Martin—Instructional coach and core teacher, San Jose, California

Susan "Ernie" Rambo—Middle school educator, Las Vegas, Nevada

Marsha Ratzel—Teacher, Leawood, Kansas

Gail V. Ritchie—K–6 instructional coach, Fairfax County, Virginia

Taylor Ross—First-grade teacher, Birmingham, Alabama

Marti Schwartz—Teacher, Smithfield, Rhode Island

Dayle Timmons—Reading coach/ K–1 special education teacher, Chets Creek Elementary School, Jacksonville, Florida

Robyn Ulzheimer—Kindergarten teacher, New York City, New York

Stephanie Van Horn—Third-grade teacher, Boulder, Colorado

Bob Williams—Colony High School mathematics teacher, Palmer, Alaska

Isabel Campos Woytek—English language acquisition teacher, Denver, Colorado

Index